WILLIAM SHAKESPEARE

THE MERCHANT OF VENICE

William Shakespeare

THE MERCHANT OF VENICE

[Including Complete Text, Summary and Analysis of Text, Critical Analysis and Historical Context]

Aditya Nandwani
B.A. English (Hons), Delhi University;
M.A. (English), IGNOU; Print Journalism (English) YMCA

ANMOL PUBLICATIONS PVT. LTD.
NEW DELHI - 110 002 (INDIA)

ANMOL PUBLICATIONS PVT. LTD.

H.O.: 4374/4B, Ansari Road, Darya Ganj,
New Delhi-110 002 (India)
Ph.: 23278000, 23261597

B.O.: No. 1015, Ist Main Road, BSK IIIrd Stage
IIIrd Phase, IIIrd Block
Bangalore - 560 085 (India)
Visit us at: www.anmolpublications.com

The Merchant of Venice

First Published, 2009

PRINTED IN INDIA

Printed at Mehra Offset Press, Delhi.

Contents

Preface

The Merchant of Venice was first printed in 1600 in quarto, of which nineteen copies survive. This was followed by a 1619 printing, and later an inclusion in the First Folio in 1623. The play was written shortly after Christopher Marlowe's immensely popular Jew of Malta (1589), a play wherein a Jew named Barabas plays a greatly exaggerated villain. The portrayal of Shakespeare's Jew was and remained comic until the late 1700s at which time he was first played as a true villain. In 1814 Shylock's role was depicted as a character to be pitied, and in 1879 he was first portrayed as a tragic character. Subsequent interpretations have varied greatly over the years, but since World War II he has most often been conceived of as tragic.

The Merchant of Venice has been described as a great commentary on the nature of racial and religious interactions. The title itself is misleading, and is often misconstrued as a reference to Shylock, the Jew. However, in reality it describes the merchant Antonio. This ambiguity and misinterpretation has not surprisingly led scholars to continue hotly debating whether Shakespeare meant to be anti-Semitic or critical of anti-Semitism. His depiction of Shylock, the Jewish moneylender, causes the audience to both hate and pity the man, and has left critics wondering what Shakespeare was really trying to achieve.

The choice of Venice can hardly have been arbitrary. The Venice of Shakespeare's day was renowned for its wealth and diversity of cultures, for it was a cosmopolitan market where

Eastern goods made their way into the West. Since Shakespeare's interactions with Jews in England would have been limited, if at all, Venice provided him with the example of tolerance and heterogeneity that he needed.

Author

Chapter 1

Introduction

The Merchant of Venice was first printed in 1600 in quarto, of which nineteen copies survive. This was followed by a 1619 printing, and later an inclusion in the First Folio in 1623. The play was written shortly after Christopher Marlowe's immensely popular Jew of Malta, a play wherein a Jew named Barabas plays a greatly exaggerated villain. The portrayal of Shakespeare's Jew was and remained comic until the late 1700s at which time he was first played as a true villain.

In 1814 Shylock's role was depicted as a character to be pitied, and in 1879 he was first portrayed as a tragic character. Subsequent interpretations have varied greatly over the years, but since World War II he has most often been conceived of as tragic.

The Merchant of Venice has been described as a great commentary on the nature of racial and religious interactions. The title itself is misleading, and is often misconstrued as a reference to Shylock, the Jew. However, in reality it describes the merchant Antonio. This ambiguity and misinterpretation has not surprisingly led scholars to continue hotly debating whether Shakespeare meant to be anti-Semitic or critical of anti-Semitism. His depiction of Shylock, the Jewish moneylender, causes the audience to both hate and pity the man, and has left critics wondering what Shakespeare was really trying to achieve.

The choice of Venice can hardly have been arbitrary. The Venice of Shakespeare's day was renowned for its wealth and diversity of cultures, for it was a cosmopolitan market where

Eastern goods made their way into the West. Since Shakespeare's interactions with Jews in England would have been limited, if at all, Venice provided him with the example of tolerance and heterogeneity that he needed.

It is interesting to note that the Christians are portrayed as being an incredibly tight, commonly bound group. Antonio rushes to grant Bassanio a loan, even though it will bankrupt him. A similar example occurs later when Graziano asks Bassanio for a favour, which is granted before Bassanio even knows exactly what Graziano is asking for. However, this central community of Christians, with all of its virtue and decency, is immediately subverted by the prodigal loss of the money by Bassanio. While it may be virtuous for Antonio to give all he has to his friend, it is clear to the audience that it is foolish for him to give to a friend who will gamble it away.

In addition, the Christian's generosity and friendship is further undermined by the racism so apparent in their actions. Antonio is proud of the fact that he kicks and spits upon Shylock, while Portia is overjoyed when the black Prince of Morocco fails to choose the correct casket, saying, "Let all of his complexion choose me so". The Christian ideals are not only undermined by this racism, this inherent distaste for anyone different from themselves, but also by their hypocrisy with respect to slavery. When the Christians exhort Shylock to release Antonio, he asks them why Antonio should be treated differently from their slaves, considering that he was bought by Shylock via the contract. Shakespeare thus plants doubt as to whether the Christians' kindness to each other is in fact as great a virtue as it would at first appear.

The nature of the religious differences has a profound impact on the way the Christians and the Jews live their lives. For Shylock, absolute adherence to the law is necessary, as evidenced by his reliance on contracts. In addition, money and possessions are things which he feels he must defend. Rather than try to increase his wealth, he struggles merely to maintain it. This economic conservatism contrasts starkly with the aristocratic, gambling nature of Bassanio and the others. The characteristic generosity of the Christians is a very aristocratic trait, based on an ideology which forces gentlemen to ignore practical monetary concerns. Thus Bassanio can truly say, "all the wealth I had ran in my veins".

Perhaps the moment of strongest contrast between Shylock and the Christians' ideals concerns the contract of a pound of flesh. Shylock directly links money and flesh as being equal, something which any Christian would consider taboo. Antonio is unable to see this link, thinking instead that the contract is some form of game for Shylock. He makes the crucial mistake of believing that the contract cannot be for real, and that Shylock must somehow have grown "kind."

There is a division between the Christian portrayal of Shylock and the words and actions of Shylock himself which cannot be overlooked. The Christians are convinced that he can only think of money, whereas Shylock actually presents a very different, even sentimental outlook. Solanio claims that Shylock ran through the street crying out for his daughter and ducats in the same breath, yet there is no evidence of this when Shylock himself appears. Later, when his daughter, Jessica, exchanges a turquoise ring for a monkey, Shylock is not upset about the monetary loss of the ring, but rather the sentimental value it held for him.

Most of Shakespeare's comedies return to the first city in which they are set. However, this type of ending is uniquely absent in The Merchant of Venice. The final scene moves away from the abandonment of Shylock in Venice, shifting instead to Belmont. Belmont, however, is not nearly as idyllic as it appears throughout the play. Indeed, it represents wealth derived from inheritance, built on the merchandising of Venice, and is therefore a paradise founded on the despised trade it claims to hate. Ending the play in Belmont serves to remind the audience that the play can be viewed as anything but a comedy, and that in fact it is in many ways a tragedy.

Chapter 2

William Shakespeare: Biography

SHAKESPEARE'S ANCESTRY

As a brief introductory detail, it should be mentioned that, during the sixteenth century, there were many families with the name Shakespeare in and around Stratford. "Shakespeare" appears countless times in town minutes and court records, spelled in a variety of ways, from Shags ere to Casper. Unfortunately, very few records reveal William Shakespeare's relationship to or with the many other Stratford Shakespeare's. Genealogists claim to have discovered one man related to Shakespeare who was hanged in Gloucestershire for theft in 1248, and Shakespeare's father, in an application for a coat of arms, claimed that his grandfather was a hero in the War of the Roses and was granted land in Warwickshire in 1485 by Henry VII. No historical evidence has been discovered to corroborate this story of the man who would be William Shakespeare's great-grandfather, but, luckily, we do have information regarding his paternal and maternal grandfathers.

The Bard's paternal grandfather was Richard Shakespeare, a farmer in Snitterfield, a village four miles northeast of Stratford. There is no record of Richard Shakespeare before 1529, but details about his life after this reveal that he was a tenant farmer, who, on occasion, would be fined for grazing too many cattle on the common grounds and for not attending manor court. There is no record of Richard Shakespeare's wife, but together they had two sons, John and Henry. Richard

Shakespeare worked on several different sections of land during his lifetime, including the land owned by the wealthy Robert Arden of Wilmecote, Shakespeare's maternal grandfather. Robert Arden was the son of Thomas Arden of Wilmecote, Shakespeare's maternal great-grandfather, who probably belonged to the aristocratic family of the Arden's of Park Hall. He was catholic and married more than once (we know the name of his second wife — Agnes Hill) and he fathered no fewer than eight daughters. He became the stepfather of Agnes' four children. Robert Arden had accumulated much property, and when he died, he named his daughter (Shakespeare's mother) Mary, only sixteen at the time, one of his executors. He left Mary some money and, in his own words, "all my land in Willmecote cawlide As byes and the crop apone the grounde, sowne and tyllide as hitt is".

SHAKESPEARE'S PARENTS

Shakespeare's father, John, came to Stratford from Snitterfield before 1532 as an apprentice glover and tanner of leathers. John Shakespeare prospered and began to deal in farm products and wool. It is recorded that he bought a house in 1552 (the date that he first appears in the town records), and bought more property in 1556. Because John Shakespeare owned one house on Greenhill Street and two houses on Henley Street, the exact location of William's birth cannot be known. Sometime between 1556 and 1558, John Shakespeare married Mary Arden, the daughter of the wealthy Robert Arden of Wilmecote and owner of the sixty-acre farm called Asbies. The wedding would have most likely taken place in Mary Arden's parish church at Aston Cantlow, the burial place of Robert Arden, and, although there is no evidence of strong piety on either side of the family, it would have been a Catholic service, since Queen Mary I was the reigning monarch.

We assume neither John nor Mary could write — John used a pair of glovers' compasses as his signature while Mary used a running horse — but it did not prevent them from becoming important members of the community. John Shakespeare was elected to a multitude of civic positions, including ale-taster of the borough (Stratford had a long-reaching reputation for its brewing) in 1557, chamberlain of the borough in 1561, alderman in 1565, (a position which came with free education for his children at the Stratford Grammar School), high bailiff, or mayor, in 1568, and chief alderman in 1571. Due to his important civic duties, he rightfully sought the title of gentleman and applied for his coat-of-arms in 1570. However, for unspecific reasons the application was abruptly withdrawn, and within the next few years, for reasons just as mystifying, John Shakespeare would go from wealthy business owner and dedicated civil servant to debtor and absentee council member. By 1578, he was behind in his taxes and stopped paying the statutory aldermanic subscription for poor relief. In 1579, he had to mortgage Mary Shakespeare's estate, Asbies, to pay his creditors. In 1580, he was fined 40 pounds for missing a court date and in 1586, the town removed him from the board of aldermen due to lack of attendance.

By 1590, John Shakespeare owned only his house on Henley Street and, in 1592, he was fined for not attending church. However, near the very end of John Shakespeare's life, it seems that his social and economic standing was again beginning to flourish. He once again applied to the College of Heralds for a coat-of-arms in 1596, and, due likely to the success of William in London, this time his wish was granted. On October 20 of that year, by permission of the Garter King of Arms (the Queen's aid in such matters) "the said John Shakespeare, Gentlemen, and...His children, issue and posterity" were lawfully entitled to display the gold coat-of-arms, with a black banner bearing a silver spear (a visual representation of the family name "Shakespeare").

The coat-of-arms could then be displayed on their door and all their personal items. The motto was "Non sans droict" or "not without right. The reason cited for granting the coat-of-arms was John Shakespeare's grandfather's faithful service to Henry VII, but no specifics were given as to what service he actually performed. The coat-of-arms appears on Shakespeare's tomb in Stratford. In 1599, John Shakespeare was reinstated on the town council, but died a short time later, in 1601. He was probably near seventy years old and he had been married for forty-four years. Mary Shakespeare died in 1608 and was buried on September 9.

SHAKESPEARE'S BIRTH

The baptismal register of the Holy Trinity parish church, in Stratford, shows the following entry for April 26, 1564: Gulielmus filius Johannes Shakespeare. The actual date of Shakespeare's birth is not known, but, traditionally, April 23, St George's Day has been Shakespeare's accepted birthday, and a house on Henley Street in Stratford, owned by William's father, John, is accepted as Shakespeare's birthplace. However, the reality is that no one really knows when the great dramatist was born. According to the Book of Common Prayer, it was required that a child be baptized on the nearest Sunday or holy day following the birth, unless the parents had a legitimate excuse. As Dennis Kay proposes in his book Shakespeare

If Shakespeare were indeed born on Sunday, April 23, the next feast day would have been St. Mark's Day on Tuesday the 25. There might well have been some cause, both reasonable and great — or perhaps, as has been suggested, St. Mark's Day was still held to be unlucky, as it had been before the Reformation, when altars and crucifixes used to be draped in black cloth, and when some claimed to see in the churchyard the spirits of those doomed to die in that year....but that does not help to explain the christening on the twenty-sixth.

No doubt, Shakespeare's true birthday will remain a mystery forever. However, the assumption that the Bard was born on the same day of the month that he died lends an exciting esoteric highlight to the otherwise mundane details of Shakespeare's life.

SHAKESPEARE'S SIBLINGS

William Shakespeare was indeed lucky to survive to adulthood in sixteenth-century England. Waves of the plague swept across the countryside, and pestilence ravaged Stratford during the hot summer months. Mary and John Shakespeare became parents for the first time in September of 1558, when their daughter Joan was born. Nothing is known of Joan Shakespeare except for the fact that she was baptized in Stratford on September 15, and succumbed to the plague shortly after. Their second child, Margaret, was born in 1562 and was baptized on December 2. She died one year later. The Shakespeare's' fourth child, Gilbert, was baptized on October 13, 1566, at Holy Trinity. It is likely that John Shakespeare named his second son after his friend and neighbor on Henley Street, Gilbert Bradley, a glover and the burgess of Stratford for a time. Records show that Gilbert Shakespeare survived the plague and reached adulthood, becoming a haberdasher, working in London as of 1597, and spending much of his time back in Stratford.

In 1609, he appeared in Stratford court in connection with a lawsuit, but we know no details regarding the matter. Gilbert Shakespeare seems to have had a long and successful career as a tradesman, and he died a bachelor in Stratford on February 3, 1612. In 1569, John and Mary Shakespeare gave birth to another girl, and named her after her first-born sister, Joan. Joan Shakespeare accomplished the wondrous feat of living to be seventy-seven years old — outliving William and all her other siblings by decades. Joan married William Hart the hatter and had four children but two of them died in childhood. Her son William Hart (1600-1639) followed in his famous uncle's footsteps and became an actor, performing with the King's Men in the mid-1630s.

His most noted role was that of Falstaff. William Hart never married, but the leading actor of the restoration period, Charles Hart, is believed to have been William Hart's illegitimate son and grandnephew to Shakespeare. Due to the fact that Shakespeare's children and his other siblings did not carry on the line past the seventeenth century, the descendants of Joan Shakespeare Hart possess the only genetic link to the great playwright. Joan Shakespeare lost her husband William a week before she lost her brother William in 1616, and she lived the rest of her life in Shakespeare's birthplace. Joan died in 1646, but her descendants stayed in Stratford until 1806.

Undoubtedly already euphoric that Joan had survived the precarious first few years of childhood, the Shakespeare's' joy was heightened with the birth of their fourth daughter, Anne, in 1571, when William was seven years old. Unfortunately, tragedy befell the family yet again when Anne died at the age of eight. The sorrow felt by the Shakespeare's' over the loss of Anne was profound, and even though they were burdened by numerous debts at the time of her death, they arranged an unusually elaborate funeral for their cherished daughter. Anne Shakespeare was buried on April 4, 1579. In 1574, Mary and John Shakespeare had another boy and they named him Richard, probably after his paternal grandfather. Richard was baptized on March 11 of that year, and nothing else is known about him, except for the fact that he died, unmarried, and was buried on February 4, 1613 — a year and a day after the death of Gilbert Shakespeare.

Mary gave birth to one more child in 1580. They christened him on May 3 and named him Edmund, probably in honour of his uncle Edmund Lambert. Edmund was eager to follow William into the acting profession, and when he was old, enough he joined William in London to embark on a career as a "player". Edmund did not make a great reputation for himself as an actor, but, in all fairness, cruel fate, and not his poor acting abilities, was likely the reason. Edmund died in 1607 — not yet thirty years old. He was buried in St. Savior's Church, in Southwark, on December 31 of that year. His funeral was costly and magnificent, with tolling bells heard across the Thames. It is most likely that William planned the funeral for his younger brother because William would have been the only Shakespeare wealthy enough to afford such an expensive tribute to Edmund. In addition, records show that the funeral was held in the morning, and as Dennis Kay points out, funerals were usually held in the afternoon. It is probable that the morning funeral was arranged so that Shakespeare's fellow actors could attend the burial of Edmund.

SHAKESPEARE'S EDUCATION AND CHILDHOOD

Shakespeare probably began his education at the age of

six or seven at the Stratford grammar school, which is still standing only a short distance from his house on Henley Street and is in the care of the Shakespeare Birthplace Trust. Although we have no record of Shakespeare attending the school, due to the official position held by John Shakespeare it seems likely that he would have decided to educate young William at the school, which was under the care of Stratford's governing body. The Stratford grammar school had been built some two hundred years before Shakespeare was born and in that time the lessons taught there were, of course dictated primarily by the beliefs of the reigning monarch. In 1553, due to a charter by King Edward VI, the school became known as the King's New School of Stratford-upon-Avon. During the years that Shakespeare attended the school, at least one and possibly three headmasters stepped down because of their devotion to the Catholic religion proscribed by Queen Elizabeth. One of these masters was Simon Hunt (b. 1551), who, in 1578, according to tradition, left Stratford to pursue his more spiritual goal of becoming a Jesuit, and relocated to the seminary at Rheims. Hunt had found his true vocation: when he died in Rome seven years later he had raised to the position of Grand Penitentiary.

Like all of the great poets and dramatists of the time, Shakespeare learned his basic reading and writing skills from an ABC, or hornbook. Robert Speight in his book, Shakespeare: The Man and His Achievement, describes this book as

a primer framed in wood and covered with a thin plate of transparent horn. It included the alphabet in small letters and in capitals, with combinations of the five vowels with b, c, and d, and the Lord's Prayer in English. The first of these alphabets, which ended with the abbreviation for 'and' began with the mark of the cross. Hence the alphabet was known as 'Christ cross row' – the cross-row of Richard III, I, i, 55. A short catechism was often included in the ABC book (the 'absey book' of King John, I, i, 196).

In 'The Merry Wives of Windsor', there is a comical scene in which the Welsh headmaster tests his pupil's knowledge, who is appropriately named William. There is little doubt that

Shakespeare was recalling his own experiences during his early school years. As was the case in all Elizabethan grammar schools, Latin was the primary language of learning. Although Shakespeare likely had some lessons in English, Latin composition and the study of Latin authors like Seneca, Cicero, Ovid, Virgil, and Horace would have been the focus of his literary training. One can see that Shakespeare absorbed much that was taught in his grammar school, for he had an impressive familiarity with the stories by Latin authors, as is evident when examining his plays and their sources. Even though scholars, basing their argument on a story told more than a century after the fact, accept that Shakespeare was removed from school around age thirteen because of his father's financial and social difficulties. There is no reason whatsoever to believe that he had not acquired a firm grasp of both English and Latin and that he had continued his studies elsewhere. The famous quotation from Nicholas Rowe's notoriously inaccurate biography of Shakespeare (written in 1709), where he claims that Shakespeare "acquired that little Latin he was Master of" and that Shakespeare was prevented by his father's poor fortune from "further Proficiency in that Language", should be read with an extremely critical eye.

There are other fragmented and dubious details about Shakespeare's life growing up in Stratford. He is supposed to have worked for a butcher, in addition to helping run his father's business. There is a fable that Shakespeare stole a deer from Sir Thomas Lucy at Charlecote, and instead of serving a prison sentence, fled from Stratford. Although this surely is a fictitious incident, a few verses of a humorous ballad mocking Lucy have been connected to Shakespeare. "Edmond Malone records a version of two verses of the Lucy Ballad collected by one of the few great English classical scholars, Joshua Barnes, at Stratford between 1687 and 1690. Barnes stopped overnight at an inn and heard an old woman singing it. He gave her a new gown for the two stanzas which were all she remembered":

Sir Thomas was so covetous
To covet so much deer

When horns enough upon his head
Most plainly did appear
Had not his worship one deer left?
What then? He had a wife
Took pains enough to find him horns
Should last him during life.

Shakespeare's daily activities after he left school and before he re-emerged as a professional actor in the late 1580s are impossible to trace. Suggestions that he might have worked as a schoolmaster or lawyer or glover with his father and brother, Gilbert, are all plausible. So too is the argument that Shakespeare studied intensely to become a master at his literary craft, and honed his acting skills while traveling and visiting playhouses outside of Stratford. However, it is from this period known as the "lost years" that we obtain one vital piece of information about Shakespeare: he married a pregnant orphan named Anne Hathaway.

SHAKESPEARE'S MARRIAGE AND CHILDREN

Recordings in the Episcopal register at Worcester on the dates of November 27 and 28, 1582, reveal that Shakespeare desired to marry a young girl named Anne. There are two different documents regarding this matter, and their contents have raised a debate over just whom Shakespeare first intended to wed. Were there two Anne's? Was Shakespeare in love with one but in lust with the other? Was Shakespeare ready to join in matrimony with the Anne of his dreams only to have an attack of conscience and marry the Anne with whom he had carnal relations? To discuss the controversy properly we should look at the documents in question. The first entry in the register is the following record of the issue of a marriage license to one Wm Shakespeare:

Anno Domini 1582...Novembers...27 die eiusdem mensis. Item eodem die supradicto emanavit Licentia inter Wm Shaxpere et Annam Whateley de Temple Grafton.1

The next entry in the episcopal register records the marriage bond granted to one Wm Shakespeare:

Noverint universi per praesentes nos Fulconem Sandells de Stratford in comitatu Warwici agricolam et Johannem Rychardson ibidem agricolam, teneri et firmiter obligari Ricardo Cosin generoso et Roberto Warmstry notario publico in quadraginta libris bonae et legalis monetae Angliae solvend. eisdem Ricardoet Roberto haered. execute. et assign at. suis ad quam quidem solucionem bene et fideliter faciend. obligamus nos et utrumque nostrum per se pro toto et in solid. haired. executor. et administrator. nostros firmiter per praesentes sigillis nostris sigillat.

Dat. 28 die Novem. Anno regni dominae nostrae Eliz. Dei gratia Angliae Franc. et Hiberniae Reginae fidei defensor &c.25.2 The condition of this obligation is such that if hereafter there shall not appear any lawful let or impediment by reason of any precontract, consanguinuity, affinity or by any other lawful means whatsoever, but that William Shagspere on the one party and Anne Hathwey of Stratford in the diocese of Worcester, maiden, may lawfully solemnize matrimony together, and in the same afterwards remain and continue like man and wife according unto the laws in that behalf provided...

Three possible conclusions can be reached from the above records: 1) The Anne Whateley in the first record and the Anne Hathwey in the second record are the same woman. Some scholars believe that the name Whateley was substituted accidentally for Hathwey into the register by the careless clerk. "The clerk was a nincompoop: he wrote Baker for Barber in his register and Darby for Bradley, and Dock for Lock and Anne Whitely for Anne Hathaway.

A lot of ingenious ink has been spilt over this error, but it is surely a simple one: the name whitely occurs in a tithe appeal by a vicar on the same page of the register; the clerk could not follow his own notes, or he was distracted" Moreover, some believe that the couple selected Temple Grafton as the place for the wedding for reasons of privacy and that is why it is recorded in the register instead of Stratford. 2) The Wm Shaper and the Anna Whateley who wished to marry in Temple Grafton were two different people entirely from the Wm Shagspere and Anne Hathwey who were married in Stratford.

This argument relies on the assumption that there was a relative of Shakespeare's living in Temple Grafton, or a man unrelated but sharing Shakespeare's name (which would be extremely unlikely), and that there is no trace of this relative after the issue of his marriage license. 3) The woman Shakespeare loved and the woman Shakespeare finally married were two different Anne's. Not many critics support this hypothesis, but those that do use it to portray Shakespeare as a young man torn between the love he felt for Anne Whateley and the obligation he felt toward Anne Hathwey and the child she was carrying, which was surely his. In Shakespeare, Anthony Burgess constructs a vivid scenario to this effect:

It is reasonable to believe that Will wished to marry a girl named Anne Whateley. The name is common enough in the Midlands and is even attached to a four-star hotel in Horse Fair, Banbury. Her father may have been a friend of John Shakespeare's, he may have sold kidskin cheap, there are various reasons why the Shakespeare's and the Whateleys, or their nubile children, might become friendly. Sent on skin-buying errands to Temple Grafton, Will could have fallen for a comely daughter, sweet as May and shy as a fawn. He was eighteen and highly susceptible. Knowing something about girls, he would know that this was the real thing. Something, perhaps, quite different from what he felt about Mistress Hathaway of Shottery.

But why, attempting to marry Anne Whateley, had he put himself in the position of having to marry the other Anne? I suggest that, to use the crude but convenient properties of the old women's-magazine morality-stories, he was exercised by love for the one and lust for the other. I find it convenient to imagine that he knew Anne Hathaway carnally, for the first time, in the spring of 1582...

Whichever argument one chooses to accept, it is fact that Shakespeare, a minor at the time, married Anne Hathaway, who was twenty-six and already several months pregnant. Anne was the eldest daughter, and one of the seven children of Richard Hathaway, a twice-married farmer in Shottery. When Richard died in 1581, he requested his son,

Bartholomew, move into the house we now know as Anne Hathaway's Cottage, and maintain the property for his mother, Richard's second wife and Anne's stepmother. Anne lived in the cottage with Bartholomew, her stepmother, and her other siblings. No doubt, she was bombarded with a barrage of household tasks to fill her days at Hew land Farm, as it was then called. After her marriage to Shakespeare, Anne left Hew land Farm to live in John Shakespeare's house on Henley Street, as was the custom of the day. Preparations for the new bride were made, and for reasons unknown, her arrival greatly bothered John Shakespeare's current tenant in the house, William Burbage. A heated fight ensued, and John refused to release Burbage from his lease, so Burbage decided to take the matter to a London court. On July 24, 1582, lawyers representing both sides met and resolved the matter — John would release William Burbage from his lease.

The Shakespeare's' first child was Susanna, christened on May 26, 1583, and twins arrived in January 1585. They were baptized on February 2 of that year and named after two very close friends of William — the baker Hamnet Sadler and his wife, Judith. The Sadlers became the godparents of the twins and, in 1598, they, in turn, named their own son William.

Not much information is known about the life of Anne and her children after this date, except for the tragic fact that Hamnet Shakespeare died of an unknown cause on August 11, 1596, at the age of eleven. By this time, Shakespeare had long since moved to London to realise his dreams on the English stage and we do not know if he was present at Hamnet's funeral in Stratford. We can only imagine how deeply the loss of his only son touched the sensitive poet, but his sorrow is undeniably reflected in his later work, and, particularly, in a passage from King John, written between 1595 and 1597:

> *Young Arthur is my son, and he is lost:*
> *I am not mad: I would to heaven I were!*
> *For then, 'tis like I should forget myself:*
> *O, if I could, what grief should I forget!*

Preach some philosophy to make me mad,
And thou shalt be canonized, cardinal;
For being not mad but sensible of grief,
My reasonable part produces reason
How I may be deliver'd of these woes,
And teaches me to kill or hang myself:
If I were mad, I should forget my son,
Or madly think a babe of clouts were he:
I am not mad; too well, too well I feel
The different plague of each calamity....
I tore them from their bonds and cried aloud
'O that these hands could so redeem my son,
As they have given these hairs their liberty!'
But now I envy at their liberty,
And will again commit them to their bonds,
Because my poor child is a prisoner.
And, father cardinal, I have heard you say
That we shall see and know our friends in heaven:
If that be true, I shall see my boy again;
For since the birth of Cain, the first male child,
To him that did but yesterday suspire,
There was not such a gracious creature born.
But now will canker-sorrow eat my bud
And chase the native beauty from his cheek
And he will look as hollow as a ghost,
As dim and meagre as an ague's fit,
And so he'll die; and, rising so again,
When I shall meet him in the court of heaven
I shall not know him: therefore never, never
Must I behold my pretty Arthur more.

Chapter 3

Shakespeare as Actor and Playwright

We know very little about Shakespeare's life during two major spans of time, commonly referred to as the "lost years." The lost years fall into two periods: 1578-82 and 1585-92. The first period covers the time after Shakespeare left grammar school until his marriage to Anne Hathaway in November of 1582. The second period covers the seven years of Shakespeare's life in which he must have been perfecting his dramatic skills and collecting sources for the plots of his plays. "What could such a genius accomplish in this direction during six or eight years? The histories alone must have required unending hours of labor to gather facts for the plots and counter-plots of these stories. When we think of the time he must have spent in reading about the pre-Tudor dynasties, we are at a loss to estimate what a day's work meant to him.

Perhaps he was one of those singular geniuses who absorb books. George Douglas Brown, when discussing Shakespeare, often used to say he knew how to 'pluck the guts' out of a tome". No one knows for certain how Shakespeare first started his career in the theatre, although several London players would visit Stratford regularly, and so, sometime between 1585 and 1592, it is probable that young Shakespeare could have been recruited by the Leicester's or Queen's men. Whether an acting troupe recruited Shakespeare in his hometown or he was forced on his own to travel to London to begin his career, he was nevertheless an established actor in the great city by the end of 1592. In this year came the first reference to Shakespeare in the world of the theatre. The dramatist Robert Greene declared in his death-bed autobiography that "There is an upstart crow, beautified with our feathers, that with his Tigers heart wrap in a Players hide supposes he is as well able to bombast out a blank verse as the best of you; and, being an absolute Johannes Factotum, is in his own conceit the only Shake-scene in a country." After Green's death, his editor, Henry Chettle, publicly apologized to Shakespeare in the Preface to his Kind-Heart's Dream:

About three months since died M. Robert Greene, leaving many papers in sundry booksellers' hands, among other his Groatsworth of Wit, in which a letter written to divers play-makers is offensively by one or two of them taken, and because on the dead they cannot be avenged, they willfully forge in their conceits a living author....With neither of them that take offence was I acquainted, and with one of them I care not if I never be. The other, whom at that time I did not so much spare as since I wish I had, for that, as I have moderated the heat of living writers and might have used my own discretion (especially in such a case, the author being dead), that I did not I am as sorry as if the original fault had been my fault, because myself have seen his demeanor no less civil than he excellent in the quality he professes. Besides, the divers of worship have reported his uprightness of dealing, which argues his honesty and his facetious grace in writing that approves his art.

Such an apology indicates that Shakespeare was already a respected player in London with influential friends and connections. Records also tell us that several of Shakespeare's plays were popular by this time, including Henry VI, The Comedy of Errors, and Titus Andronicus. The company that staged most of the early productions of these plays was Pembroke's Men, sponsored by the Earl of Pembroke, Henry Herbert. The troupe was very popular and performed regularly at the court of Queen Elizabeth. Most critics conclude that Shakespeare spent time as both a writer and an actor for Pembroke's Men before 1592. The turning point in

Shakespeare's career came in 1593. The theatres had been closed since 1592 due to an outbreak of the plague and, although it is possible that Shakespeare toured the outlying areas of London with acting companies like Pembroke's Men or Lord Strange's Men, it seems more likely that he left the theatre entirely during this time to work on his non-dramatic poetry. The hard work paid off, for by the end of 1593, Shakespeare had caught the attention of the Earl of Southampton.

Southampton became Shakespeare's patron, and on April 18, 1593, Venus and Adonis were entered for publication. Shakespeare had made his formal debut as a poet. The dedication Shakespeare wrote to Southampton at the beginning of the poem is impassioned and telling, "phrased with courtly deference"

To the right Honorable henry wriothesley, eary of southampton, and baron of tichfield.

RIGHT HONORABLE,

I KNOW not how I shall offend in dedicating my unpolished lines to your lordship, nor how the world will censure me for choosing so strong a prop to support so weak a burden only, if your honour seem but pleased, I account myself highly praised, and vow to take advantage of all idle hours, till I have honoured you with some graver labour. But if the first heir of my invention prove deformed, I shall be sorry it had so noble a god-father, and never after ear so barren a land, for fear it yield me still so bad a harvest.

I leave it to your honourable survey, and your honour to your heart's content; which I wish may always answer your own wish and the world's hopeful expectation.

Your honour's in all duty,

Although there is no concrete proof that Shakespeare had a long and close friendship with Southampton, most scholars agree that this was the case, based on Shakespeare's writings, particularly the early sonnets.

Shakespeare returned to the theatre in 1594, and became a leading member of the Lord Chamberlain's Men, formally known as Lord Strange's Men. The manuscript account of the treasurer of the royal chamber in the public records office tells us the following:

To William Kempe, William Shakespeare, and Richard Burbage, servants to the Lord Chamberlain, upon the council's warrant dated at Whitehall xv die March 1594 for two several comedies or interludes showed by them before her Majesty in Christmas time last past, viz; upon St. Stephan's day and Innocent's day, xiiij li. vj s. viij d. and by way of her Majesty's reward...

This is proof that Shakespeare had performed with the Chamberlain's Men before Elizabeth I on several occasions. As payment for their performance, the actors each received 10 pounds. During his time with the Chamberlain's Men Shakespeare wrote many plays, including Romeo and Juliet, Richard II, King John, and Love's Labour's Lost. As G.E. Bentley points out in Shakespeare and the Theatre, Shakespeare had by this time become immersed in his roles as actor and writer. He was "more completely and more continuously involved in theatres and acting companies than any other Elizabethan dramatist. [Shakespeare is] "the only one known who not only wrote plays for his company, acted in the plays, and shared the profits, but who was also one of the housekeepers who owned the building. For seventeen years he was one of the owners of the Globe theatre and for eight years he was one of the housekeepers of the company's second theatre, the Black friars, as well". During the years Shakespeare performed with the Chamberlain's Men, before their purchase of the Globe in 1599, they played primarily at the well-established theatres like the Swan, the Curtain, and the Theatre. The troupe would also give regular performances before Elizabeth I and her court, and tour the surrounding areas of London. Some important events in Shakespeare's personal life also take place during this period. The Shakespeare has finally received a coat of arms 1596 (see "Shakespeare's Parents" for more information on the coat-of-arms), and on August 11 of the same year, Shakespeare's son, Hamnet, died at the age of eleven. Shakespeare no doubt returned to Stratford for the burial, although we have no documented proof. In 1597, Shakespeare purchased the second largest house in Stratford: New Place. The house stood at the corner of Chapel Lane and Chapel Street, north of the Guild Chapel and right across from the very school he attended in his youth. He bought it from William Underhill for the low price of 60 pounds. And below is the actual deed transferring New Place from Underhill to Shakespeare on May 4, 1597.

Between William Shakespeare, complainant, and William Underhill, deforciant [wrongful occupier, supposed by the legal fiction on which the fine method of transfer was based to be keeping the complainant out of his rightful property], concerning one dwelling house, two barns, and two gardens with their appurtenances in Stratford-on-Avon, in regard to which a plea of agreement was broached in the same court: Namely, that the said William Underhill acknowledged the said tenements with their appurtenances to be the right of W. Shakespeare as being those which the same William Shakespeare has by gift of the said W. U., and remitted and waived claim to them from himself and his heirs to the said W.S. and his heirs forever....and agreement the same W.S. has given the foresaid W./U. sixty pounds sterling.

Many theorize that Shakespeare renewed his interest in Stratford only after the death of Hamnet and that, for the many years he was away in London, he neglected his family back home. However, it is just as likely that he made frequent yet unrecorded trips to Stratford while he was trying to find success in London.

SHAKESPEARE'S FELLOW ACTORS

Richard Burbage (b.1567 d.1619)

Richard Burbage is considered to be the first great actor in the English theatre. He was the son of James Burbage, the theatrical entrepreneur who built "the Theatre" in Shore ditch on the outskirts of London, and the brother of another famous actor of the day, Cuthbert Burbage. Richard Burbage achieved success as performer by the age of 20 and during his career, he appeared in plays by Jonson, Kyd, Beaumont and Fletcher, and John Webster. He also played many of the major Shakespearean characters, including Othello, Hamlet, Lear, and Richard III. "It is likely that Richard III was the most popular of all Shakespeare's plays with the Elizabethan public; it provided a superlative part for Burbage". Legend tells us that a woman fell in love with Burbage when she saw him play Richard III and begged him to come to her chambers that night under the name of King Richard. But Shakespeare overheard the proposition and, as a joke, left the theatre early to take Burbage's place. Shakespeare was 'at his game ere Burbage came. Then, message being brought that Richard III was at the door, Shakespeare caused return to be made that "William the Conqueror" was before Richard III". Early in his career Burbage probably would have been a member of both Lord Strange's Men and the Admiral's Men. Both companies performed at James Burbage's Theatre between 1590 and 1591. We do know that Burbage was a member of the Chamberlain's Men after 1594 and stayed with the group through its evolution into the King's Men in 1603. Although his last recorded performance was in 1610, he remained with the King's Men until his death in 1619.

In addition to acting, Richard Burbage was also an entrepreneur much like his father. When James Burbage died in 1597, he left the Theatre to Richard and his brother. Together they disassembled the Theatre and built the Globe in 1599. The Burbages kept half the shares in the new theatre and the rest were assigned equally to Shakespeare and other members of the Chamberlain's Men. James Burbage also left another theatre to Richard - the Blackfriars Theatre. Richard Burbage leased it to an acting company called the Children of the Chapel, but, after they could not make the payments, Burbage bought back the lease with his brother and four new partners from the King's Men - Shakespeare, Henry Condell, William Sly, and John Heminge. Richard Burbage was also a wonderful painter. Some believe that the anonymous oil painting of Burbage seen above is actually a self-portrait, and he has often been credited with painting the Chandos portrait of Shakespeare, seen on the right. Burbage's skills as an artist were often in demand. With Shakespeare as his partner, providing the commemorative words, Burbage designed an impresa, or personal badge, for the Earl of Rutland (1578-1632). The badge was to be worn on the Earl's shield at a tournament on March 24, 1613 to honour James I. When Shakespeare died in 1616, he left his dear friend Burbage money to buy a mourning-ring in his memory. Burbage died on March 9, 1619, and "the true sound of Shakespeare's lines, as he had conceived them [and] Burbage had interpreted them, was silenced forever".

William Kempe (b.1560 d.1603)

William Kempe was one of the most beloved clowns in the Elizabethan theatre. Records tell us that Kempe was an actor with Leicester's Men on a tour of the Netherlands and Denmark in 1585-86. By 1593, Kempe was a member of Strange's Men, and theatregoers and fellow actors were beginning to recognize his comedic talent. Thomas Nashe declared him the successor to the great Elizabethan performer, Richard Tarlton. Kempe joined the Chamberlain's Men in 1594 and acted in many of Shakespeare's plays. He was the original portrayer of Dogberry in Much Ado about Nothing, Peter in Romeo and Juliet, and possibly Falstaff. He also likely played Lancelot Gobbo in The Merchant of Venice and Bottom in A Midsummer Night's Dream. However, it appears that Kempe suddenly left the Chamberlain's Men in 1599. The reason for his departure is not documented, although many believe that he was asked to leave due to his chronic improvising, and that Shakespeare referred to this in Hamlet:

And let those that play
your clowns speak no more than is
set down for them;
for there be of them that will themselves laugh, to
set on some quantity of barren spectators to laugh
too.

Once Kempe left the troupe, Shakespeare's comic characters changed dramatically, indicating that earlier parts were written to fit Kempe's unique style. Examining Shakespeare's changes provides us with even more information about Kempe's stage presence. "He was a big man who specialized in Plebian clowns who spoke in earthly language...Kempe's characters have a tendency to confuse and mispronounce their words, and contemporary references to his dancing and ability to "make a scurvy face" suggest a physical brand of humour."Now finished with Shakespeare's troupe and looking for another way to entertain the people of London, Kempe planned a wild publicity stunt. In 1600, he danced a morris dance from London to Norwich, almost 100 miles north. He wrote his own account of the event called Kempe's Nine Days Wonder, and the picture above is from the cover of the original copy. Kempe returned to acting in 1601 when he left England to tour Europe. When he arrived home in 1602 he joined Worchester's Men, but he disappears from the records shortly after. Some scholars conclude that he died from the 1603 plague in London - the year of one of the largest outbreaks of the disease during Shakespeare's life.

Chapter 4

William Shakespeare – Timeline

1564	Born in Stratford-upon-Avon to tanner and glove maker, John Shakespeare and his wife, Mary. His actual birthday is unknown but assumed to be April the 23 rd. His baptism was recorded in the Parish register of Holy Trinity Church on April the 26th.	
1571	If Shakespeare went to school this is when he would have started because children in Stratford began their schooling at the age of seven. He would have gone to the local grammar school.	
1582	Shakespeare marries Anne Hathaway November the 27th at Temple Grafton, a village near Stratford.	
1583	Susanna, his first child is born	
1585	Judith and Hamnet, twins, are born, February 2 nd. Shakespeare goes to London and starts his theatrical career.	
1589-92	Shakespeare establishes his career and begins to make a name for himself.	Henry VI, 1,2,3 The Comedy of Errors Titus

		Andronicus The Taming of the Shrew Richard III
1593	Dedicates *Venus and Adonis* and *The Rape of Lucrece* to Henry Wriothsley, Earl of Southampton - thought to be the beautiful youth of the Sonnets,	1593 Venus and Adonis Begins writing the Sonnets Two Gentlemen of Verona Love's Labour's Lost
1594	Founding member of the Lord Chamberlain's Men , an acting company.	The Rape of Lucrece (published)
1596-97	Hamnet dies 1597 Shakespeare purchases New Place, a large house in Stratford, 1597.	A Midsummer Night's Dream Romeo and Juliet Richard II Merchant of Venice
1597-99	The Globe Theater built on Bankside 1599. Shakespeare is a shareholder.	Henry IV,1,2 The Merry Wives ofWindsor As You Like It Much Ado About Nothing Henry V Julius Caesar
1600-08	The Great Tragedies 1601 Shakespeare's father dies 1603 The Lord Chamberlain's Men become The King's Men and perform regularly at court. 1607 Susanna Shakespeare marries Dr. John Hall 1608 The King's Men begin playing at the Blackfriars 1608 Shakespeare's mother dies.	Twelfth Night Hamlet Troilus & Cressida Alls Well That Ends Well Measure for Measure Othello King Lear Macbeth Antony and Clepatra Coriolanus Timon of Athens

1609-16	1609 the Sonnets published. The Romances	Pericles Prince of Tyre Cymbeline The Winter's Tale The Tempest
1612-16	Shakespeare retires from the theatre and returns to live in Stratford. Works on new plays with his friend, John Fletcher 1616 Judith Shakespeare married Thomas Quiney.	Henry VIII The Two Noble Kinsmen Cardenio
1616	Shakespeare dies 23 rd April (on his birthday) and is buried in Holy Trinity Church.	

Chapter 5

William Shakespeare: List of Works

Comedy

- All's Well That Ends Well
- As You Like It
- The Comedy of Errors
- Cymbeline
- Love's Labours Lost
- Measure for Measure
- The Merry Wives of Windsor
- The Merchant of Venice
- A Midsummer Night's Dream
- Much Ado About Nothing
- Pericles, Prince of Tyre
- Taming of the Shrew
- The Tempest
- Troilus and Cressida
- Twelfth Night
- Two Gentlemen of Verona
- Winter's Tale

History

- Henry IV, part 1
- Henry IV, part 2
- Henry V
- Henry VI, part 1
- Henry VI, part 2
- Henry VI, part 3
- Henry VIII
- King John
- Richard II
- Richard III

Tragedy

- Antony and
- Cleopatra
- Coriolanus
- Hamlet
- Julius Caesar
- King Lear
- Macbeth
- Othello
- Romeo and Juliet
- Timon of Athens
- Titus Andronicus

Poetry

- The Sonnets
- A Lover's
- Complaint
- The Rape of
- Lucrece
- Venus and Adonis
- Funeral Elegy by W.S.

Chapter 6

Important Aspects of Elizabethan Drama

The Elizabethan Age in the world occurred in the sixteenth and seventeenth century in England. It is named for Queen Elizabeth, who is known mainly for her love of religion of the arts. The Elizabethan Age was most influential through its drama.

The Elizabethan Age in England showered the world with a burst of brilliant playwrights. Four of the most well known of early Elizabethan playwrights were John Lyly, Thomas Kyd, Robert Greene, and Christopher Marlowe. John Lyly's most famous work is "Endimion, Man in Moon." Thomas Kyd is the author of "Spanish Tragedy." Robert Greene is best known for "Friar Bacon Friar Bungay." Many people think that Christopher Marlowe was the greatest of early Elizabethan writers. His most well known play is "Doctor Faustus." This play is about a man named Faustus who sells his soul to the devil in exchange for power on earth. Christopher Marlowe was born shortly before William Shakespeare.

He was supposed to be a shoemaker. The Archbishop of Canterbury offered him a scholarship to Cambridge University, but Christopher avoided becoming shoemaker to enter the theater. He started writing plays for an acting company called the Admiral's Men. His major literary works were tragedies, as lots of Elizabethan dramas were. Other than "Doctor Faustus", his other two greatest works were "Tamburlaine" and "Jew of Malta." Marlowe's major literary achievements are the use of refined blank verse, spiritual drama, dramatic action, and the Renaissance hero. He loved learning and hated ignorance. This was apparent in many of his literary works. Marlowe was a friend of Sir Walter Raleigh and a favourite of Queen Elizabeth, even though records show that Marlowe was not gentleman. Christopher Marlowe's roommate accused him of atheism and treason, which were crimes in that time. Records show that he was involved in two tavern brawls. In one of the brawls, a man lost his life. In the other brawl, Marlowe was stabbed in the eye. He died three days later. Conspiracy has been suspected about his death. Marlowe, Lyly, Kyd, Greene are known as the University Wits. They defined the London Theater.

William Shakespeare wrote in the middle of the Elizabethan Period, and he is the most famous writer in the era; maybe the greatest of all time. His plays have very good plots, characterization, and backgrounds. Other than tragedy, which was the most common drama of the time, Shakespeare wrote great comedies, tragicomedies, and histories. His characters come alive, and they are admired and even envied by people. His plots are full of action. "Hamlet" was the most popular of his tragedies. Shakespeare's most successful comedy was "A Midsummer Night's Dream." Perhaps his most famous tragicomedy was "The Tempest". "Richard III" and Henry V" are two of Shakespeare's histories that have been made into motion pictures. Shakespeare combined the best aspects of Elizabethan drama with classic drama. This enriched his imagination and humour. The age of Shakespeare was a great time in English history.

There are many important events that occurred during the Elizabethan Period. In approximately 1477, Caxton set up a printing press, and he printed the first books in England. Around 1500, "Everyman", a morality play, was written and performed. In 1533, John Heywood's "The Play of the Weather" was performed. A poetry collection called "Tottle's Miscellany" was published in 1557. This work included Wyatt and Surrey's sonnets. Besides drama, the sonnet is the epitome of literature in the Elizabethan period. In 1564, William

Shakespeare and Christopher Marlowe were born. "The Theatre", the first permanent structure for plays in England, was constructed in 1576. Christopher Marlowe directed his first play, "Tamburlaine", in 1587. In 1590, Shakespeare directed his first play, "The Comedy of Errors." Christopher Marlowe wrote "The Jew of Malta"a year later. He was killed in 1593. Shakespeare wrote "The Merchant of Venice" in 1597. In 1599, the Globe Theater was constructed. Shakespeare wrote "Macbeth" in 1605. He died in 1616.

Another very important aspect of Elizabethan Drama was the audiences. The audiences were always large and very excited at plays. The common people paid an equivalent to one penny to sit in the front of the theater. Unless it was raining, these people had the best seats in the theater. The audience would participate in the play by cheering, hissing, or even throwing rotten vegetables. The audience would know that plays were about to be performed by a flag that rose over the theater.

The theater played an important role in this era. Without theaters, there would be nowhere for the play to be performed. There were two types of theaters: indoor and outdoor. Outdoor theaters were public theaters. "The Theatre" is an example of an outdoor theater. Indoor theaters were private theaters.

Elizabethan Actors were all male. Females were not allowed to act in the theater. All female parts were played by men whose voices had not changed yet. Actors had to have good memories, strong voices, and the ability to fence. Actors also had to have the ability to sing and dance. The costumes that the actors wore were very elaborate, but not historic.

Many special effects were used in the theater. Death scenes were very gory and realistic. To show an eye falling out, a grape would fall to the floor. Animal organs were used to show scenes where organs fell out of actors' bodies.

The stage was the centre of the theater. It had several levels. The lowest level of the stage was used for a number of things. Devils, ghosts, graves, and ditched are a few of them. The second level was the main stage. This is where the most important scenes were. The third level of the stage was a balcony. It was used for a number of things such as mountains or city walls. The fourth level of the stage was a series of pulleys where angels, birds, and thunderbolts could be sent down from the main stage. The highest level was a room where the musicians were.

There is one aspect of Elizabethan Drama that still remains a mystery. Vocabulary in the Elizabethan Era was very different than it is now. Modern historians are not sure about all of the word meanings. This is why some of the phrases used are hard to understand.

Elizabethan Drama is a very important addition to the literature world and to England. Drama is part of England's heritage, and helps make them who they are.

The most important aspects of Elizabethan Drama are is playwrights, events, audiences, theaters, actors, speech, special effects, and the stage. These things make it up, and help keep it alive. Elizabethan Drama is very important in literature.

Chapter 7

The History of the Globe Theater

History of Elizabethan London Theaters - including the Globe Theatre

The first proper theater as we know it was called the Theatre, built at Shoreditch, London in 1576 and the owner was James Burbage. James Burbage had obtained a 21 year lease with permission to build the first playhouse, aptly named ' The Theatre '. Before this time plays were performed in the courtyard of inns or inn-yards, or sometimes, in the houses of noblemen or in extreme circumstances on open ground. After the Theatre, further open-air playhouses (theaters) opened in the London area, including the Rose Theatre (1587), and the Hope Theatre (1613). The most famous Elizabethan playhouse (theater) was the Globe Theatre (1599) built by the company in which Shakespeare had a stake - now often referred to as the Shakespearean Globe. The full history of the Elizabethan Theater with all its theaters, playhouses and inn-yards is available by clicking the Elizabethan Theatre link, which provides comprehensive information about Elizabethan Inn-Yards, Theaters and Playhouses.

THE LEASE OF THE ' THEATRE ' EXPIRES

The 21 year lease for the ground upon which The Theatre had been built was due to expire at the end of 1597. The ground landlord of The Theater was called Giles Allen. A grasping man, he disapproved of theatrical productions, the theatre in general, and raised the price of the lease of The Theatre to an exorbitant level. The troupe failed to agree new terms and when the lease of The Theatre finally expired, the Chamberlain's men were forced to move to The Curtain Theater, another public playing house near The Theatre. All attempts to negotiate the new tenancy and lease agreement of The Theatre failed and Giles Allen planned to pull down the Theatre and capitalize on the building materials. But Burbage found a clause in their former lease allowing them to dismantle the Theatre building. The players decided to pull down The Theatre and transport the timber to a new Theater site on Bankside in Southwark. The work of demolishing the Theatre and transporting the timber across the River Thames was noisily undertaken by the Acting Troupe themselves. Giles Allen was absolutely furious. A new theatre would be built learning from both the mistakes and successes of the original ' Theatre '. The new theater was called The Globe.

THE GLOBE THEATER, BANKSIDE IN SOUTHWARD, LONDON

The Globe, built by carpenter Peter Smith and his workers, was the most magnificent theater that London had ever seen and built in 1597 -1598. This theatre could hold several thousand people! The Globe Theatre didn't just show plays. It was also reputed to be a brothel and gambling house. It was situated on the South bank of the river Thames in Southward. The old Globe Theatre was a magnificent amphitheatre, as shown in the picture at the top of the page. Maps of London clearly show the architecture of the Globe Theatre, and these have enabled an approximate picture of the old Globe Theatre to be drawn. Not one inside picture of the old Globe Theatre is in existence, however, a picture of another amphitheatre, the Swan, has survived. The amphitheatres were similar in design, so the picture of the Swan Theatre can be used a good guide to the structure of the old Globe.

THE GLOBE THEATER IS A HUGE SUCCESS

The Globe Theatre was a huge success and as it had been built in close proximity to the Bear Garden. The profits of the Bear Garden slumped and in 1614, Henslowe and Edward

Alleyn (the most famous actor in Elizabethan England) had it demolished and replaced with a new playhouse, which they called The Hope Theatre (aptly named!). Edward Alleyn returned to the stage in an attempt to lure the crowds from The Globe Theatre.

THE GLOBE THEATER - THE PLAYS

Plays were big! There was money to be made! There was a constant demand for new material! Rivalry between the Theatres Playhouses was enormous! As soon as a play had been written it was immediately produced - printing followed productions! So the actors initially used 'foul papers' or prompts. Rival theater companies would send their members to attend plays to produce unauthorized copies of plays - notes were made and copied as quickly as possible. In Shakespeare's time, copyright did not exist.

Alternative versions of Shakespearean plays were produced! These unauthorized and inferior text copies of Shakespeare's plays are called Quarto Texts. The success of the Elizabethan theaters, including the Globe, was such that other forms of Elizabethan entertainment were being seriously affected. In 1591, the growing popularity of theatres led to a law closing all theaters on Thursdays so that the bull and bear bating industries would not be neglected!

THE GLOBE THEATER - THE EVENT

Days out at the Globe Theater would have been an exciting event. The grounds surrounding the Globe Theater would have been bustling with people. There would be Stalls selling merchandise and refreshments creating a market day atmosphere. Non-playgoers would flock to the Globe Theater to go to the market stalls and 'soak in ' the holiday-like atmosphere. The Globe would have particularly attracted young people and the were many complaints of apprentices avoiding work in order to go to the theater. A trumpet was sounded to announce to people that the play was about to begin at the Globe Theatre in order for people to take their final places.

ELIZABETHAN ADVERTISING

Towering above the Globe was a small tower with a flagpole. Flags were used as a form of Elizabethan Advertising! Flags were erected on the day of the performance, which sometimes displayed a picture advertising the next play to be performed. Colour-coding was also used - a black flag meant a tragedy, white a comedy and red a history. Elizabethan and Shakespearean Advertising

THE GLOBE THEATRE'S CREST AND MOTTO

To announce the arrival of the new playhouse, the Lord Chamberlain's Men flew a flag featuring the figure of Hercules carrying a Globe on his shoulders to announce the imminent performance of their first performance, Julius Caesar. This theme was displayed above the main entrance of the Globe Theater. A crest displaying Hercules bearing the globe on his shoulders together with the motto "Totus mundus

agit histrionem" (the whole world is a playhouse). This phrase was slightly re-worded in the William Shakespeare play As You Like It - "All the world's a stage" which was performed at the Globe Theater.

THE GLOBE THEATER - THE PRODUCTIONS

The purpose built Globe theatre allowed stage productions to become quite sophisticated with the use of massive props such as fully working canons, although it would of course had to be left on stage for the entire performance of the play. Special effects at the Globe were also a spectacular addition at the theater allowing for smoke effects, the firing of a real canon, fireworks (for dramatic battle scenes) and spectacular 'flying' entrances from the rigging in the 'heavens'. The stage floor had trap doors allowing for additional surprising incidents. Music was another addition to the Globe productions. It was no wonder that the Globe Theater and this form of Elizabethan entertainment were so popular. The sight of Shakespearean actors apparently flying must have been quite amazing to the discerning Elizabethan Theater audiences.

THE GLOBE THEATER - THE ACTORS

The Globe Theater audience never had time to get bored. In just two weeks, Elizabethan theaters could often present "eleven performances of ten different plays". The Shakespearean Actors generally only got their lines as the play was in progress. Parts were often allocated on the day of the performance. Many times the actors didn't even get their own lines. They did "cue acting ", which meant that there was a person backstage who whispered the lines to the actor just before he was going to say them. This rapid turnover led to another technique called "cue scripting", where each actor was given only his own lines. The complete scene of the play was not explained to the actors until it was actually being performed. This technique allowed for zero rehearsal time, thus enabling a fast turnover in terms of new productions at the Globe Theater and a huge portfolio of different roles. There were no actresses. Female characters had to be played by young boys. The acting profession was not a credible one and it was unthinkable that any woman would appear in a play. Two of the most notable actors of the Elizabethan era were Edward Alleyn and Will Kempe. Edward Alleyn became immensely wealthy due to stake holding in a theatre company (the Admiral's men).

THE GLOBE THEATER AUDIENCES

The Elizabethan general public (the Commoners) referred to, as groundlings would pay 1 penny to stand in the 'Pit' of the Globe Theater. The gentry would pay to sit in the galleries often using cushions for comfort! Rich nobles could watch the play from a chair set on the side of the Globe stage itself. Theatre performances were held in the afternoon, because, of course, there was no artificial lighting. Men and women attended plays, but often the prosperous women would wear a mask to disguise their identity.

The plays were extremely popular and attracted vast audiences to the Globe. The audiences only dropped during outbreaks of the bubonic plague, which was unfortunately an all too common occurrence during the Elizabethan era. This happened in 1593, 1603 and 1608 when all theaters were closed due to the Bubonic Plague (The Black Death). The Shakespearean actors were therefore temporary out of work and left London to stay in other parts of England. William Shakespeare no doubt used these periods of closure to write more plays and go home to Stratford.

THE 'BOX OFFICE'

Globe audiences had to put one penny in a box by the door, which would pay for a view of the play by standing on the ground, in front of the stage. To sit on the first gallery would cost another penny in the box, which was held by a collector on the front of the stairs. To sit on the second gallery, you put another penny in the box held by the man at the second flight of stairs. Then when the show started, the men went and put the boxes in a room backstage - the Elizabethan box office. Profits there were shared between members of the Globe company as such and the owners of the theatre (called "housekeepers"), who included the James and his son the actor Richard Burbage and five others, one of them was William Shakespeare. Shakespeare received approximately 10% of the profit although he had a 20% stake holding in the troupe, as James Burbage owned the lease for the land that the Globe Theater was built on.

SHAKESPEARE THE ACTOR

William Shakespeare had a stake holding in the Globe Theatre and also acted in some of the productions of the plays. It is not known exactly how many roles Shakespeare played himself, although we do have some documented information. Shakespeare had began his career on the stage by 1592, because there is a surviving document by Robert Greene' Groatsworth. It is probable that Shakespeare played the title role in Edward I (a play by Edward Peele) in 1593. It is also assumed that Shakespeare played smaller roles in a variety of his own plays, including As You Like It (Adam), Macbeth (King Duncan), Henry IV (King Henry), and Hamlet (Hamlet's father). Shakespeare's first biographer, Nicholas Rowe, referring to a role by William Shakespeare as "the Ghost in his own Hamlet" and was "the top of his performance".

PLAYS AND PROPAGANDA

Strolling players of actors had been popular for centuries in England but as there were no initial regulations it was possible to use plays as a vehicle for propaganda. Plays could be used to encourage criticism of the state and freedom of thought in terms of both religion and politics. Queen Elizabeth, ever concerned about her popularity with the people, realised that although it would be prudent to enforce some regulations that it would be foolhardy to apply too many restrictions. She had controlled the troupes of strolling players in 1572 by granting a license by royal patent to organized acting companies, thus initiating legitimate troupes such as Earl of Leicester's Men. Any Elizabethan players might at any time be required to show their credentials.

And under Queen Elizabeth, political and religious subjects were forbidden on the stage. Plays still however often led to heated debates in the theaters and arguments erupted. The subject matter of the plays would often be vulgar and bawdy. The behaviour of some the audience was the worse! The theatres didn't just show plays. Some also served as a bear pit, brothel and gambling house. Crime increased at the theaters and following the performances, the crowds were noisy and unruly. The vast crowds and the popularity of the London Theaters needed some additional controls. Published plays soon required a license, which provided a form of censorship by the state.

THE THEATERS ARE BANNED FROM LONDON CITY LIMITS

The objections to the theaters escalated and the Church, London Officials and respectable citizens raised even more objections to the theatres. Theaters were not only used to show plays. There was gambling and in some there was even bear baiting. Not only were there objections about the bawdy nature of some of the plays, the rise in crime but there was also the real risk of the crowded theatres encouraging the spread of the plague. The reputation of actors was remained disreputable, a legacy from the rogues and vagabonds who had previously roamed the country putting on plays and their classification as "vagabonds and sturdy beggars," in a 1572 act of Parliament. In December 1574, the Common Council of London, under the influences of puritanical factions, issued a statement describing:

" great disorder rampant in the city by the inordinate haunting of great multitudes of people, especially youth, to plays, interludes, namely occasion of frays and quarrels, evil practices of incontinency in great inns having chambers and secret places adjoining to their open stages and galleries, inveigling and alluring of maids, especially of orphans and good citizens' children under age, to privy and unmeet contracts, the publishing of unchaste, uncomely, and unshamefast speeches and doings... uttering of popular, busy, and seditious matters, and many other corruptions of youth and other enormities... [Thus] from henceforth no play, comedy, tragedy, interlude, not public show shall be openly played or showed within the liberties of the City... and that no innkeeper, tavernkeeper, nor other person whatsoever within the liberties of this City shall openly show or play... any interlude, comedy, tragedy, matter, or show which shall not be first perused and allowed... "

The outcry continued and grew so much that in 1596 London's authorities banned the public presentation of plays and all theaters within the city limits of London. All theaters located in the City were forced to move to the South side of the River Thames.

THE GLOBE THEATER - THE FIRE AND THE RE-BUILDING OF THE GLOBE THEATRE

The Globe was only in use until 1613, when on June 29 a fire broke out at the Globe Theatre. The canon used for special affects, such as heralding great entrances, was loaded with gunpowder and wadding. The thatched roof caught on fire and the Globe Theatre burned to the ground. It is not known whether there were any casualties but there must have been some panic. In 1614, the Globe Theatre was rebuilt (referred to as Globe 2).

THE END OF THE GLOBE THEATER - THE PURITANS

In 1642, under the force of the Puritans, the English Parliament issued an ordinance suppressing all stage plays in the theatres. The Puritans were a religious faction and the term came into general usage at the end of the reign of Queen Mary I (Bloody Mary). A broad definition of the puritans is 'those who wanted to completely change the Church of England, with its Roman Catholic type of structure and traditions, for another reformed and plain church model'. This strict religious view spread to encompass many social activities within England moving to a stricter code of conduct, which deplored any kind of finery or flippant behaviours. .

1642 was a truly eventful year for England. The Puritans, lead by Oliver Cromwell, who had been elected to Parliament came into total conflict with the Royalists lead by King Charles I. The English Civil war broke out. In 1644, the Puritans demolished the Globe Theatre. In 1647, even stricter rules were passed regarding stage plays and theatres. This culminated in 1648 when all playhouses were ordered to be pulled down. All players were to be seized and whipped, and anyone caught attending a play to be fined five shillings.

In 1649, the Civil War finally leads to the terrible execution of King Charles I. In 1653, Oliver Cromwell becomes Lord Protector of England. In 1658, Cromwell dies and the power of the Puritan starts to decline. In 1660, King Charles II is restored to the throne of England. With the Restoration of the English monarchy and, and the demise in the power of the Puritans in 1660 the theatres finally open again. But the Globe is never re-built. Please click the appropriate link to access a.

TIMELINE OF THE OLD GLOBE THEATRE.

The site of the old Globe theatre was rediscovered in the 20th century and a reconstruction of a New Globe Theatre has been built near the spot.

Chapter 8

William Shakespeare and Existentialism

One may find it ridiculous to contrast between Shakespeare and existentialism in its 20th century form, however one must keep in mind, that existentialism does not appear as a single philosophical system. It is more an attitude of life, a General vision - existentialist Jean-Paul Sartre is known to have stated that existentialism was never invented, it has always existed as the ultimate foundation. Upon that light, why not seek the foundations from the work of the forefather of all dramatists?

It is above all naïve to claim Prospero's epilogue in Shakespeare's play The Tempest a mere conventional appeal for applause or the stripping of the imaginary glamour built up by the plays magic. Even the greatest of artists would rather give away his life than surrender his art to be judged solely by the public. Art for an artistic genius is practiced for its own sake, art for the purpose of art. Existence for the sake of existence itself - stripped of meaning, of value and of subjective interpretation. In its bear meaningless form, something still remains the necessary Natural Law, a philosophical concept considered the basis of human well-being, a system of the values that determine human existence.

Throughout The Tempest Prospero's character portrays an image of a nearly Nietzchean superhuman capable of disclaiming authority, killing God. He is in control of every situation and event as if the chain of causes and effects would be a conductible melody waiting for an artist's touch. On the other hand, he is very human: a wronged duke and a father, a symbiosis which Shakespeare displayed with the use of Prospero's garment as a theatrical tool. An artist is the creator, the maker of realities yet he remains human, an animal with feelings and urges, ties only waiting to be cut. The view implied is not far from the ideologies that emerged from the great suffering of the second world war: a man is capable of constructing himself a framework of personal and social meaning, but his true animal nature remains unchanged. In the heart of existence, life has no predefined meaning, it is a mere passage of survival from necessary birth to necessary death. Prospero's and his daughter's situation on the island was hopeless, however Prospero had chosen a function for his life - revenge.

Prospero created a meaning for his life, built a synthetic reality to keep him sane on the path towards the finality of human death. Early existentialism begins to appear.

The literatory image behind The Epilogue of The Tempest greatly involves the attitude and interpretation of art. Having constructed a window or more or less a door to an imaginary world for the audience, Shakespeare has succeeded in fusing art and reality. Upon that light, it is incomprehensible to assume his need to address the subjective yet neutral third party, the audience - shatter the synthetic reality. However, The Epilogue is a beautiful and humble ending to a story filled with strong magical elements - the control is given to the audience, they are given Prospero's magical garment. The passive third party is given a choice of interaction, chance to rise beyond spectatorship. An interesting aspect to The Epilogue of The Tempest is the fact that it was Shakespeare's last play - the final words of a great artist. Due to the lack of historically trustworthy biographical information of Shakespeare's character, it is difficult if not impossible to determine the effect of his life situation to the message itself. Whether justified or not, The Epilogue seems like a farewell a humble artist handing over his life to the audience to which he has dedicated his entire life.

When examining The Epilogue with the restriction of intertextuality, one is forced to focus on the character of Prospero. Why does he leave a farewell, why does he become the ultimate link from the world of the play to the world of the third party, the audience. His importance as the narrator of The Epilogue creates a third dimension to his character traits, he becomes the God-figure that seems limited to living on an island yet he can

Perform metaphysical leaps between dimensions. The person speaking is the author himself, for in his art he has become God.

Rhythmically and structurally, The Epilogue follows the same style and pattern as the entire play, rich in Rhyme and in wording. The passage can be more or less distinctly separated into three equal parts. However, every detail gives space for wide interpretation.

Now my charms are all o'erthrown, / And what strength I have's mine own, Whish is most faint: now, 'tis true, / I must be here confin'd by you, Or sent to Naples. Let me not, / Since I have my dukedom got, The main structure of The Epilogue can be interpreted as the passage of a life. First the narrator enters the game of existence, appears from the womb: "And what strength I have's my own." As strongly claimed by Jean-Paul Sartre's metaphysics, birth to a person is a subjectively chosen process, emerged from the "charms" that are now, after birth "all o'erthrown". Using the presented division birth is followed by life itself, a search for a meaning and true freedom: "But release me from my bands." The narrator realises his situation on the island of life, in the world derived of meaning and purpose. He wants to be released from his misery - the only way he can achieve that is making his life worthwhile - giving up life would be a crime against Natural Law.

And pardon'd the deceiver, dwell / In this bear island by your spell; But release me from my bands / With the help of your good hands: The last segment of The Epilogue requests freedom by final death. The narrator has realised the purpose he has constructed for his life has been fully fulfilled. He wants to die with peace - he seeks acknowledgement for his life's successful passage. "As you from crimes would pardon'd be, / Let your indulgence set me free." Gentle breathe of yours my sails / Must fill, or else my project fails, Which was to please. Now I want / Spirits to enforce, Art to enchant;

And my ending in despair, / Unless I be reliev'd by prayer, Which pierces so, that it assaults / Mercy itself, and frees all faults. As you from crimes would pardon'd be, / Let your indulgence set me free.

One view The Epilogue can be examined upon is the fact that the artist, be it Shakespeare or Prospero as his creation declares himself detached from moral ties directed to towards the third party and, with reference to Prospero's use of power, the other characters of the play. This is a very important aspect in both the general basis of human nature and as the driving force of the artist, in this case Shakespeare. The Epilogue clearly claims that the cause-effect event-chain created by the artist was built free of ties - therefore to be judged with the appropriate honesty and freedom of attitude. One may question the necessity for such a statement, but considering the importance of theatre during Shakespeare's era, it has certain logicality. Just as a true human, the human of the Natural Laws, is justified to assume a superhuman position, an artist, the creator, is justified to practice unconditional freedom.

Freedom is and element of the Natural Law - the system of necessities to justify a meaningful existence. However, as the French philosopher Jean-Paul Sartre stated, freedom necessarily involves the property of responsibility. Man has unconditional freedom and self-defined moral ties yet he is responsible for following his own will with regard to his own value system. If responsibility is not utilized, man takes s step towards animal qualities, he does not fulfill the Natural Law. A similar pattern of freedom and responsibilities is presented in The Epilogue. Shakespeare has utilized unconditional freedom not only in his art but also in giving respect to the audience as the object of amusement: "Gentle breathe of yours my sails / Must fill, or else my project fails, / which was to please. Now I want / Spirits to enforce, Art to enchant."

Chapter 9

The Bible and The Merchant of Venice

PATRICK GRANT: FROM "THE BIBLE AND THE MERCHANT OF VENICE HERMENEUTICS, IDEOLOGY, AND DISPLACED PERSONS"

When his daughter runs off with Lorenzo and becomes a Christian, and when conversion is forced upon Shylock himself after the trial, the entire general issue of the relationship between Christian revelation and the Hebrew scriptures, and between Gentiles and Jews, is pressingly upon us. Shakespeare keeps circling these ideas, which, as we see, are closely associated with the two attitudes to money.

The binary structure of these various elements is fairly obvious: mercy—justice; revenge—love; Jew—Gentile; the value of money—the value of relationship. And, indeed, as if to confirm this design, the play is just as obviously built up in sets of linked yet opposed pairs. This is evident first of all in the two main settings. On the one hand is the enchanted, golden world of Belmont, with its touches of harmony, its brimming silence and haunting moonlight, where the heavens are inlaid with patens of gold, and mysterious longings brought provocatively to the rim of consciousness through the fairytale motif of the caskets, are fulfilled at last in surprise and delight: "You are all amazed," says Portia (v.i.266). On the other hand is Venice, a centre of nascent capitalism, opulent and hard. "I know not why I am so sad," says Antonio in the play's very first line, but Salerio and Solanio, Antonio's so-called friends, help to remind him why. His mind is "tossing on the ocean," they say; his "argosies with portly sail" are "like signiors and rich burghers on the flood", and yet they are at risk, for Antonio's merchant venture involves committing his capital to the vagaries of foreign trade and the dangers of sea-voyaging. . . .

The basic contrast between Belmont and Venice could not be stronger, and is repeated in a whole series of further oppositions. Thus, there are two trials, one in Venice, the other (involving the rings) in Belmont. There are two daughters, the first, Portia, under the rule of a magically benign father; the second, Jessica, under the rule of the father as ogre. There are two "venturing" lovers, Bassanio and Gratiano, who make two pairs with Portia and Nerissa; there are even two merchants, Antonio and Shylock. When we put all this along with the thematic twofoldness I have outlined (mercy against justice, and so on), it seems easy to conclude that Shakespeare's play asks to be read through a series of oppositions, within which we are invited to assess the Biblical themes. Several critics have dealt with the general question of Biblical allusion in *The Merchant of Venice,* and I would like for a moment to have Barbara Lewalski stand as their representative.

Briefly, Lewalski argues that *The Merchant of Venice is* about Christian love and its antitheses. Antonio is a Christ figure, ready to give his life to redeem his friend's debt. Shylock sinks further into vengefulness and evil, the opposite of redemptive love. The casket plot represents Everyman's choice of spiritual life and death, and is about the soul's worthiness to wed Christ. At the courtroom scene, Antonio's plight resembles the crucifixion, and Portia represents Mercy. This is the allegorical side of Lewalski's argument: the other side deals with specific Biblical allusions. For instance, the venture theme is associated with Christian love through Matt. "Lay not up treasures for yourselves upon the earth. . . / But lay up treasures for yourselves in heaven." Gratiano's speech on loss and gain ("You have too much respect upon the world; / They lose it that do buy it with much care" recalls Matt. "Whosoever will save his life, shall lose it. . . / For what shall it profit a man, though he should winne the whole world, if he lose his owne soule?". The Sermon on the Mount, calling for forgiveness and love of one's enemies, is exemplified by Antonio's eventual patient submission to Shylock, and Matthew's exhortation, "do good to them that hate you" is what Antonio attempts to enact. In laying down his life for his friend, Antonio also brings to mind John 15:13 ("Greater love hath no man than this, that a man lay down his life for his friends.". Matthew's version of the Lord's Prayer in the Bishops' and Geneva versions has the words, "Forgive us our dettes, as we forgive our detters", and is alluded to twice in the trial scene, when Portia pleads with Shylock to "render / The deeds of mercy", rather than demand exact justice.

Her famous speech on the quality of mercy that "droppeth as the gentle rain from heaven" closely follows Ecclesiasticus 25:19 ("O how faire a thyng is mercy in the tyme of anguish and trouble: it is like a cloud of rayne that commeth in the tyme of drought"). Shylock's cry, "The curse never fell upon our nation till now, I never felt it till now", alludes to the curse pronounced on Jerusalem itself in Matt. 23:38. And when Shylock says, "I have a daughter; / Would any of the stock of Barabbas / Had been her husband" (IV.i.294-96), he alludes to the choice of Barabbas over Christ described in Matt. 27:16-21 (no doubt mediated by way of Marlowe). There are clear allusions also to the Book of Daniel, and a good deal else of the same sort, on the strength of which Lewalski concludes that in *The Merchant of Venice* "patterns of Biblical allusion and imagery" are "so precise and pervasive as to be patently deliberate".

Many of these passages are cited also by other critics and editors, and it is hard to deny their relevance. But as far as I can tell, nobody has done much with the simple fact that the preponderance of such allusions derives from the Gospel according to Matthew. This is the case with practically all of the examples I have cited from the New Testament. It is Matthew who gives us the Sermon on the Mount and the Lord's Prayer, and Matthew is more concerned than any other gospel with the relationship between Jewish law and the new

Christian church. Moreover, Matthew's gospel is more explicitly concerned with money than any of the others, a fact commonly noticed by Biblical scholars. Matthew's special material, by which he is distinguished from the other synoptics, shows a marked emphasis on people dealing with money: the stories of the treasure in the field (13:44), the pearl of great price (13:45), the labourers in the vineyard (20:1-16), and the wise and foolish maidens (25:1-13) occur only in Matthew. In the broadest sense, Shakespeare's play is, in turn, quite clearly concerned with relationships between law and charity, and of course with money. . . .

Everywhere he insists on symmetry and balance, and everywhere he is fond of rhetorical structures exploring relationships between opposites. Thus the Sermon on the Mount is developed within the antithetical framework, "You have heard that it was said. . . But I say unto you" (5:27 ff.). Two senses of fire are opposed in John the Baptist's promise that the Holy Spirit will baptize with fire, but also that "unquenchable fire" will burn up the chaff when the wheat is separated out (3:11-12). A man cannot have two masters (6:24), and houses built on rock and sand are compared (7:24-27), as are the fruits of good and corrupt trees (12:33), and so on. . . . This emphasis on binary structures is unique to Matthew, and it seems to me to be connected to the fact that Matthew alone among the synoptics gives an account of the Last Judgment, in which the Lord's pronouncement divides the opposites: on the one hand, "Come, o blessed of my Father, inherit the kingdom prepared for you from the foundation of the world" (25:34); on the other, "Depart from me you cursed, into the eternal fire prepared for the devil and his angels" (25:41).

Matthew is fierce on this matter, and insists that in the final accounting, the difference between these opposites is absolute and terrible. And yet there is also the parable of the wheat and the tares, which again is unique to Matthew (13:24-30). In it, you will recall, the weeds (or tares) are allowed to grow along with the wheat, for fear that uprooting the young weeds would also uproot the wheat. Only at the harvest will two piles be made, and the weeds burned. The idea is, then, that fierce and final as the last judgment will be, we are not in a position to make it yet, while we are alive and kicking along the furrows of human existence. . . .

Clearly, God's ways remain seismic, disconcerting, surprising to our expectation, and yet the measure of such disturbance is precisely that there is a foundation of expectation, a pattern to fulfil. Matthew thus seems quite aware of presenting us simultaneously with order—with clearly defined pairs, antitheses and doubles—and then with a disturbing *tertium quid*, the unsettler of our best-laid rhetoric.

To my mind, this effect is prominent also in Matthew's money stories. His little parables about investments and riches and treasures and so on are in fact awkward bits of subversive narration when we look at them closely. The parable of the labourers in the vineyard (20:1-11) is an example. You'll recall how it tells of workers who are hired early in the morning, and who work all day. Then, at the eleventh hour, some new workers are hired, and at the end of the day everyone is paid the same wage—one denarius. To me, that is bothersome, and if the householder is God, then he acts unfairly. Exegetes of course try to find a solution by saying that the parable really describes how the Gentiles came late into Israel's history through Jesus, but are no less worthy. Or, since one denarius is a subsistence wage, the employer really wanted to be sure nobody starved. I don't know: I have never been able to like that story much.

The parable of the ten maidens provides another example, though I will not dwell on it, except to notice that we are asked to sympathize with the selfish young women who will not share their oil, and this strikes me as being in flat contradiction to the Sermon on the Mount: "Give to him that begs from you, and do not refuse him who would borrow from you" (5:42). Again, there are hermeneutic explanations, but at the last I am not sure if my opinion is much changed regarding those selfish ones who refuse to share. . . .

As I mentioned earlier, uncomfortable money stories are Matthew's specialty, and they belong with the general tendency in his gospel to deflect us from plain, symmetrically arranged pairs of opposites, which nonetheless we need to know about. And you can see that I am about to bring this back to *The Merchant of Venice* by claiming that Shakespeare's play also is an uncomfortable money story, which upsets the binary symmetries of his structure and themes. . . . I am not sure how interested Shakespeare would have been in studying Matthew's doublets. But the money stories are another thing, and, as I have shown, they link with everything else, including the parable of the wheat and the tares. And it does seem clear that Shakespeare knew the moralizing glosses on the parables that we find in the Geneva Bible and Tomson's New Testament, the Bishops' Bible, and perhaps the Rheims New Testament, and with the kind of spirituality that informs these, deriving from Calvin and Beza, in contention with various shades of Catholic opinion. It is therefore highly instructive to watch how these commentators paper over the cracks between the gospel narrative and their own special, often politically interested interpretations.

In his commentary on the parable of the labourers, Calvin dodges and weaves from the start. "If any man should resolve to sift out with exactness every portion of this parable, his curiosity would be useless," he tells us. And yet, he goes on to say that "there will be no harm in examining the words, that the doctrine may be more clearly evinced" (II.409). There is some evident, self-conscious throat-clearing here, and it suggests that Calvin feels pressure, and well he might. The parable for him, it turns out, means simply that the Lord "owes no man anything": that is, God's dealings have nothing in common with the laws governing human economic practice. Calvin draws this tough conclusion without flinching, even though it does threaten to leave God the unabashed exploiter of human labour, but Calvin prefers to avoid "all subtleties" (II.410), as he says, pertaining to issues like that. It might not come as a surprise for us to learn that Calvin was advanced for his times in arguing that taking interest on the principal of a loan was not un-Christian: in other words, he defended what was known as usury. And there is a consistency in all this, for if redemptive love is indeed so far transcendent and above economic calculation, then economic practice must in turn be allowed to work according to its own laws.

By contrast, the kinds of subtlety Calvin hopes to avoid are made conspicuous in the gloss to the Rheims New Testament of 1582, which claims that the denarius (or "penny") is "life everlasting," and that different kinds and degrees of labour contribute to earning it. Calvin at least sticks to the story and allows the penny to be a penny. Rheims tries to rescue a hard case by making it a different case: the penny is not a penny, but something else. . . .

As in all these commentaries, we are forced here again uncomfortably upon the difference between worldly calculus and spiritual economy, and confronted with the simultaneous awareness that the two seem more distinct than they are. Clearly, Shakespeare was exposed to a variety of such fitful and floundering attempts to make seemingly plain meanings come clear, and to separate sheep from goats, good from bad, wheat from tares, in a manner that often only confirms how problematic such an enterprise is.

Nor was all this made any simpler by the strenuous debate about usury in Shakespeare's day, in response to the Elizabethan act of 1571, repealing the 1552 act of Edward VI, and allowing the taking of interest up to ten percent. For the sake of clarity, I should point out that usury was traditionally understood as contracting intentionally for more than the principal of a loan without risk to the lender. Interestingly, the Elizabethan statute unequivocally condemned all interest taking, even though in effect it permitted what it was unable to prevent, thereby offering what in practice became a highly complex compromise position. . . .

In fact, taking interest on loans was contrived in Elizabethan England by innumerable pretences, evasions, subterfuges, and hypocrisies. People knew *how* the world went, no matter what they thought fit to say about it. Theoretically, charity is everywhere praised, and usury condemned: that is the official, ideological position, everywhere dominant, and so these opposites—charity and usury—are conveniently and ubiquitously mounted as shibboleths, while concealing a wilderness of evasive behaviours and sharp practices. And everywhere the tracts keep struggling for a solution, but mainly instead they keep reproducing an enmeshment that I can see only as a parodic inverse of that seismic reconstitution of the whole question of God and Mammon that fractures the tombstone sealing up the Christ in Matthew, and which also, I will want to say, explodes the allegory in Shakespeare.

But what is the equivalent of this seismic effect in *The Merchant of Venice?* For a start, the series of pairs in *The Merchant of Venice* that I outlined earlier sits uncertainly in relationship to a relatively undeveloped yet insistently subtending interest in threes. Shylock's three thousand ducats are loaned for three months, and of course there are three caskets, and three suitors make choices. At the end, three pairs of lovers are united, with Lorenzo and Jessica turning up in Belmont on their own recognizance, as it were, to support the principal two pairs. Although the ring trial at the end parallels the courtroom trial, it is possible to see the casket scenes also as a trial, thus making three. And it has recently been argued that the really effective merchant, in the play is neither Antonio nor Shylock, but Portia, who, because she is a woman, is even more subversive in her rewriting all the male bonds, financial and otherwise. In short, the play has a way of making us aware of a *tertium quid,* even in the midst of its foregrounded display of opposites.

You might recall that I suggested how the most obvious of Shakespeare's pairs of opposites is the setting at Belmont and Venice. The first is a golden, enchanted world, the second, where Antonio finds himself unaccountably sad, is the real world of financial anxiety and venture capital. Yet, when we move from act I, sc. i (that is, Venice), to act I, sc. ii (Belmont), we move from a scene written entirely in poetry to one entirely in prose. It is not exactly what we might expect: the poetry, surely, should belong to Belmont. Moreover, Portia's first words are "By my troth, Nerissa, my little body is aweary of this great world." The tone is at once brisk and deflated, and the line echoes Antonio's lament about being sad. Shakespeare thus obscures the contrast between Venice and Belmont even as he draws it. Indeed, the more we think about it, the interdependency between these two worlds becomes increasingly, and uncomfortably, obvious.

For instance, despite her golden fleece and caskets, mysterious music and enchanted ambience, Portia is well-moneyed, resilient, capable of vindictiveness, cosily vigorous in the conduct of character assassination from within her protected estate, and an accomplished entrepreneur. Certainly, she can knock the stuffing out of the Venetians at their own hard games. Moreover, her glamorous, eloquent, and true lover, Bassanio, explains to Antonio that he is off to Belmont because a lady there is "richly left," is "fair," and has "wondrous virtues" (I.i.161-63). That is, she has an inheritance, is good looking, and happens also to be virtuous: Bassanio's order of priorities is a markedly disenchanted one, and again we see that values in Belmont and in Venice are not as distinct as we might want them to be. The very Venetian worldliness of Portia's attractions is, apparently, necessary for her to find the true romantic love that ought (apparently) to be above such venality.

The unsettling effect of all this is aggravated in several further ways. For instance, Bassanio is not really at risk in the casket trial, if only because Morocco and Aragon have already made the wrong choices of gold and silver. By the fairytale law of threes, it is quite clear that Bassanio will choose correctly. Indeed, the main action at Belmont is so perfectly and poetically just (each of the suitors chooses in character, and true love is vindicated) that we suspect our own self-indulgence in such a fantasy, as W.H. Auden has pointed out. On the other hand, Shylock's bond for the pound of flesh is itself an age-old fairy-tale motif, so that the supposedly real and threatening prospect of Shylock using the knife he whets before us is effectively absorbed. But again we feel this is evasive, for so powerful is Shylock's resolve, and so ferocious the animus he expresses, that we hesitate somehow to commute it by a structural subterfuge into just another fairytale motif. The opposition between Belmont and Venice that would, on the surface, provoke our moral judgments on the issue of money and human relationships is thus repeatedly unsettled and destabilized.

Something of the same effect accompanies the play's best-known speeches. Portia's famous words on mercy in the courtroom scene of act IV, sc. i introduce an amazing, momentary stillness into the tense, half-demented atmosphere of the trial:

The quality of mercy is nct strained;
It droppeth as the gentle rain from heaven
Upon the place beneath....

And so on. The feeling of release and refreshment is unmistakable, and unmistakably welcome as soft rain, and as a gift. Such mercy is "mightiest in the mightiest," and is more powerful than the power of monarchs. It is greater even than that, and yet "It is enthroned in the hearts of kings": it is concealed at the centre, in the secret heart of things where overarching transcendence and vulnerable interiority are presented as mysteriously at one. We pray for that quality of mercy, says Portia, "And that same prayer doth teach us all to render / The deeds of mercy." There is a kind of confidence, here, that in its very defencelessness is free from anxiety, and

Portia recommends it. But then, even in mid-line, she snaps out of it.

I have spoke thus much
To mitigate the justice of thy plea;
Which if thou follow, this strict court of Venice
Must needs give sentence 'gainst the merchant there.
(IV.i.201-04)

It is back to business: she knows that he will want the bond, and she knows already how she will trip him up on a technicality. The mercy speech is beautiful, but is oddly dislocated from what precedes and follows, abruptly relinquished, almost a kind of move, we might suspect, designed to drive another nail into Shylock's coffin, for he will soon learn that he has not listened. But she knows he will not listen, and the speech rounds out the design of an accomplished entrapment. She goes on to enclose him entirely.

Or take Shylock's famous plea in act III, sc. i, in reply to Salerio, who asks what good taking a pound of flesh will do.

Hath not a Jew eyes? Hath not a Jew hands, organs, dimensions, senses, affections, passions?—fed with the same food, hurt with the same weapons, subject to the same diseases, healed by the same means, warmed and cooled by the same winter and summer as a Christian is? If you prick us, do we not bleed? If you tickle us, do we not laugh? If you poison us, do we not die? And if you wrong us, shall we not revenge.

Indeed, these words enliven us to our common condition—we all have senses, blood, are vulnerable to disease, and so on. Shylock is one of us, and in the name of the body's vitality, basis of all human community, he makes his demand. And yet, the very meagreness of Shylock's scope, here, is menacing: he sees only the reflex actions of the autonomic nervous system as our common inheritance. And the aggressive questioning expresses an antagonism that comes to light at last, again in the riveting conclusion: "And if you wrong us, shall we not revenge?" There is no real distinction between the account of hands, organs, bleeding, disease, and the moral issue of revenge. For Shylock they appear the same (or he makes them appear so): revenge is as instinctive as eating. Perhaps we had thought revenge to be another kind of thing—and yet, the miserable vindictiveness of the play's Christian gentlemen and husbands is also much as Shylock describes it. As with Portia's speech, we are stopped at the very moment when we might extend a degree of unguarded sympathy, and we are thrown back on something altogether less self-indulgent, less secure.

Much else in the play resembles these examples, but I would like to move toward a conclusion by citing one brief point that highlights again the theme of material and spiritual wealth. The annoying and verbose Gratiano has just told Bassanio and Portia that their success with the casket test has enabled his betrothal to Nerissa. He turns then enthusiastically to his bride-to-be, his heart full (presumably), and, dumbfoundingly, he says to her, "We'll play with them the first boy for a thousand ducats". That is, let's make a bet of a thousand ducats on which of us couples produces the first baby boy. It is another bargain, another bond, this time dealing with a few extra pounds of flesh, but never mind. It seems obvious that we are meant to see this in relation to the pound of flesh story in Venice, but this Belmont version, though in one way a merrier bond than Shylock's, is a tainted enough thing, and it seems that love and money, charity and revenge, accountability and accountancy, are not after all distinct, however pleasing it might be to think of them that way. . . .

Chapter 10

Shylock and History

Towering over Shakespeare's romantic comedy *The Merchant of Venice* is the tragic figure of Shylock. Before we can begin to understand Shylock, though, we must understand the historical and dramatic influences under which Shakespeare wrote.

Although Shakespeare wrote possibly the most famous Jew in English literature, there were virtually no Jews in England during his lifetime. It isn't known whether Shakespeare would have come into contact with anyone who was Jewish. It would also be impossible to surmise how detailed his knowledge of the historical facts about Jews in England was, but fact and myth were certainly handed down through the ages, and it is safe to assume that he would have been aware of his country's historical folklore.

JEWS IN EARLY ENGLAND: ASSIMILATION TO EXPULSION

One of the first documented groups of Jews residing in England comes from Oxford in 1075. For more than a century, English Jews were not confined to ghettos, unlike many of their European counterparts. Eyewitness accounts report that Jews and non-Jews visited each other's houses, indicating that they lived side by side in relative harmony. Jews, however, were not citizens. They were viewed as outsiders, and were often barred from many professions because of their religion. Only Christians could belong to the artisan guilds — the professional associations of the era — and own land, which left Jews with few means of earning a living. Christians, however, could not lend money with interest, and many Jews earned a lucrative living as usurers. This profession was not a sure path to riches, as debts often had a way of going unpaid. The Jewish lender often had to become his own debt collector, and in trying to regain the debt owed to him, he frequently became the target of resentment. As usury was a profession comprised exclusively of Jews, religion eventually became the focus of much of this bad feeling.

In the late 12th century, preparation for the Third Crusade brought a heightened level of anti-Jewish sentiment. Anti-Semitic violence culminated in two massacres, one at the coronation of Richard I in 1189, when 30 Jews were killed, and the other in 1190 in the city of York, when 150 Jews were massacred. The Magna Carta, the basis for English constitutional law, is itself a testament to the growing unpopularity of Jewish money-lending activities. Two clauses in the 1215 document state that if a debtor dies before his debt is paid, neither his heir nor his widow will be responsible for repaying the debt.

Repressive measures against Jews continued to grow as the century wore on until finally, in 1275, they were forbidden to be money-lenders. Several more edicts against Jews were implemented at this time, including the taxation of any Jew over the age of 12 and the wearing of badges that identified people as Jewish. With the loss of their primary source of income, and thus their value to the King's coffers, Jews became expendable to the Crown and were expelled from England in 1290, not to be readmitted until 1655.

After the Expulsion, the English view of Jews began to be formed by several myths that grew in popularity through the centuries. The strongest of these myths was undoubtedly that of ritual murder (or "blood libel"), which remained in circulation in England long after the Jews had been expelled. There were several variations of this ritual murder legend, the most prevalent one being that of Jews kidnapping children at Easter and using them in ritual practices. It was also believed that adult Christians would be killed and their blood used for

Passover ceremonies. Not one of these myths had any basis in fact; instead they stemmed from fear of an unknown culture and, yet, they were regarded as truth by many.

JEWS IN ELIZABETHAN SOCIETY

The world in which Shakespeare lived was an exceedingly dangerous one. The threat of a civil war was never far away. When Elizabeth ascended the throne in 1558, she staved off the threat of rebellion by dealing ruthlessly with any hint of treason. Many of her enemies — perceived or actual — were beheaded.

Much of the plotting against Elizabeth I had its origins in the religious intolerance of the era, begun when Elizabeth's father, Henry VIII, broke with the Catholic Church. Desperate for a male heir to guarantee the Tudor succession, Henry was eager to divorce his then-wife and marry Anne Boleyn, whom he hoped would give him an heir. The Pope refused to grant him a divorce, and Henry VIII's solution to this conundrum was to break from the Catholic Church and create the Church of England, installing himself as head of a new Protestant religion.

A religious war for the soul of England then developed. By the time Elizabeth was Queen, the threat was not just internal but international, as the Pope and Catholic European countries plotted against the Protestant monarch in the hope of returning a Catholic to the throne of England. Elizabeth was forced into a series of reprisals against recusant Catholics (people who outwardly seemed to be Protestant, but who secretly practiced Catholicism), many of whom were murdered.

Elizabeth, however, was by no means the first Tudor monarch to engage in such actions. Her own father was guilty of similar intolerance, and her Catholic sister, Mary, had imprisoned Elizabeth herself in the Tower of London when it became clear that she was the focus of Protestant insurrections against Mary, then queen. She soon earned the epithet "Bloody Mary" because of her murderous actions against the Protestants. It would be no understatement to say that religion was serious business in Elizabethan England.

Where do the Jews fit in this climate of religious intolerance? Despite their expulsion 300 years earlier, small groups of Jews sought refuge in England from the Spanish Inquisition and were living quietly during Elizabeth's reign. These Jews, known as *Marranos* or *Conversos,* people who had converted to Christianity from Judaism, and though they outwardly appeared to be Christians, many retained their Jewish heritage, even if they did not actively participate in Jewish religious practices. Another small group of Jews made its way to London in the 1500s and became musicians at the Court of King Henry VIII. Some scholars have even suggested that the "Dark Lady" of Shakespeare's sonnets was one Emilia Bassano, descended from these same musicians.

Most people of Jewish descent living in England in the 16th century were not persecuted by their Christian neighbors. But there was one notorious event which could hardly have escaped Shakespeare's notice. In 1593, a few years before *The Merchant of Venice* was written, Queen Elizabeth I's physician Roderigo Lopez was accused of trying to poison her. Lopez, allegedly in league with the King of Spain, was convicted of treason, hung, and drawn and quartered in 1594. His was a very public execution, and the fact that he was a Marrano led to an outbreak of anti-Jewish sentiment in the country. He was taunted by slurs on the scaffold as he died, still proclaiming his innocence. It was a clear but unfortunate sign that there was a latent anti-Semitism within the English public. Suspicion was not reserved for Jews alone, though. At this time all foreigners were regarded with suspicion and distrust, at this time, because they were seen as a threat to the security of the English nation. Anti-Spanish sentiment, for instance, was even more prevalent than anti-Semitism at the time of Lopez's death.

SHAKESPEARE AND SHYLOCK

William Shakespeare, being a man of the theatre, would have been heavily influenced not only by history, but also by the theatre that had preceded him. He was also an exceptionally good businessman with a keen sense of what his audience wanted. Portrayals of Jews in drama were a long-standing tradition by the time Shakespeare wrote *The Merchant of Venice.* The Jew seems to have been the guy audiences loved to hate in medieval and Renaissance drama — the equivalent to Americans' glee at watching the television exploits of the fictional J.R. Ewing two decades ago.

The roots of Shakespearean drama begin with mystery and miracle plays. During the Middle Ages, touring troupes primarily sponsored by the church performed the stories of the Old and New Testaments for a largely illiterate audience. Within these performances lurked the medieval dichotomy of feeling about the Jewish race that had dogged Christianity. On the one hand, Jewish patriarchs such as Moses were admired, while on the other Jews were often seen to be responsible for Christ's crucifixion.

With the coming of the Renaissance this strictly biblical, if somewhat biased, portrayal of Jews gave way to an overly melodramatic perception. Jews became the evil villains of Elizabethan drama. Frequently portrayed as Machiavellian or greedy or both, they were not complex characters. In fact, many of Shakespeare's contemporaries simply told a story, rather than added any psychological layers to characters and their motives. Even Christopher Marlowe, Shakespeare's greatest rival, fell into the one-dimensional trap in his play *The Jew of Malta,* written in 1589 — nearly a decade before *The Merchant of Venice.* Both Barabas in *The Jew of Malta* and Shylock are money-lenders and they both have daughters who leave home with their father's money, but there the similarity ends. Barabas is an over-the-top villain who steals, cheats, and indulges in murder until he finally meets a gruesome end — boiling in oil. Shakespeare's characterization of Shylock broke with theatrical tradition. Shylock is a complex man, whose every action can be understood and who, finally, elicits understanding from his audience.

Shylock

Elements of all these influences — historical, societal, and theatrical — helped to mold Shylock's character. What we can draw from the play regarding Shakespeare's ideas about the

Jewish people, however, is pure supposition. Shakespeare left no journals, no lifetime correspondence from which a biographer could draw a full picture of the author and his work. It is even questionable his plays would have survived if it weren't for a band of actors pooling their memories together seven years after his death to publish the First Folio.

Shylock began the play much as an Elizabethan audience would expect: He exhibited every sign of being the piece's villain. As the money-hungry Jewish usurer that had become a stock character in Elizabethan drama, Shylock made himself thoroughly unpleasant, with asides to the audience stating that he hated Antonio because Antonio was a Christian — "but more" he continued, because he lent money without interest, thus competing with Shylock's business and threatening Shylock's sole means of supporting himself and his family.

In Shylock's final scene, Shakespeare had him act out another stereotype: a ritual murder. Of course, there is no mention in the play that Shylock would use Antonio's blood in any religious ritual. But the audience would have immediately associated the stage action with the myth. Shakespeare seemed to be giving his audience exactly what they expect from a stage Jew. In Portia, the audience got the means to stop the ritual murder because she would not let the Jew shed one drop of Christian blood. The text specifically says "Christian," reinforcing the "blood libel" legends.

While he perpetuated received notions of Jews, Shakespeare also did an extraordinary thing for an Elizabethan playwright: He created a Jewish character who was flawed, and human, *and* oppressed by the Christians surrounding him. The audience was told time and again of Shylock's encounters with Christians and how they spat upon him, called him nasty epithets, and spurned him. Shylock was the very picture of a man who suffered much at the hands of his fellow men and who had finally reached his breaking point. Growing scholarship points to the possibility that Shakespeare's family were themselves recusant Catholics, oppressed in Stratford and fallen from their high place in local society while Shakespeare was still a boy. If this is true, then perhaps

Shylock's oppression was a metaphor for England's religious oppression during Shakespeare's lifetime. His forced conversion also fits with this notion, as it was not only Jews being forced to become Christians, but also Catholics forced to become Protestants and vice versa, depending on who was in control of the throne at the time. They had to convert or lose their lives. This theory is pure speculation, but it would hardly be the first time — or the last — that theatre was used to make a covert political statement.

Viewing the play through modern eyes, Shylock can be seen as both an Elizabethan stereotype and a fully drawn human being. Ironically, it is precisely because of the stereotypical elements in Shylock's character that many people argue against *The Merchant of Venice,* viewing it as an anti-Semitic work — an understandable reaction in a post-Holocaust era. Shakespeare, however, did not write a one-dimensional villain, but a complex character who defies explanation and who will probably never be fully understood.

Chapter 11

List of Characters

Shylock

A Jewish moneylender in Venice. Angered by his mistreatment at the hands of Venice's Christians, particularly Antonio, Shylock schemes to eke out his revenge by ruthlessly demanding as payment a pound of Antonio's flesh. Although seen by the rest of the play's characters as an inhuman monster, Shylock at times diverges from stereotype and reveals himself to be quite human. These contradictions, and his eloquent expressions of hatred, have earned Shylock a place as one of Shakespeare's most memorable characters.

Shylock (In-Depth Analysis)

Although critics tend to agree that Shylock is The Merchant of Venice's most noteworthy figure, no consensus has been reached on whether to read him as a bloodthirsty bogeyman, a clownish Jewish stereotype, or a tragic figure whose sense of decency has been fractured by the persecution he endures. Certainly, Shylock is the play's antagonist, and he is menacing enough to seriously imperil the -happiness of Venice's businessmen and young lovers alike. Shylock is also, however, a creation of circumstance; even in his single-minded pursuit of a pound of flesh, his frequent mentions of the cruelty he has endured at Christian hands make it hard for us to label him a natural born monster.

In one of Shakespeare's most famous monologues, for example, Shylock argues that Jews are humans and calls his quest for vengeance the product of lessons taught to him by the cruelty of Venetian citizens. On the other hand, Shylock's coldly calculated attempt to revenge the wrongs done to him by murdering his persecutor, Antonio, prevents us from viewing him in a primarily positive light. Shakespeare gives us unmistakably human moments, but he often steers us against Shylock as well, painting him as a miserly, cruel, and prosaic figure.

PORTIA

A wealthy heiress from Belmont. Portia's beauty is matched only by her intelligence. Bound by a clause in her father's will that forces her to marry whichever suitor chooses correctly among three caskets, Portia is nonetheless able to marry her true love, Bassanio. Far and away the most clever of the play's characters, it is Portia, in the disguise of a young law clerk, who saves Antonio from Shylock's knife.

Portia (In-Depth Analysis)

Portia Quick-witted, wealthy, and beautiful, Portia embodies the virtues that are typical of Shakespeare's heroines—it is no surprise that she emerges as the antidote to Shylock's malice. At the beginning of the play, however, we do not see Portia's potential for initiative and resourcefulness, as she is a near prisoner, feeling herself absolutely bound to follow her father's dying wishes. This opening appearance, however, proves to be a revealing introduction to Portia, who emerges as that rarest of combinations—a free spirit who abides rigidly by rules. Rather than ignoring the stipulations of her father's will, she watches a stream of suitors pass her by, happy to see these particular suitors go, but sad that she has no choice in the matter.

When Bassanio arrives, however, Portia proves herself to be highly resourceful, begging the man she loves to stay a while before picking a chest, and finding loopholes in the will's provision that we never thought possible. Also, in her defeat of Shylock Portia prevails by applying a more rigid standard than Shylock himself, agreeing that his contract very much entitles him to his pound of flesh, but adding that it does not allow for any loss of blood. Anybody can break the rules, but Portia's effectiveness comes from her ability to make the law work for her.

Portia rejects the stuffiness that rigid adherence to the law might otherwise suggest. In her courtroom appearance, she vigorously applies the law, but still flouts convention by appearing disguised as a man. After depriving Bassanio of his ring, she stops the prank before it goes to far, but still takes it far enough to berate Bassanio and Graziano for their callousness, and she even insinuates that she has been unfaithful.

Antonio

The merchant whose love for his friend Bassanio prompts him to sign Shylock's contract and almost lose his life. Antonio is something of a mercurial figure, often inexplicably melancholy and, as Shylock points out, possessed of an incorrigible dislike of Jews. Nonetheless, Antonio is beloved of his friends and proves merciful to Shylock, albeit with conditions.

Antonio (In-Depth Analysis)

Although the play's title refers to him, Antonio is a rather lackluster character. He emerges in Act I, scene i as a hopeless depressive, someone who cannot name the source of his melancholy and who, throughout the course of the play, devolves into a self-pitying lump, unable to muster the energy required to defend himself against execution. Antonio never names the cause of his melancholy, but the evidence seems to point to his being in love, despite his denial of this idea in Act I, scene i. The most likely object of his affection is Bassanio, who takes full advantage of the merchant's boundless feelings for him. Antonio has risked the entirety of his fortune on overseas trading ventures, yet he agrees to guarantee the potentially lethal loan Bassanio secures from Shylock.

In the context of his unrequited and presumably unconsummated relationship with Bassanio, Antonio's willingness to offer up a pound of his own flesh seems particularly important, signifying a union that grotesquely alludes to the rites of marriage, where two partners become "one flesh."

Further evidence of the nature of Antonio's feelings for Bassanio appears later in the play, when Antonio's proclamations resonate with the hyperbole and self-satisfaction of a doomed lover's declaration: "Pray God Bassanio come / To see me pay his debt, and then I care not" (III.iii.35–36). Antonio ends the play as happily as he can, restored to wealth even if not delivered into love.

Without a mate, he is indeed the "tainted wether"—or castrated ram—of the flock, and he will likely return to his favourite pastime of moping about the streets of Venice (IV.i.113). After all, he has effectively disabled himself from pursuing his other hobby—abusing Shylock—by insisting that the Jew convert to Christianity. Although a sixteenth-century audience might have seen this demand as merciful, as Shylock is saving himself from eternal damnation by converting, we are less likely to be convinced. Not only does Antonio's reputation as an anti-Semite precede him, but the only instance in the play when he breaks out of his doldrums is his "storm" against Shylock (I.iii.132). In this context, Antonio proves that the dominant threads of his character are melancholy and cruelty.

Bassanio

A gentleman of Venice, and a kinsman and dear friend to Antonio. Bassanio's love for the wealthy Portia leads him to borrow money from Shylock with Antonio as his guarantor. An ineffectual businessman, Bassanio proves himself a worthy suitor, correctly identifying the casket that contains Portia's portrait.

Graziano

A friend of Bassanio's who accompanies him to Belmont. A coarse and garrulous young man, Graziano is Shylock's most vocal and insulting critic during the trial. While Bassanio courts Portia, Graziano falls in love with and eventually weds Portia's lady-in-waiting, Nerissa.

Jessica

Although she is Shylock's daughter, Jessica hates life in her father's house, and elopes with the young Christian gentleman, Lorenzo. The fate of her soul is often in doubt: the play's characters wonder if her marriage can overcome the fact that she was born a Jew, and we wonder if her sale of a ring given to her father by her mother is excessively callous.

Lorenzo

A friend of Bassanio and Antonio, Lorenzo is in love with Shylock's daughter, Jessica. He schemes to help Jessica escape from her father's house, and he eventually elopes with her to Belmont.

Nerissa

Portia's lady-in-waiting and confidante. She marries Graziano and escorts Portia on Portia's trip to Venice by disguising herself as her law clerk.

Lancelot Gobbo

Bassanio's servant. A comical, clownish figure who is especially adept at making puns, Lancelot leaves Shylock's service in order to work for Bassanio.

The prince of Morocco

A Moorish prince who seeks Portia's hand in marriage. The prince of Morocco asks Portia to ignore his dark countenance and seeks to win her by picking one of the three caskets. Certain that the caskets reflect Portia's beauty and stature, the prince of Morocco picks the gold chest, which proves to be incorrect.

The prince of Aragon [SSH

An arrogant Spanish nobleman who also attempts to win Portia's hand by picking a casket. Like the prince of Morocco, however, the prince of Aragon chooses unwisely. He picks the silver casket, which gives him a message calling him an idiot instead of Portia's hand.

Salerio

A Venetian gentleman, and friend to Antonio, Bassanio, and Lorenzo. Salerio escorts the newlyweds Jessica and Lorenzo to Belmont, and returns with Bassanio and Graziano for Antonio's trial. He is often almost indistinguishable from his companion Solanio.

Solanio

A Venetian gentleman, and frequent counterpart to Salerio.

The duke of Venice—The ruler of Venice, who presides over Antonio's trial. Although a powerful man, the duke's state is built on respect for the law, and he is unable to help Antonio.

Old Gobbo

Lancelot's father, also a servant in Venice.

Tubal A

Jew in Venice, and one of Shylock's friends.

Doctor Bellario

A wealthy Paduan lawyer and Portia's cousin. Doctor Bellario never appears in the play, but he gives Portia's servant the letters of introduction needed for her to make her appearance in court.

Balthasar

Portia's servant, whom she dispatches to get the appropriate materials from Doctor Bellario.

Chapter 12

Plot Synopsis

The Merchant of Venice opens with Antonio, a Christian merchant, in a depressed state. His friends try to cheer him up, but nothing works to make him feel better. Finally his friend Bassanio, an aristocrat who has lost all of his money, comes and asks Antonio to loan him some money.

Antonio, who has tied up all of his money is seafaring ventures, is unable to give Bassanio a direct loan. Instead he offers to use his good credit to get a loan for Bassanio. Bassanio finds Shylock, a Jewish moneylender, and convinces him to give a loan of three thousand ducats as long as Antonio will sign the contract. In a rather unusual twist, instead of charging the Christian men interest, Shylock agrees to waive it as long as Antonio promises him a pound of his flesh as collateral. Antonio, thinking this is a "merry sport," accepts the condition of the bond (contract) and signs it.

Bassanio takes the money and prepares to go visit Portia, a wealthy heiress living in Belmont. She is unmarried because her father has decreed that all suitors must first select one of three caskets in order to marry her. The caskets, one made of gold, one of silver, and one of base lead, all contain different messages. Only one of these caskets contains a picture of Portia. The suitor who picks that casket will be granted permission to marry her.

Prior to Bassanio's arrival the Prince of Morocco tries his luck in choosing among the caskets. He picks the gold casket because it contains an inscription reading "what every man desires." Instead of Portia's picture, he finds a skull which symbolizes the fact that gold hides corruption. As part of losing the suit, he is further sworn to never propose marriage to any other woman, and must return to Morocco immediately. The next suitor, the Prince of Aragon, selects the silver casket which bears an inscription stating that it will give a man what he deserves. Inside is a picture of an idiot, indicating that his self-centreed approach was foolish. He too leaves in shame.

Back in Venice, Jessica, the daughter of Shylock, has fallen in love with Lorenzo. They plan to escape one night when Shylock is invited to eat at Bassanio's house. After Shylock leaves Lorenzo goes to his house with two friends. Jessica appears at a window dressed as a boy and tosses a chest of money and jewels down to them. She then emerges from the house and runs away with Lorenzo.

Shylock, upon discovering that his daughter has run away with a lot of his money, blames Antonio for helping her escape. At the same time there are rumors developing in Venice that many of Antonio's ships, with which he expected to repay Shylock for the loan, have sunk or been lost at sea. Shylock begins to revel in the news that Antonio is losing everything because he wants to exact his pound of flesh in revenge for the many insults Antonio has dealt him throughout the years.

Bassanio arrives in Belmont and meets Portia. She remembers him as the dashing soldier with whom she fell in love several years earlier. Portia begs Bassanio to wait before choosing among the caskets, but he demands the right to start immediately. Without even properly reading the inscriptions, Bassanio selects the lead one because he considers it a threatening casket. Portia is overjoyed when he finds her portrait inside. She gives him a ring to seal their engagement and they prepare to get married the next day. Graziano, who has accompanied Bassanio to Belmont, tells him that he and Nerissa (Portia's friend) wish to be married as well.

A messenger arrives and hands Bassanio a letter from Antonio in which he informs Bassanio that he has lost all his money and must forfeit a pound of flesh to Shylock. Bassanio immediately tells Portia what has happened. She orders him to take six thousand ducats and return to Venice where he can pay Shylock and cancel the contract. After Bassanio and Graziano have left, Nerissa and Portia depart for Venice disguised as men.

Shylock has Antonio arrested and brought before the Duke of Venice, who presides over a court of justice. The Duke pleads with Shylock to forgive the contract and let Antonio go free. When he refuses, the Duke asks him how he expects any mercy if he is unable to offer it. The Duke then tells the gathered men that he is waiting for a doctor of the law to arrive.

Nerissa enters the court and hands a letter to the Duke which notifies him that a Doctor Bellario has sent an educated young doctor in his place. Portia arrives disguised as the Doctor Balthasar. She informs the Duke that she has studied the case and will preside over it.

She first asks Shylock for the contract and looks it over. Bassanio offers to pay Shylock the six thousand ducats, but he refuses to accept the money, preferring instead the revenge of killing Antonio. Unable to find any loopholes, Portia grants Shylock his pound of flesh. Shylock, overjoyed at winning his case, holds a knife ready to cut into Antonio's breast. Portia stops him by asking if he has a surgeon present to suppress the flow of blood. Shylock tells her that the bond said nothing about providing a doctor. She informs him that he may have his pound of flesh, but that if he sheds a single drop of blood then Venice can take away his lands and wealth according to the law. Shylock, clearly unable to comply with this law, asks instead that he be given the six thousand ducats. Portia refuses his request, explaining that she has already ruled according to the contract, and that it must be carried out.

Portia then starts to read the contract literally, reaffirming that Shylock must take exactly one pound of flesh, no more and no less, or he will violate the contract and die. Shylock tells the court that he wishes to completely drop his case and forgive Antonio the entire three thousand ducats. Portia again refuses his request, explaining that the law in Venice states that if any foreigner conspires against the life of a Venetian, half his wealth is to be given to the man against whom he conspired, and half is taken as a fine by the state. In addition, the Duke is granted the power of life and death over him.

When Shylock is pardoned by the Duke, he informs the court that he would prefer death rather than lose everything he owns. Antonio asks the court to return the fine of half of Shylock's wealth provided Shylock converts to Christianity. In addition, Antonio declares he will keep his share in a trust for Jessica and Lorenzo. Portia agrees to this, and also makes Shylock promise to give all his money to Lorenzo upon his death.

After the trial Bassanio thanks "Dr. Balthasar" (Portia) for "his" good work and offers "him" anything "he" desires. Portia asks him for the ring she had given him earlier as a token of their love. He is upset about giving it to her since he thinks she is "Balthasar." However, after Antonio points out that he nearly lost his life for Bassanio, Bassanio pulls off the ring and hands it to her.

Portia and Nerissa return to Belmont dressed normally. Lorenzo and Jessica have been living there, enjoying the comfortable life Belmont offers. Soon after the two women arrive, Bassanio and Graziano also return from Venice. The happy reunion is destroyed when Portia asks Bassanio about the ring (which he gave away). She forgives him only after Antonio vouches for Bassanio's fidelity.

Portia then gives Antonio the ring and has him hand it to Bassanio. He is shocked to see it is the same ring he gave "Balthasar". Portia finally tells him the truth about Balthasar. The play ends with three happy couples: namely Lorenzo and Jessica, Nerissa and Graziano, as well as Portia and Bassanio. However, Antonio and Shylock remain outcasts, separated from the happy ending.

Chapter 13

Complete Text

ACT I

SCENE I. Venice. A street.

Enter ANTONIO, SALARINO, and SALANIO

ANTONIO

In sooth, I know not why I am so sad:
It wearies me; you say it wearies you;
But how I caught it, found it, or came by it,
What stuff 'tis made of, whereof it is born,
I am to learn;
And such a want-wit sadness makes of me,
That I have much ado to know myself.

SALARINO

Your mind is tossing on the ocean;
There, where your argosies with portly sail,
Like signiors and rich burghers on the flood,
Or, as it were, the pageants of the sea,
Do overpeer the petty traffickers,
That curtsy to them, do them reverence,
As they fly by them with their woven wings.

SALANIO

Believe me, sir, had I such venture forth,
The better part of my affections would
Be with my hopes abroad. I should be still
Plucking the grass, to know where sits the wind,
Peering in maps for ports and piers and roads;
And every object that might make me fear

Misfortune to my ventures, out of doubt
Would make me sad.
SALARINO
My wind cooling my broth
Would blow me to an ague, when I thought
What harm a wind too great at sea might do.
I should not see the sandy hour-glass run,
But I should think of shallows and of flats,
And see my wealthy Andrew dock'd in sand,
Vailing her high-top lower than her ribs
To kiss her burial. Should I go to church
And see the holy edifice of stone,
And not bethink me straight of dangerous rocks,
Which touching but my gentle vessel's side,
Would scatter all her spices on the stream,
Enrobe the roaring waters with my silks,
And, in a word, but even now worth this,
And now worth nothing? Shall I have the thought
To think on this, and shall I lack the thought
That such a thing bechanced would make me sad?
But tell not me; I know, Antonio
Is sad to think upon his merchandise.
ANTONIO
Believe me, no: I thank my fortune for it,
My ventures are not in one bottom trusted,
Nor to one place; nor is my whole estate
Upon the fortune of this present year:
Therefore my merchandise makes me not sad.
SALARINO
Why, then you are in love.
ANTONIO
Fie, fie!
SALARINO
Not in love neither? Then let us say you are sad,
Because you are not merry: and 'twere as easy
For you to laugh and leap and say you are merry,
Because you are not sad. Now, by two-headed Janus,
Nature hath framed strange fellows in her time:

Some that will evermore peep through their eyes
And laugh like parrots at a bag-piper,
And other of such vinegar aspect
That they'll not show their teeth in way of smile,
Though Nestor swear the jest be laughable.
Enter BASSANIO, LORENZO, and GRATIANO
SALANIO
Here comes Bassanio, your most noble kinsman,
Gratiano and Lorenzo. Fare ye well:
We leave you now with better company.
SALARINO
I would have stay'd till I had made you merry,
If worthier friends had not prevented me.
ANTONIO
Your worth is very dear in my regard.
I take it, your own business calls on you
And you embrace the occasion to depart.
SALARINO
Good morrow, my good lords.
BASSANIO
Good signiors both, when shall we laugh? say, when?
You grow exceeding strange: must it be so?
SALARINO
We'll make our leisures to attend on yours.
Exeunt Salarino and Salanio
LORENZO
My Lord Bassanio, since you have found Antonio,
We two will leave you: but at dinner-time,
I pray you, have in mind where we must meet.
BASSANIO
I will not fail you.
GRATIANO
You look not well, Signior Antonio;
You have too much respect upon the world:
They lose it that do buy it with much care:
Believe me, you are marvellously changed.
ANTONIO
I hold the world but as the world, Gratiano;

A stage where every man must play a part,
And mine a sad one.

GRATIANO

Let me play the fool:
With mirth and laughter let old wrinkles come,
And let my liver rather heat with wine
Than my heart cool with mortifying groans.
Why should a man, whose blood is warm within,
Sit like his grandsire cut in alabaster?
Sleep when he wakes and creep into the jaundice
By being peevish? I tell thee what, Antonio—
I love thee, and it is my love that speaks—
There are a sort of men whose visages
Do cream and mantle like a standing pond,
And do a wilful stillness entertain,
With purpose to be dress'd in an opinion
Of wisdom, gravity, profound conceit,
As who should say 'I am Sir Oracle,
And when I ope my lips let no dog bark!'
O my Antonio, I do know of these
That therefore only are reputed wise
For saying nothing; when, I am very sure,
If they should speak, would almost damn those ears,
Which, hearing them, would call their brothers fools.
I'll tell thee more of this another time:
But fish not, with this melancholy bait,
For this fool gudgeon, this opinion.
Come, good Lorenzo. Fare ye well awhile:
I'll end my exhortation after dinner.

LORENZO

Well, we will leave you then till dinner-time:
I must be one of these same dumb wise men,
For Gratiano never lets me speak.

GRATIANO

Well, keep me company but two years moe,
Thou shalt not know the sound of thine own tongue.

ANTONIO

Farewell: I'll grow a talker for this gear.

GRATIANO
Thanks, i' faith, for silence is only commendable
In a neat's tongue dried and a maid not vendible.
Exeunt GRATIANO and LORENZO
ANTONIO
Is that any thing now?
BASSANIO
Gratiano speaks an infinite deal of nothing, more than any man in all Venice. His reasons are as two grains of wheat hid in two bushels of chaff: you shall seek all day ere you find them, and when you have them, they are not worth the search.
ANTONIO
Well, tell me now what lady is the same
To whom you swore a secret pilgrimage,
That you to-day promised to tell me of?
BASSANIO
'Tis not unknown to you, Antonio,
How much I have disabled mine estate,
By something showing a more swelling port
Than my faint means would grant continuance:
Nor do I now make moan to be abridged
From such a noble rate; but my chief care
Is to come fairly off from the great debts
Wherein my time something too prodigal
Hath left me gaged. To you, Antonio,
I owe the most, in money and in love,
And from your love I have a warranty
To unburden all my plots and purposes
How to get clear of all the debts I owe.
ANTONIO
I pray you, good Bassanio, let me know it;
And if it stand, as you yourself still do,
Within the eye of honour, be assured,
My purse, my person, my extremest means,
Lie all unlock'd to your occasions.
BASSANIO
In my school-days, when I had lost one shaft,

I shot his fellow of the self-same flight
The self-same way with more advised watch,
To find the other forth, and by adventuring both
I oft found both: I urge this childhood proof,
Because what follows is pure innocence.
I owe you much, and, like a wilful youth,
That which I owe is lost; but if you please
To shoot another arrow that self way
Which you did shoot the first, I do not doubt,
As I will watch the aim, or to find both
Or bring your latter hazard back again
And thankfully rest debtor for the first.

ANTONIO

You know me well, and herein spend but time
To wind about my love with circumstance;
And out of doubt you do me now more wrong
In making question of my uttermost
Than if you had made waste of all I have:
Then do but say to me what I should do
That in your knowledge may by me be done,
And I am prest unto it: therefore, speak.

BASSANIO

In Belmont is a lady richly left;
And she is fair, and, fairer than that word,
Of wondrous virtues: sometimes from her eyes
I did receive fair speechless messages:
Her name is Portia, nothing undervalued
To Cato's daughter, Brutus' Portia:
Nor is the wide world ignorant of her worth,
For the four winds blow in from every coast
Renowned suitors, and her sunny locks
Hang on her temples like a golden fleece;
Which makes her seat of Belmont Colchos' strand,
And many Jasons come in quest of her.
O my Antonio, had I but the means
To hold a rival place with one of them,
I have a mind presages me such thrift,
That I should questionless be fortunate!

ANTONIO

Thou know'st that all my fortunes are at sea;
Neither have I money nor commodity
To raise a present sum: therefore go forth;
Try what my credit can in Venice do:
That shall be rack'd, even to the uttermost,
To furnish thee to Belmont, to fair Portia.
Go, presently inquire, and so will I,
Where money is, and I no question make
To have it of my trust or for my sake.

Exeunt

SCENE II: Belmont. A room in PORTIA'S house.

Enter PORTIA and NERISSA

PORTIA

By my troth, Nerissa, my little body is aweary of this great world.

NERISSA

You would be, sweet madam, if your miseries were in the same abundance as your good fortunes are: and yet, for aught I see, they are as sick that surfeit with too much as they that starve with nothing. It is no mean happiness therefore, to be seated in the mean: superfluity comes sooner by white hairs, but competency lives longer.

PORTIA

Good sentences and well pronounced.

NERISSA

They would be better, if well followed.

PORTIA

If to do were as easy as to know what were good to do, chapels had been churches and poor men's cottages princes' palaces. It is a good divine that follows his own instructions: I can easier teach twenty what were good to be done, than be one of the twenty to follow mine own teaching. The brain may devise laws for the blood, but a hot temper leaps o'er a cold decree: such a hare is madness the youth, to skip o'er the meshes of good counsel the cripple. But this reasoning is not in the fashion to choose me a husband. O me, the word 'choose!' I may neither choose whom I would nor refuse whom I dislike; so is the will of a living daughter curbed by the will of a dead father. Is it not hard, Nerissa, that I cannot choose one nor refuse none?

NERISSA

Your father was ever virtuous; and holy men at their death have good inspirations: therefore the lottery, that he hath devised in these three chests of gold, silver and lead, whereof who chooses his meaning chooses you, will, no doubt, never be chosen by any rightly but one who shall rightly love. But what warmth is there in your affection towards any of these princely suitors that are already come?

PORTIA

I pray thee, over-name them; and as thou namest them, I will describe them; and, according to my description, level at my affection.

NERISSA

First, there is the Neapolitan prince.

PORTIA

Ay, that's a colt indeed, for he doth nothing but talk of his horse; and he makes it a great appropriation to his own good parts, that he can shoe him himself. I am much afeard my lady his mother played false with a smith.

NERISSA

Then there is the County Palatine.

PORTIA

He doth nothing but frown, as who should say 'If you will not have me, choose:' he hears merry tales and smiles not: I fear he will prove the weeping philosopher when he grows old, being so full of unmannerly sadness in his youth. I had rather be married to a death's-head with a bone in his mouth than to either of these. God defend me from these two!

NERISSA

How say you by the French lord, Monsieur Le Bon?

PORTIA

God made him, and therefore let him pass for a man. In truth, I know it is a sin to be a mocker: but, he! why, he hath a horse better than the Neapolitan's, a better bad habit of frowning than the Count Palatine; he is every man in no man; if a throstle sing, he falls straight a capering: he will fence with his own shadow: if I should marry him, I should marry twenty husbands. If he would despise me I would forgive him, for if he love me to madness, I shall never requite him.

NERISSA

What say you, then, to Falconbridge, the young baron of England?

PORTIA

You know I say nothing to him, for he understands not me, nor I him: he hath neither Latin, French, nor Italian, and you will come into the court and swear that I have a poor pennyworth in the English. He is a proper man's picture, but, alas, who can converse with a dumb-show? How oddly he is suited! I think he bought his doublet in Italy, his round hose in France, his bonnet in Germany and his behaviour every where.

NERISSA

What think you of the Scottish lord, his neighbour?

PORTIA

That he hath a neighbourly charity in him, for he borrowed a box of the ear of the Englishman and swore he would pay him again when he was able: I think the Frenchman became his surety and sealed under for another.

NERISSA

How like you the young German, the Duke of Saxony's nephew?

PORTIA

Very vilely in the morning, when he is sobre, and most vilely in the afternoon, when he is drunk: when he is best, he is a little worse than a man, and when he is worst, he is little better than a beast: and the worst fall that ever fell, I hope I shall make shift to go without him.

NERISSA

If he should offer to choose, and choose the right casket, you should refuse to perform your father's will, if you should refuse to accept him.

PORTIA

Therefore, for fear of the worst, I pray thee, set a deep glass of rhenish wine on the contrary casket, for if the devil be within and that temptation without, I know he will choose it. I will do any thing, Nerissa, ere I'll be married to a sponge.

NERISSA

You need not fear, lady, the having any of these lords: they have acquainted me with their determinations; which is, indeed, to return to their home and to trouble you with no more suit, unless you may be won by some other sort than your father's imposition depending on the caskets.

PORTIA

If I live to be as old as Sibylla, I will die as chaste as Diana, unless I be obtained by the manner of my father's will. I am glad this parcel of wooers are so reasonable, for there is not one among them but I dote on his very absence, and I pray God grant them a fair departure.

NERISSA

Do you not remember, lady, in your father's time, a Venetian, a scholar and a soldier, that came hither in company of the Marquis of Montferrat?

PORTIA

Yes, yes, it was Bassanio; as I think, he was so called.

NERISSA

True, madam: he, of all the men that ever my foolish eyes looked upon, was the best deserving a fair lady.

PORTIA

I remember him well, and I remember him worthy of thy praise.

Enter a Serving-man

How now! what news?

SERVANT

The four strangers seek for you, madam, to take their leave: and there is a forerunner come from a fifth, the Prince of Morocco, who brings word the prince his master will be here to-night.

PORTIA

If I could bid the fifth welcome with so good a heart as I can bid the other four farewell, I should be glad of his approach: if he have the condition of a saint and the complexion of a devil, I had rather he should shrive me than wive me. Come, Nerissa. Sirrah, go before.

Whiles we shut the gates
upon one wooer, another knocks at the door.

Exeunt

SCENE III. Venice. A public place.

Enter BASSANIO and SHYLOCK

SHYLOCK

Three thousand ducats; well.

BASSANIO

Ay, sir, for three months.

SHYLOCK

For three months; well.

BASSANIO

For the which, as I told you, Antonio shall be bound.

SHYLOCK

Antonio shall become bound; well.

BASSANIO

May you stead me? will you pleasure me? shall I know your answer?

SHYLOCK

Three thousand ducats for three months and Antonio bound.

BASSANIO

Your answer to that.

SHYLOCK

Antonio is a good man.

BASSANIO

Have you heard any imputation to the contrary?

SHYLOCK

Oh, no, no, no, no: my meaning in saying he is a good man is to have you understand me that he is sufficient. Yet his means are in supposition: he hath an argosy bound to Tripolis, another to the Indies; I understand moreover, upon the Rialto, he hath a third at Mexico, a fourth for England, and other ventures he hath, squandered abroad. But ships are but boards, sailors but men: there be land-rats and water-rats, water-thieves and land-thieves, I mean pirates, and then there is the peril of waters, winds and rocks. The man is, notwithstanding, sufficient. Three thousand ducats; I think I may take his bond.

BASSANIO

Be assured you may.

SHYLOCK

I will be assured I may; and, that I may be assured, I will bethink me. May I speak with Antonio?

BASSANIO

If it please you to dine with us.

SHYLOCK

Yes, to smell pork; to eat of the habitation which your prophet the Nazarite conjured the devil into. I will buy with you, sell with you, talk with you, walk with you, and so following, but I will not eat with you, drink with you, nor pray with you. What news on the Rialto? Who is he comes here?

Enter ANTONIO

BASSANIO
This is Signior Antonio.
SHYLOCK
[Aside] How like a fawning publican he looks!
I hate him for he is a Christian,
But more for that in low simplicity
He lends out money gratis and brings down
The rate of usance here with us in Venice.
If I can catch him once upon the hip,
I will feed fat the ancient grudge I bear him.
He hates our sacred nation, and he rails,
Even there where merchants most do congregate,
On me, my bargains and my well-won thrift,
Which he calls interest. Cursed be my tribe,
If I forgive him!
BASSANIO
Shylock, do you hear?
SHYLOCK
I am debating of my present store,
And, by the near guess of my memory,
I cannot instantly raise up the gross
Of full three thousand ducats. What of that?
Tubal, a wealthy Hebrew of my tribe,
Will furnish me. But soft! how many months
Do you desire?
To *ANTONIO*
Rest you fair, good signior;
Your worship was the last man in our mouths.
ANTONIO
Shylock, although I neither lend nor borrow
By taking nor by giving of excess,
Yet, to supply the ripe wants of my friend,
I'll break a custom. Is he yet possess'd
How much ye would?
SHYLOCK
Ay, ay, three thousand ducats.
ANTONIO
And for three months.

SHYLOCK
I had forgot; three months; you told me so.
Well then, your bond; and let me see; but hear you;
Methought you said you neither lend nor borrow
Upon advantage.
ANTONIO
I do never use it.
SHYLOCK
When Jacob grazed his uncle Laban's sheep—
This Jacob from our holy Abram was,
As his wise mother wrought in his behalf,
The third possessor; ay, he was the third—
ANTONIO
And what of him? did he take interest?
SHYLOCK
No, not take interest, not, as you would say,
Directly interest: mark what Jacob did.
When Laban and himself were compromised
That all the eanlings which were streak'd and pied
Should fall as Jacob's hire, the ewes, being rank,
In the end of autumn turned to the rams,
And, when the work of generation was
Between these woolly breeders in the act,
The skilful shepherd peel'd me certain wands,
And, in the doing of the deed of kind,
He stuck them up before the fulsome ewes,
Who then conceiving did in eaning time
Fall parti-colour'd lambs, and those were Jacob's.
This was a way to thrive, and he was blest:
And thrift is blessing, if men steal it not.
ANTONIO
This was a venture, sir, that Jacob served for;
A thing not in his power to bring to pass,
But sway'd and fashion'd by the hand of heaven.
Was this inserted to make interest good?
Or is your gold and silver ewes and rams?
SHYLOCK

I cannot tell; I make it breed as fast:
But note me, signior.
ANTONIO
Mark you this, Bassanio,
The devil can cite Scripture for his purpose.
An evil soul producing holy witness
Is like a villain with a smiling cheek,
A goodly apple rotten at the heart:
O, what a goodly outside falsehood hath!
SHYLOCK
Three thousand ducats; 'tis a good round sum.
Three months from twelve; then, let me see; the rate—
ANTONIO
Well, Shylock, shall we be beholding to you?
SHYLOCK
Signior Antonio, many a time and oft
In the Rialto you have rated me
About my moneys and my usances:
Still have I borne it with a patient shrug,
For sufferance is the badge of all our tribe.
You call me misbeliever, cut-throat dog,
And spit upon my Jewish gaberdine,
And all for use of that which is mine own.
Well then, it now appears you need my help:
Go to, then; you come to me, and you say
'Shylock, we would have moneys:' you say so;
You, that did void your rheum upon my beard
And foot me as you spurn a stranger cur
Over your threshold: moneys is your suit
What should I say to you? Should I not say
'Hath a dog money? is it possible
A cur can lend three thousand ducats?' Or
Shall I bend low and in a bondman's key,
With bated breath and whispering humbleness, Say this;
'Fair sir, you spit on me on Wednesday last;
You spurn'd me such a day; another time
You call'd me dog; and for these courtesies
I'll lend you thus much moneys'?

ANTONIO
I am as like to call thee so again,
To spit on thee again, to spurn thee too.
If thou wilt lend this money, lend it not
As to thy friends; for when did friendship take
A breed for barren metal of his friend?
But lend it rather to thine enemy,
Who, if he break, thou mayst with better face
Exact the penalty.
SHYLOCK
Why, look you, how you storm!
I would be friends with you and have your love,
Forget the shames that you have stain'd me with,
Supply your present wants and take no doit
Of usance for my moneys, and you'll not hear me:
This is kind I offer.
BASSANIO
This were kindness.
SHYLOCK
This kindness will I show.
Go with me to a notary, seal me there
Your single bond; and, in a merry sport,
If you repay me not on such a day,
In such a place, such sum or sums as are
Express'd in the condition, let the forfeit
Be nominated for an equal pound
Of your fair flesh, to be cut off and taken
In what part of your body pleaseth me.
ANTONIO
Content, i' faith: I'll seal to such a bond
And say there is much kindness in the Jew.
BASSANIO
You shall not seal to such a bond for me:
I'll rather dwell in my necessity.
ANTONIO
Why, fear not, man; I will not forfeit it:
Within these two months, that's a month before

This bond expires, I do expect return
Of thrice three times the value of this bond.
SHYLOCK
O father Abram, what these Christians are,
Whose own hard dealings teaches them suspect
The thoughts of others! Pray you, tell me this;
If he should break his day, what should I gain
By the exaction of the forfeiture?
A pound of man's flesh taken from a man
Is not so estimable, profitable neither,
As flesh of muttons, beefs, or goats. I say,
To buy his favour, I extend this friendship:
If he will take it, so; if not, adieu;
And, for my love, I pray you wrong me not.
ANTONIO
Yes Shylock, I will seal unto this bond.
SHYLOCK
Then meet me forthwith at the notary's;
Give him direction for this merry bond,
And I will go and purse the ducats straight,
See to my house, left in the fearful guard
Of an unthrifty knave, and presently
I will be with you.
ANTONIO
Hie thee, gentle Jew.
Exit Shylock
The Hebrew will turn Christian: he grows kind.
BASSANIO
I like not fair terms and a villain's mind.
ANTONIO
Come on: in this there can be no dismay;
My ships come home a month before the day.
Exeunt

ACT II

SCENE I. Belmont. A room in PORTIA'S house.

Flourish of cornets. Enter the PRINCE OF MOROCCO and his train; PORTIA, NERISSA, and others attending
MOROCCO

Mislike me not for my complexion,
The shadow'd livery of the burnish'd sun,
To whom I am a neighbour and near bred.
Bring me the fairest creature northward born,
Where Phoebus' fire scarce thaws the icicles,
And let us make incision for your love,
To prove whose blood is reddest, his or mine.
I tell thee, lady, this aspect of mine
Hath fear'd the valiant: by my love I swear
The best-regarded virgins of our clime
Have loved it too: I would not change this hue,
Except to steal your thoughts, my gentle queen.

PORTIA

In terms of choice I am not solely led
By nice direction of a maiden's eyes;
Besides, the lottery of my destiny
Bars me the right of voluntary choosing:
But if my father had not scanted me
And hedged me by his wit, to yield myself
His wife who wins me by that means I told you,
Yourself, renowned prince, then stood as fair
As any comer I have look'd on yet
For my affection.

MOROCCO

Even for that I thank you:
Therefore, I pray you, lead me to the caskets
To try my fortune. By this scimitar
That slew the Sophy and a Persian prince
That won three fields of Sultan Solyman,
I would outstare the sternest eyes that look,
Outbrave the heart most daring on the earth,
Pluck the young sucking cubs from the she-bear,
Yea, mock the lion when he roars for prey,
To win thee, lady. But, alas the while!
If Hercules and Lichas play at dice
Which is the better man, the greater throw
May turn by fortune from the weaker hand:
So is Alcides beaten by his page;

And so may I, blind fortune leading me,
Miss that which one unworthier may attain,
And die with grieving.

PORTIA

You must take your chance,
And either not attempt to choose at all
Or swear before you choose, if you choose wrong
Never to speak to lady afterward
In way of marriage: therefore be advised.

MOROCCO

Nor will not. Come, bring me unto my chance.

PORTIA

First, forward to the temple: after dinner
Your hazard shall be made.

MOROCCO

Good fortune then!
To make me blest or cursed'st among men.

Cornets, and exeunt

SCENE II. Venice. A street.

Enter LAUNCELOT

LAUNCELOT

Certainly my conscience will serve me to run from this Jew my master. The fiend is at mine elbow and tempts me saying to me 'Gobbo, Launcelot Gobbo, good Launcelot,' or 'good Gobbo,' or good Launcelot Gobbo, use your legs, take the start, run away. My conscience says 'No; take heed,' honest Launcelot; take heed, honest Gobbo, or, as aforesaid, 'honest Launcelot Gobbo; do not run; scorn running with thy heels.' Well, the most courageous fiend bids me pack: 'Via!' says the fiend; 'away!' says the fiend; 'for the heavens, rouse up a brave mind,' says the fiend, 'and run.' Well, my conscience, hanging about the neck of my heart, says very wisely to me 'My honest friend Launcelot, being an honest man's son,' or rather an honest woman's son; for, indeed, my father did something smack, something grow to, he had a kind of taste; well, my conscience says 'Launcelot, budge not.' 'Budge,' says the fiend. 'Budge not,' says my conscience. 'Conscience,' say I, 'you counsel well;' ' Fiend,' say I, 'you counsel well:' to be ruled by my conscience, I should stay with the Jew my master, who, God bless the mark, is a kind of devil; and, to run away from the Jew, I should be ruled by the fiend, who, saving your reverence, is the devil himself. Certainly the Jew is the very devil incarnal; and, in my conscience, my conscience is but a kind of hard conscience, to offer to counsel me to stay with the Jew. The fiend gives the more friendly counsel: I will run, fiend; my heels are at your command; I will run.

Enter Old GOBBO, with a basket

GOBBO

Master young man, you, I pray you, which is the way to master Jew's?

LAUNCELOT

[Aside] O heavens, this is my true-begotten father! who, being more than sand-blind, high-gravel blind, knows me not: I will try confusions with him.

GOBBO

Master young gentleman, I pray you, which is the way to master Jew's?

LAUNCELOT

Turn up on your right hand at the next turning, but, at the next turning of all, on your left; marry, at the very next turning, turn of no hand, but turn down indirectly to the Jew's house.

GOBBO

By God's sonties, 'twill be a hard way to hit. Can you tell me whether one Launcelot, that dwells with him, dwell with him or no?

LAUNCELOT

Talk you of young Master Launcelot?

Aside

Mark me now; now will I raise the waters. Talk you of young Master Launcelot?

GOBBO

No master, sir, but a poor man's son: his father, though I say it, is an honest exceeding poor man and, God be thanked, well to live.

LAUNCELOT

Well, let his father be what a' will, we talk of young Master Launcelot.

GOBBO

Your worship's friend and Launcelot, sir.

LAUNCELOT

But I pray you, ergo, old man, ergo, I beseech you, talk you of young Master Launcelot?

GOBBO

Of Launcelot, an't please your mastership.

LAUNCELOT

Ergo, Master Launcelot. Talk not of Master Launcelot, father; for the young gentleman, according to Fates and Destinies and such odd sayings, the Sisters Three and such branches of learning, is indeed deceased, or, as you would say in plain terms, gone to heaven.

GOBBO

Marry, God forbid! the boy was the very staff of my age, my very prop.

LAUNCELOT

Do I look like a cudgel or a hovel-post, a staff or a prop? Do you know me, father?

GOBBO

Alack the day, I know you not, young gentleman: but, I pray you, tell me, is my boy, God rest his soul, alive or dead?

LAUNCELOT

Do you not know me, father?

GOBBO

Alack, sir, I am sand-blind; I know you not.

LAUNCELOT

Nay, indeed, if you had your eyes, you might fail of the knowing me: it is a wise father that knows his own child. Well, old man, I will tell you news of your son: give me your blessing: truth will come to light; murder cannot be hid long; a man's son may, but at the length truth will out.

GOBBO

Pray you, sir, stand up: I am sure you are not Launcelot, my boy.

LAUNCELOT

Pray you, let's have no more fooling about it, but give me your blessing: I am Launcelot, your boy that was, your son that is, your child that shall be.

GOBBO

I cannot think you are my son.

LAUNCELOT

I know not what I shall think of that: but I am Launcelot, the Jew's man, and I am sure Margery your wife is my mother.

GOBBO

Her name is Margery, indeed: I'll be sworn, if thou be Launcelot, thou art mine own flesh and blood. Lord worshipped might he be! what a beard hast thou got! thou hast got more hair on thy chin than Dobbin my fill-horse has on his tail.

LAUNCELOT

It should seem, then, that Dobbin's tail grows backward: I am sure he had more hair of his tail than I have of my face when I last saw him.

GOBBO

Lord, how art thou changed! How dost thou and thy master agree? I have brought him a present. How 'gree you now?

LAUNCELOT

Well, well: but, for mine own part, as I have set up my rest to run away, so I will not rest till I have run some ground. My master's a very Jew: give him a present! give him a halter: I am famished in his service; you may tell every finger I have with my ribs. Father, I am glad you are come: give me your present to one Master Bassanio, who, indeed, gives rare new liveries: if I serve not him, I will run as far as God has any ground. O rare fortune! here comes the man: to him, father; for I am a Jew, if I serve the Jew any longer.

Enter BASSANIO, with LEONARDO and other followers

BASSANIO

You may do so; but let it be so hasted that supper be ready at the farthest by five of the clock. See these letters delivered; put the liveries to making, and desire Gratiano to come anon to my lodging.

Exit a Servant

LAUNCELOT

To him, father.

GOBBO

God bless your worship!

BASSANIO

Gramercy! wouldst thou aught with me?

GOBBO

Here's my son, sir, a poor boy,—

LAUNCELOT

Not a poor boy, sir, but the rich Jew's man; that would, sir, as my father shall specify—

GOBBO

He hath a great infection, sir, as one would say, to serve—

LAUNCELOT

Indeed, the short and the long is, I serve the Jew, and have a desire, as my father shall specify—

GOBBO

His master and he, saving your worship's reverence, are scarce cater-cousins—

LAUNCELOT

To be brief, the very truth is that the Jew, having done me wrong, doth cause me, as my father, being, I hope, an old man, shall frutify unto you—

GOBBO

I have here a dish of doves that I would bestow upon your worship, and my suit is—

LAUNCELOT

In very brief, the suit is impertinent to myself, as your worship shall know by this honest old man; and, though I say it, though old man, yet poor man, my father.

BASSANIO

One speak for both. What would you?

LAUNCELOT

Serve you, sir.

GOBBO

That is the very defect of the matter, sir.

BASSANIO

I know thee well; thou hast obtain'd thy suit:
Shylock thy master spoke with me this day,
And hath preferr'd thee, if it be preferment
To leave a rich Jew's service, to become
The follower of so poor a gentleman.

LAUNCELOT

The old proverb is very well parted between my master Shylock and you, sir: you have the grace of God, sir, and he hath enough.

BASSANIO

Thou speak'st it well. Go, father, with thy son.
Take leave of thy old master and inquire
My lodging out. Give him a livery
More guarded than his fellows': see it done.

LAUNCELOT

Father, in. I cannot get a service, no; I have ne'er a tongue in my head. Well, if any man in Italy have a fairer table which doth offer to swear upon a book, I shall have good fortune. Go to, here's a simple line of life: here's a small trifle of wives: alas, fifteen wives is nothing! eleven widows and nine maids is a simple coming-in for one man: and then to 'scape drowning thrice, and to be in peril of my life with the edge of a feather-bed;

here are simple scapes. Well, if Fortune be a woman, she's a good wench for this gear. Father, come; I'll take my leave of the Jew in the twinkling of an eye.

Exeunt Launcelot and Old Gobbo

BASSANIO

I pray thee, good Leonardo, think on this:
These things being bought and orderly bestow'd,
Return in haste, for I do feast to-night
My best-esteem'd acquaintance: hie thee, go.

LEONARDO

My best endeavours shall be done herein.

Enter GRATIANO

GRATIANO

Where is your master?

LEONARDO

Yonder, sir, he walks.

Exit

GRATIANO

Signior Bassanio!

BASSANIO

Gratiano!

GRATIANO

I have a suit to you.

BASSANIO

You have obtain'd it.

GRATIANO

You must not deny me: I must go with you to Belmont.

BASSANIO

Why then you must. But hear thee, Gratiano;
Thou art too wild, too rude and bold of voice;
Parts that become thee happily enough
And in such eyes as ours appear not faults;
But where thou art not known, why, there they show
Something too liberal. Pray thee, take pain
To allay with some cold drops of modesty
Thy skipping spirit, lest through thy wild behaviour

I be misconstrued in the place I go to,
And lose my hopes.

GRATIANO

Signior Bassanio, hear me:
If I do not put on a sobre habit,
Talk with respect and swear but now and then,
Wear prayer-books in my pocket, look demurely,
Nay more, while grace is saying, hood mine eyes
Thus with my hat, and sigh and say 'amen,'
Use all the observance of civility,
Like one well studied in a sad ostent
To please his grandam, never trust me more.

BASSANIO

Well, we shall see your bearing.

GRATIANO

Nay, but I bar to-night: you shall not gauge me
By what we do to-night.

BASSANIO

No, that were pity:
I would entreat you rather to put on
Your boldest suit of mirth, for we have friends
That purpose merriment. But fare you well:
I have some business.

GRATIANO

And I must to Lorenzo and the rest:
But we will visit you at supper-time.

Exeunt

SCENE III. The same. A room in SHYLOCK'S house.

Enter JESSICA and LAUNCELOT

JESSICA

I am sorry thou wilt leave my father so:
Our house is hell, and thou, a merry devil,
Didst rob it of some taste of tediousness.
But fare thee well, there is a ducat for thee:
And, Launcelot, soon at supper shalt thou see
Lorenzo, who is thy new master's guest:
Give him this letter; do it secretly;

And so farewell: I would not have my father
See me in talk with thee.

LAUNCELOT

Adieu! tears exhibit my tongue. Most beautiful pagan, most sweet Jew! if a Christian did not play the knave and get thee, I am much deceived. But, adieu: these foolish drops do something drown my manly spirit: adieu.

JESSICA

Farewell, good Launcelot.

Exit Launcelot

Alack, what heinous sin is it in me
To be ashamed to be my father's child!
But though I am a daughter to his blood,
I am not to his manners. O Lorenzo,
If thou keep promise, I shall end this strife,
Become a Christian and thy loving wife.

Exit

SCENE IV. The same. A street.

Enter GRATIANO, LORENZO, SALARINO, and SALANIO

LORENZO

Nay, we will slink away in supper-time,
Disguise us at my lodging and return,
All in an hour.

GRATIANO

We have not made good preparation.

SALARINO

We have not spoke us yet of torchbearers.

SALANIO

'Tis vile, unless it may be quaintly order'd,
And better in my mind not undertook.

LORENZO

'Tis now but four o'clock: we have two hours
To furnish us.

Enter LAUNCELOT, with a letter

Friend Launcelot, what's the news?

LAUNCELOT

An it shall please you to break up
this, it shall seem to signify.
LORENZO
I know the hand: in faith, 'tis a fair hand;
And whiter than the paper it writ on
Is the fair hand that writ.
GRATIANO
Love-news, in faith.
LAUNCELOT
By your leave, sir.
LORENZO
Whither goest thou?
LAUNCELOT
Marry, sir, to bid my old master the
Jew to sup to-night with my new master the Christian.
LORENZO
Hold here, take this: tell gentle Jessica
I will not fail her; speak it privately.
Go, gentlemen,
Exit Launcelot
Will you prepare you for this masque tonight?
I am provided of a torch-bearer.
SALANIO
Ay, marry, I'll be gone about it straight.
SALANIO
And so will I.
LORENZO
Meet me and Gratiano
At Gratiano's lodging some hour hence.
SALARINO
'Tis good we do so.
Exeunt SALARINO and SALANIO
GRATIANO
Was not that letter from fair Jessica?
LORENZO
I must needs tell thee all. She hath directed
How I shall take her from her father's house,
What gold and jewels she is furnish'd with,

What page's suit she hath in readiness.
If e'er the Jew her father come to heaven,
It will be for his gentle daughter's sake:
And never dare misfortune cross her foot,
Unless she do it under this excuse,
That she is issue to a faithless Jew.
Come, go with me; peruse this as thou goest:
Fair Jessica shall be my torch-beare r.
Exeunt
SCENE V. The same. Before SHYLOCK'S house.
Enter SHYLOCK and LAUNCELOT
SHYLOCK
Well, thou shalt see, thy eyes shall be thy judge,
The difference of old Shylock and Bassanio:—
What, Jessica!—thou shalt not gormandise,
As thou hast done with me:—What, Jessica!—
And sleep and snore, and rend apparel out;—
Why, Jessica, I say!
LAUNCELOT
Why, Jessica!
SHYLOCK
Who bids thee call? I do not bid thee call.
LAUNCELOT
Your worship was wont to tell me that
I could do nothing without bidding.
Enter Jessica
JESSICA
Call you? what is your will?
SHYLOCK
I am bid forth to supper, Jessica:
There are my keys. But wherefore should I go?
I am not bid for love; they flatter me:
But yet I'll go in hate, to feed upon
The prodigal Christian. Jessica, my girl,
Look to my house. I am right loath to go:
There is some ill a-brewing towards my rest,
For I did dream of money-bags to-night.
LAUNCELOT

I beseech you, sir, go: my young master doth expect your reproach.

SHYLOCK

So do I his.

LAUNCELOT

An they have conspired together, I will not say you shall see a masque; but if you do, then it was not for nothing that my nose fell a-bleeding on Black-Monday last at six o'clock i' the morning, falling out that year on Ash-Wednesday was four year, in the afternoon.

SHYLOCK

What, are there masques? Hear you me, Jessica:
Lock up my doors; and when you hear the drum
And the vile squealing of the wry-neck'd fife,
Clamber not you up to the casements then,
Nor thrust your head into the public street
To gaze on Christian fools with varnish'd faces,
But stop my house's ears, I mean my casements:
Let not the sound of shallow foppery enter
My sobre house. By Jacob's staff, I swear,
I have no mind of feasting forth to-night:
But I will go. Go you before me, sirrah;
Say I will come.

LAUNCELOT

I will go before, sir. Mistress, look out at window, for all this, There will come a Christian boy, will be worth a Jewess' eye.

Exit

SHYLOCK

What says that fool of Hagar's offspring, ha?

JESSICA

His words were 'Farewell mistress;' nothing else.

SHYLOCK

The patch is kind enough, but a huge feeder;
Snail-slow in profit, and he sleeps by day
More than the wild-cat: drones hive not with me;
Therefore I part with him, and part with him

To one that would have him help to waste
His borrow'd purse. Well, Jessica, go in;
Perhaps I will return immediately:
Do as I bid you; shut doors after you:
Fast bind, fast find;
A proverb never stale in thrifty mind.
Exit
JESSICA
Farewell; and if my fortune be not crost,
I have a father, you a daughter, lost.
Exit
SCENE VI. The same.
Enter GRATIANO and SALARINO, masqued
GRATIANO
This is the pent-house under which Lorenzo
Desired us to make stand.
SALARINO
His hour is almost past.

GRATIANO
And it is marvel he out-dwells his hour,
For lovers ever run before the clock.
SALARINO
O, ten times faster Venus' pigeons fly
To seal love's bonds new-made, than they are wont
To keep obliged faith unforfeited!
GRATIANO
That ever holds: who riseth from a feast
With that keen appetite that he sits down?
Where is the horse that doth untread again
His tedious measures with the unbated fire
That he did pace them first? All things that are,
Are with more spirit chased than enjoy'd.
How like a younker or a prodigal
The scarfed bark puts from her native bay,
Hugg'd and embraced by the strumpet wind!
How like the prodigal doth she return,

With over-weather'd ribs and ragged sails,
Lean, rent and beggar'd by the strumpet wind!
SALARINO
Here comes Lorenzo: more of this hereafter.
Enter LORENZO
LORENZO
Sweet friends, your patience for my long abode;
Not I, but my affairs, have made you wait:
When you shall please to play the thieves for wives,
I'll watch as long for you then. Approach;
Here dwells my father Jew. Ho! who's within?
Enter JESSICA, above, in boy's clothes
JESSICA
Who are you? Tell me, for more certainty,
Albeit I'll swear that I do know your tongue.
LORENZO
Lorenzo, and thy love.
JESSICA
Lorenzo, certain, and my love indeed,
For who love I so much? And now who knows
But you, Lorenzo, whether I am yours?
LORENZO
Heaven and thy thoughts are witness that thou art.
JESSICA
Here, catch this casket; it is worth the pains.
I am glad 'tis night, you do not look on me,
For I am much ashamed of my exchange:
But love is blind and lovers cannot see
The pretty follies that themselves commit;
For if they could, Cupid himself would blush
To see me thus transformed to a boy.
LORENZO
Descend, for you must be my torchbearer.
JESSICA
What, must I hold a candle to my shames?
They in themselves, good-sooth, are too too light.
Why, 'tis an office of discovery, love;
And I should be obscured.

LORENZO
So are you, sweet,
Even in the lovely garnish of a boy.
But come at once;
For the close night doth play the runaway,
And we are stay'd for at Bassanio's feast.
JESSICA
I will make fast the doors, and gild myself
With some more ducats, and be with you straight.
Exit above
GRATIANO
Now, by my hood, a Gentile and no Jew.
LORENZO
Beshrew me but I love her heartily;
For she is wise, if I can judge of her,
And fair she is, if that mine eyes be true,
And true she is, as she hath proved herself,
And therefore, like herself, wise, fair and true,
Shall she be placed in my constant soul.
Enter JESSICA, below
What, art thou come? On, gentlemen; away!
Our masquing mates by this time for us stay.
Exit with Jessica and Salarino
Enter ANTONIO
ANTONIO
Who's there?
GRATIANO
Signior Antonio!
ANTONIO
Fie, fie, Gratiano! where are all the rest?
'Tis nine o'clock: our friends all stay for you.
No masque to-night: the wind is come about;
Bassanio presently will go aboard:
I have sent twenty out to seek for you.
GRATIANO
I am glad on't: I desire no more delight
Than to be under sail and gone to-night.
Exeunt

SCENE VII. Belmont. A room in PORTIA'S house.

Flourish of cornets. Enter PORTIA, with the PRINCE OF MOROCCO, and their trains

PORTIA

Go draw aside the curtains and discover
The several caskets to this noble prince.
Now make your choice.

MOROCCO

The first, of gold, who this inscription bears,
'Who chooseth me shall gain what many men desire;'
The second, silver, which this promise carries,
'Who chooseth me shall get as much as he deserves;'
This third, dull lead, with warning all as blunt,
'Who chooseth me must give and hazard all he hath.'
How shall I know if I do choose the right?

PORTIA

The one of them contains my picture, prince:
If you choose that, then I am yours withal.

MOROCCO

Some god direct my judgment! Let me see;
I will survey the inscriptions back again.
What says this leaden casket?
'Who chooseth me must give and hazard all he hath.'
Must give: for what? for lead? hazard for lead?
This casket threatens. Men that hazard all
Do it in hope of fair advantages:
A golden mind stoops not to shows of dross;
I'll then nor give nor hazard aught for lead.
What says the silver with her virgin hue?
'Who chooseth me shall get as much as he deserves.'
As much as he deserves! Pause there, Morocco,
And weigh thy value with an even hand:
If thou be'st rated by thy estimation,
Thou dost deserve enough; and yet enough
May not extend so far as to the lady:
And yet to be afeard of my deserving
Were but a weak disabling of myself.
As much as I deserve! Why, that's the lady:

I do in birth deserve her, and in fortunes,
In graces and in qualities of breeding;
But more than these, in love I do deserve.
What if I stray'd no further, but chose here?
Let's see once more this saying graved in gold
'Who chooseth me shall gain what many men desire.'
Why, that's the lady; all the world desires her;
From the four corners of the earth they come,
To kiss this shrine, this mortal-breathing saint:
The Hyrcanian deserts and the vasty wilds
Of wide Arabia are as thoroughfares now
For princes to come view fair Portia:
The watery kingdom, whose ambitious head
Spits in the face of heaven, is no bar
To stop the foreign spirits, but they come,
As o'er a brook, to see fair Portia.
One of these three contains her heavenly picture.
Is't like that lead contains her? 'Twere damnation
To think so base a thought: it were too gross
To rib her cerecloth in the obscure grave.
Or shall I think in silver she's immured,
Being ten times undervalued to tried gold?
O sinful thought! Never so rich a gem
Was set in worse than gold. They have in England
A coin that bears the figure of an angel
Stamped in gold, but that's insculp'd upon;
But here an angel in a golden bed
Lies all within. Deliver me the key:
Here do I choose, and thrive I as I may!
PORTIA
There, take it, prince; and if my form lie there,
Then I am yours.
He unlocks the golden casket
MOROCCO
O hell! what have we here?
A carrion Death, within whose empty eye
There is a written scroll! I'll read the writing.
Reads

All that glitters is not gold;
Often have you heard that told:
Many a man his life hath sold
But my outside to behold:
Gilded tombs do worms enfold.
Had you been as wise as bold,
Young in limbs, in judgment old,
Your answer had not been inscroll'd:
Fare you well; your suit is cold.
Cold, indeed; and labour lost:
Then, farewell, heat, and welcome, frost!
Portia, adieu. I have too grieved a heart
To take a tedious leave: thus losers part.
Exit with his train. Flourish of cornets
PORTIA
A gentle riddance. Draw the curtains, go.
Let all of his complexion choose me so.
Exeunt
SCENE VIII. Venice. A street.
Enter SALARINO and SALANIO
SALARINO
Why, man, I saw Bassanio under sail:
With him is Gratiano gone along;
And in their ship I am sure Lorenzo is not.
SALANIO
The villain Jew with outcries raised the duke,
Who went with him to search Bassanio's ship.
SALARINO
He came too late, the ship was under sail:
But there the duke was given to understand
That in a gondola were seen together
Lorenzo and his amorous Jessica:
Besides, Antonio certified the duke
They were not with Bassanio in his ship.
SALANIO
I never heard a passion so confused,
So strange, outrageous, and so variable,
As the dog Jew did utter in the streets:

'My daughter! O my ducats! O my daughter!
Fled with a Christian! O my Christian ducats!
Justice! the law! my ducats, and my daughter!
A sealed bag, two sealed bags of ducats,
Of double ducats, stolen from me by my daughter!
And jewels, two stones, two rich and precious stones,
Stolen by my daughter! Justice! find the girl;
She hath the stones upon her, and the ducats.'

SALARINO
Why, all the boys in Venice follow him,
Crying, his stones, his daughter, and his ducats.

SALANIO
Let good Antonio look he keep his day,
Or he shall pay for this.

SALARINO
Marry, well remember'd.
I reason'd with a Frenchman yesterday,
Who told me, in the narrow seas that part
The French and English, there miscarried
A vessel of our country richly fraught:
I thought upon Antonio when he told me;
And wish'd in silence that it were not his.

SALANIO
You were best to tell Antonio what you hear;
Yet do not suddenly, for it may grieve him.

SALARINO
A kinder gentleman treads not the earth.
I saw Bassanio and Antonio part:
Bassanio told him he would make some speed
Of his return: he answer'd, 'Do not so;
Slubber not business for my sake, Bassanio
But stay the very riping of the time;
And for the Jew's bond which he hath of me,
Let it not enter in your mind of love:
Be merry, and employ your chiefest thoughts
To courtship and such fair ostents of love
As shall conveniently become you there:'
And even there, his eye being big with tears,

Turning his face, he put his hand behind him,
And with affection wondrous sensible
He wrung Bassanio's hand; and so they parted.
SALANIO
I think he only loves the world for him.
I pray thee, let us go and find him out
And quicken his embraced heaviness
With some delight or other.
SALARINO
Do we so.
Exeunt
SCENE IX. Belmont. A room in PORTIA'S house.
Enter NERISSA with a Servitor
NERISSA
Quick, quick, I pray thee; draw the curtain straight:
The Prince of Arragon hath ta'en his oath,
And comes to his election presently.
Flourish of cornets. Enter the PRINCE OF ARRAGON, PORTIA, and their trains
PORTIA
Behold, there stand the caskets, noble prince:
If you choose that wherein I am contain'd,
Straight shall our nuptial rites be solemnized:
But if you fail, without more speech, my lord,
You must be gone from hence immediately.
ARRAGON
I am enjoin'd by oath to observe three things:
First, never to unfold to any one
Which casket 'twas I chose; next, if I fail
Of the right casket, never in my life
To woo a maid in way of marriage: Lastly,
If I do fail in fortune of my choice,
Immediately to leave you and be gone.
PORTIA
To these injunctions every one doth swear
That comes to hazard for my worthless self.
ARRAGON
And so have I address'd me. Fortune now

To my heart's hope! Gold; silver; and base lead.
'Who chooseth me must give and hazard all he hath.'
You shall look fairer, ere I give or hazard.
What says the golden chest? ha! let me see:
'Who chooseth me shall gain what many men desire.'
What many men desire! that 'many' may be meant
By the fool multitude, that choose by show,
Not learning more than the fond eye doth teach;
Which pries not to the interior, but, like the martlet,
Builds in the weather on the outward wall,
Even in the force and road of casualty.
I will not choose what many men desire,
Because I will not jump with common spirits
And rank me with the barbarous multitudes.
Why, then to thee, thou silver treasure-house;
Tell me once more what title thou dost bear:
'Who chooseth me shall get as much as he deserves:'
And well said too; for who shall go about
To cozen fortune and be honourable
Without the stamp of merit? Let none presume
To wear an undeserved dignity.
O, that estates, degrees and offices
Were not derived corruptly, and that clear honour
Were purchased by the merit of the wearer!
How many then should cover that stand bare!
How many be commanded that command!
How much low peasantry would then be glean'd
From the true seed of honour! and how much honour
Pick'd from the chaff and ruin of the times
To be new-varnish'd! Well, but to my choice:
'Who chooseth me shall get as much as he deserves.'
I will assume desert. Give me a key for this,
And instantly unlock my fortunes here.
He opens the silver casket
PORTIA
Too long a pause for that which you find there.
ARRAGON
What's here? the portrait of a blinking idiot,

Presenting me a schedule! I will read it.
How much unlike art thou to Portia!
How much unlike my hopes and my deservings!
'Who chooseth me shall have as much as he deserves.'
Did I deserve no more than a fool's head?
Is that my prize? are my deserts no better?
PORTIA
To offend, and judge, are distinct offices
And of opposed natures.
ARRAGON
What is here?
Reads
The fire seven times tried this:
Seven times tried that judgment is,
That did never choose amiss.
Some there be that shadows kiss;
Such have but a shadow's bliss:
There be fools alive, I wis,
Silver'd o'er; and so was this.
Take what wife you will to bed,
I will ever be your head:
So be gone: you are sped.
Still more fool I shall appear
By the time I linger here
With one fool's head I came to woo,
But I go away with two.
Sweet, adieu. I'll keep my oath,
Patiently to bear my wroth.
Exeunt Arragon and train
PORTIA
Thus hath the candle singed the moth.
O, these deliberate fools! when they do choose,
They have the wisdom by their wit to lose.
NERISSA
The ancient saying is no heresy,
Hanging and wiving goes by destiny.
PORTIA
Come, draw the curtain, Nerissa.

Enter a Servant

Servant

Where is my lady?

PORTIA

Here: what would my lord?

Servant

Madam, there is alighted at your gate
A young Venetian, one that comes before
To signify the approaching of his lord;
From whom he bringeth sensible regreets,
To wit, besides commends and courteous breath,
Gifts of rich value. Yet I have not seen
So likely an ambassador of love:
A day in April never came so sweet,
To show how costly summer was at hand,
As this fore-spurrer comes before his lord.

PORTIA

No more, I pray thee: I am half afeard
Thou wilt say anon he is some kin to thee,
Thou spend'st such high-day wit in praising him.
Come, come, Nerissa; for I long to see
Quick Cupid's post that comes so mannerly.

NERISSA

Bassanio, lord Love, if thy will it be!

Exeunt

ACT III

SCENE I. Venice. A street.

Enter SALANIO and SALARINO

SALANIO

Now, what news on the Rialto?

SALARINO

Why, yet it lives there uncheck'd that Antonio hath
a ship of rich lading wrecked on the narrow seas;
the Goodwins, I think they call the place; a very
dangerous flat and fatal, where the carcasses of many
a tall ship lie buried, as they say, if my gossip
Report be an honest woman of her word.

SALANIO

I would she were as lying a gossip in that as ever knapped ginger or made her neighbours believe she wept for the death of a third husband. But it is true, without any slips of prolixity or crossing the plain highway of talk, that the good Antonio, the honest Antonio,—O that I had a title good enough to keep his name company!—

SALARINO

Come, the full stop.

SALANIO

Ha! what sayest thou? Why, the end is, he hath lost a ship.

SALARINO

I would it might prove the end of his losses.

SALANIO

Let me say 'amen' betimes, lest the devil cross my prayer, for here he comes in the likeness of a Jew.

Enter SHYLOCK

How now, Shylock! what news among the merchants?

SHYLOCK

You know, none so well, none so well as you, of my daughter's flight.

SALARINO

That's certain: I, for my part, knew the tailor that made the wings she flew withal.

SALANIO

And Shylock, for his own part, knew the bird was fledged; and then it is the complexion of them all to leave the dam.

SHYLOCK

She is damned for it.

SALANIO

That's certain, if the devil may be her judge.

SHYLOCK

My own flesh and blood to rebel!

SALANIO

Out upon it, old carrion! rebels it at these years?

SHYLOCK
I say, my daughter is my flesh and blood.
SALARINO
There is more difference between thy flesh and hers than between jet and ivory; more between your bloods than there is between red wine and rhenish. But tell us, do you hear whether Antonio have had any loss at sea or no?
SHYLOCK
There I have another bad match: a bankrupt, a prodigal, who dare scarce show his head on the Rialto; a beggar, that was used to come so smug upon the mart; let him look to his bond: he was wont to call me usurer; let him look to his bond: he was wont to lend money for a Christian courtesy; let him look to his bond.
SALARINO
Why, I am sure, if he forfeit, thou wilt not take his flesh: what's that good for?
SHYLOCK
To bait fish withal: if it will feed nothing else, it will feed my revenge. He hath disgraced me, and hindered me half a million; laughed at my losses, mocked at my gains, scorned my nation, thwarted my bargains, cooled my friends, heated mine enemies; and what's his reason? I am a Jew. Hath not a Jew eyes? hath not a Jew hands, organs, dimensions, senses, affections, passions? fed with the same food, hurt with the same weapons, subject to the same diseases, healed by the same means, warmed and cooled by the same winter and summer, as a Christian is? If you prick us, do we not bleed? if you tickle us, do we not laugh? if you poison us, do we not die? and if you wrong us, shall we not revenge? If we are like you in the rest, we will resemble you in that. If a Jew wrong a Christian, what is his humility? Revenge. If a Christian wrong a Jew, what should his sufferance be by

Christian example? Why, revenge. The villany you teach me, I will execute, and it shall go hard but I will better the instruction.

Enter a Servant

SERVANT

Gentlemen, my master Antonio is at his house and desires to speak with you both.

SALARINO

We have been up and down to seek him.

Enter TUBAL

SALANIO

Here comes another of the tribe: a third cannot be matched, unless the devil himself turn Jew.

Exeunt SALANIO, SALARINO, and Servant

SHYLOCK

How now, Tubal! what news from Genoa? hast thou found my daughter?

TUBAL

I often came where I did hear of her, but cannot find her.

SHYLOCK

Why, there, there, there, there! a diamond gone, cost me two thousand ducats in Frankfort! The curse never fell upon our nation till now; I never felt it till now: two thousand ducats in that; and other precious, precious jewels. I would my daughter were dead at my foot, and the jewels in her ear! would she were hearsed at my foot, and the ducats in her coffin! No news of them? Why, so: and I know not what's spent in the search: why, thou loss upon loss! the thief gone with so much, and so much to find the thief; and no satisfaction, no revenge: nor no in luck stirring but what lights on my shoulders; no sighs but of my breathing; no tears but of my shedding.

TUBAL

Yes, other men have ill luck too: Antonio, as I heard in Genoa,—

SHYLOCK

What, what, what? ill luck, ill luck?

TUBAL

Hath an argosy cast away, coming from Tripolis.

SHYLOCK

I thank God, I thank God. Is't true, is't true?

TUBAL

I spoke with some of the sailors that escaped the wreck.

SHYLOCK

I thank thee, good Tubal: good news, good news!
ha, ha! where? in Genoa?

TUBAL

Your daughter spent in Genoa, as I heard, in one
night fourscore ducats.

SHYLOCK

Thou stickest a dagger in me: I shall never see my
gold again: fourscore ducats at a sitting!
fourscore ducats!

TUBAL

There came divers of Antonio's creditors in my
company to Venice, that swear he cannot choose but
break.

SHYLOCK

I am very glad of it: I'll plague him; I'll torture
him: I am glad of it.

TUBAL

One of them showed me a ring that he had of your
daughter for a monkey.

SHYLOCK

Out upon her! Thou torturest me, Tubal: it was my
turquoise; I had it of Leah when I was a bachelor:
I would not have given it for a wilderness of monkeys.

TUBAL

But Antonio is certainly undone.

SHYLOCK

Nay, that's true, that's very true. Go, Tubal, fee
me an officer; bespeak him a fortnight before. I
will have the heart of him, if he forfeit; for, were

he out of Venice, I can make what merchandise I will. Go, go, Tubal, and meet me at our synagogue; go, good Tubal; at our synagogue, Tubal.

Exeunt

SCENE II. Belmont. A room in PORTIA'S house.

Enter BASSANIO, PORTIA, GRATIANO, NERISSA, and Attendants

PORTIA

I pray you, tarry: pause a day or two
Before you hazard; for, in choosing wrong,
I lose your company: therefore forbear awhile.
There's something tells me, but it is not love,
I would not lose you; and you know yourself,
Hate counsels not in such a quality.
But lest you should not understand me well,—
And yet a maiden hath no tongue but thought,—
I would detain you here some month or two
Before you venture for me. I could teach you
How to choose right, but I am then forsworn;
So will I never be: so may you miss me;
But if you do, you'll make me wish a sin,
That I had been forsworn. Beshrew your eyes,
They have o'erlook'd me and divided me;
One half of me is yours, the other half yours,
Mine own, I would say; but if mine, then yours,
And so all yours. O, these naughty times
Put bars between the owners and their rights!
And so, though yours, not yours. Prove it so,
Let fortune go to hell for it, not I.
I speak too long; but 'tis to peize the time,
To eke it and to draw it out in length,
To stay you from election.

BASSANIO

Let me choose
For as I am, I live upon the rack.

PORTIA

Upon the rack, Bassanio! then confess
What treason there is mingled with your love.

BASSANIO
None but that ugly treason of mistrust,
Which makes me fear the enjoying of my love:
There may as well be amity and life
'Tween snow and fire, as treason and my love.
PORTIA
Ay, but I fear you speak upon the rack,
Where men enforced do speak anything.
BASSANIO
Promise me life, and I'll confess the truth.
PORTIA
Well then, confess and live.
BASSANIO
'Confess' and 'love'
Had been the very sum of my confession:
O happy torment, when my torturer
Doth teach me answers for deliverance!
But let me to my fortune and the caskets.
PORTIA
Away, then! I am lock'd in one of them:
If you do love me, you will find me out.
Nerissa and the rest, stand all aloof.
Let music sound while he doth make his choice;
Then, if he lose, he makes a swan-like end,
Fading in music: that the comparison
May stand more proper, my eye shall be the stream
And watery death-bed for him. He may win;
And what is music then? Then music is
Even as the flourish when true subjects bow
To a new-crowned monarch: such it is
As are those dulcet sounds in break of day
That creep into the dreaming bridegroom's ear,
And summon him to marriage. Now he goes,
With no less presence, but with much more love,
Than young Alcides, when he did redeem
The virgin tribute paid by howling Troy
To the sea-monster: I stand for sacrifice
The rest aloof are the Dardanian wives,

With bleared visages, come forth to view
The issue of the exploit. Go, Hercules!
Live thou, I live: with much, much more dismay
I view the fight than thou that makest the fray.
Music, whilst BASSANIO comments on the caskets to himself
SONG.
Tell me where is fancy bred,
Or in the heart, or in the head?
How begot, how nourished?
Reply, reply.
It is engender'd in the eyes,
With gazing fed; and fancy dies
In the cradle where it lies.
Let us all ring fancy's knell
I'll begin it,—Ding, dong, bell.
ALL
Ding, dong, bell.
BASSANIO
So may the outward shows be least themselves:
The world is still deceived with ornament.
In law, what plea so tainted and corrupt,
But, being seasoned with a gracious voice,
Obscures the show of evil? In religion,
What damned error, but some sobre brow
Will bless it and approve it with a text,
Hiding the grossness with fair ornament?
There is no vice so simple but assumes
Some mark of virtue on his outward parts:
How many cowards, whose hearts are all as false
As stairs of sand, wear yet upon their chins
The beards of Hercules and frowning Mars;
Who, inward search'd, have livers white as milk;
And these assume but valour's excrement
To render them redoubted! Look on beauty,
And you shall see 'tis purchased by the weight;
Which therein works a miracle in nature,
Making them lightest that wear most of it:
So are those crisped snaky golden locks

Which make such wanton gambols with the wind,
Upon supposed fairness, often known
To be the dowry of a second head,
The skull that bred them in the sepulchre.
Thus ornament is but the guiled shore
To a most dangerous sea; the beauteous scarf
Veiling an Indian beauty; in a word,
The seeming truth which cunning times put on
To entrap the wisest. Therefore, thou gaudy gold,
Hard food for Midas, I will none of thee;
Nor none of thee, thou pale and common drudge
'Tween man and man: but thou, thou meagre lead,
Which rather threatenest than dost promise aught,
Thy paleness moves me more than eloquence;
And here choose I; joy be the consequence!

PORTIA

[Aside] How all the other passions fleet to air,
As doubtful thoughts, and rash-embraced despair,
And shuddering fear, and green-eyed jealousy! O love,
Be moderate; allay thy ecstasy,
In measure rein thy joy; scant this excess.
I feel too much thy blessing: make it less,
For fear I surfeit.

BASSANIO

What find I here?

Opening the leaden casket

Fair Portia's counterfeit! What demi-god
Hath come so near creation? Move these eyes?
Or whether, riding on the balls of mine,
Seem they in motion? Here are sever'd lips,
Parted with sugar breath: so sweet a bar
Should sunder such sweet friends. Here in her hairs
The painter plays the spider and hath woven
A golden mesh to entrap the hearts of men,
Faster than gnats in cobwebs; but her eyes,—
How could he see to do them? having made one,
Methinks it should have power to steal both his
And leave itself unfurnish'd. Yet look, how far

The substance of my praise doth wrong this shadow
In underprizing it, so far this shadow
Doth limp behind the substance. Here's the scroll,
The continent and summary of my fortune.
Reads
You that choose not by the view,
Chance as fair and choose as true!
Since this fortune falls to you,
Be content and seek no new,
If you be well pleased with this
And hold your fortune for your bliss,
Turn you where your lady is
And claim her with a loving kiss.
A gentle scroll. Fair lady, by your leave;
I come by note, to give and to receive.
Like one of two contending in a prize,
That thinks he hath done well in people's eyes,
Hearing applause and universal shout,
Giddy in spirit, still gazing in a doubt
Whether these pearls of praise be his or no;
So, thrice fair lady, stand I, even so;
As doubtful whether what I see be true,
Until confirm'd, sign'd, ratified by you.
PORTIA
You see me, Lord Bassanio, where I stand,
Such as I am: though for myself alone
I would not be ambitious in my wish,
To wish myself much better; yet, for you
I would be trebled twenty times myself;
A thousand times more fair, ten thousand times more rich;
That only to stand high in your account,
I might in virtue, beauties, livings, friends,
Exceed account; but the full sum of me
Is sum of something, which, to term in gross,
Is an unlesson'd girl, unschool'd, unpractised;
Happy in this, she is not yet so old
But she may learn; happier than this,
She is not bred so dull but she can learn;

Happiest of all is that her gentle spirit
Commits itself to yours to be directed,
As from her lord, her governor, her king.
Myself and what is mine to you and yours
Is now converted: but now I was the lord
Of this fair mansion, master of my servants,
Queen o'er myself: and even now, but now,
This house, these servants and this same myself
Are yours, my lord: I give them with this ring;
Which when you part from, lose, or give away,
Let it presage the ruin of your love
And be my vantage to exclaim on you.
BASSANIO
Madam, you have bereft me of all words,
Only my blood speaks to you in my veins;
And there is such confusion in my powers,
As after some oration fairly spoke
By a beloved prince, there doth appear
Among the buzzing pleased multitude;
Where every something, being blent together,
Turns to a wild of nothing, save of joy,
Express'd and not express'd. But when this ring
Parts from this finger, then parts life from hence:
O, then be bold to say Bassanio's dead!
NERISSA
My lord and lady, it is now our time,
That have stood by and seen our wishes prosper,
To cry, good joy: good joy, my lord and lady!
GRATIANO
My lord Bassanio and my gentle lady,
I wish you all the joy that you can wish;
For I am sure you can wish none from me:
And when your honours mean to solemnize
The bargain of your faith, I do beseech you,
Even at that time I may be married too.
BASSANIO
With all my heart, so thou canst get a wife.
GRATIANO

I thank your lordship, you have got me one.
My eyes, my lord, can look as swift as yours:
You saw the mistress, I beheld the maid;
You loved, I loved for intermission.
No more pertains to me, my lord, than you.
Your fortune stood upon the casket there,
And so did mine too, as the matter falls;
For wooing here until I sweat again,
And sweating until my very roof was dry
With oaths of love, at last, if promise last,
I got a promise of this fair one here
To have her love, provided that your fortune
Achieved her mistress.

PORTIA

Is this true, Nerissa?

NERISSA

Madam, it is, so you stand pleased withal.

BASSANIO

And do you, Gratiano, mean good faith?

GRATIANO

Yes, faith, my lord.

BASSANIO

Our feast shall be much honour'd in your marriage.

GRATIANO

We'll play with them the first boy for a thousand ducats.

NERISSA

What, and stake down?

GRATIANO

No; we shall ne'er win at that sport, and stake down.
But who comes here? Lorenzo and his infidel? What,
and my old Venetian friend Salerio?

Enter LORENZO, JESSICA, and SALERIO, a Messenger from Venice

BASSANIO

Lorenzo and Salerio, welcome hither;
If that the youth of my new interest here
Have power to bid you welcome. By your leave,

I bid my very friends and countrymen,
Sweet Portia, welcome.
PORTIA
So do I, my lord:
They are entirely welcome.
LORENZO
I thank your honour. For my part, my lord,
My purpose was not to have seen you here;
But meeting with Salerio by the way,
He did entreat me, past all saying nay,
To come with him along.
SALERIO
I did, my lord;
And I have reason for it. Signior Antonio
Commends him to you.
Gives Bassanio a letter
BASSANIO
Ere I ope his letter,
I pray you, tell me how my good friend doth.
SALERIO
Not sick, my lord, unless it be in mind;
Nor well, unless in mind: his letter there
Will show you his estate.
GRATIANO
Nerissa, cheer yon stranger; bid her welcome.
Your hand, Salerio: what's the news from Venice?
How doth that royal merchant, good Antonio?
I know he will be glad of our success;
We are the Jasons, we have won the fleece.
SALERIO
I would you had won the fleece that he hath lost.
PORTIA
There are some shrewd contents in yon same paper,
That steals the colour from Bassanio's cheek:
Some dear friend dead; else nothing in the world
Could turn so much the constitution
Of any constant man. What, worse and worse!
With leave, Bassanio: I am half yourself,

And I must freely have the half of anything
That this same paper brings you.
BASSANIO
O sweet Portia,
Here are a few of the unpleasant'st words
That ever blotted paper! Gentle lady,
When I did first impart my love to you,
I freely told you, all the wealth I had
Ran in my veins, I was a gentleman;
And then I told you true: and yet, dear lady,
Rating myself at nothing, you shall see
How much I was a braggart. When I told you
My state was nothing, I should then have told you
That I was worse than nothing; for, indeed,
I have engaged myself to a dear friend,
Engaged my friend to his mere enemy,
To feed my means. Here is a letter, lady;
The paper as the body of my friend,
And every word in it a gaping wound,
Issuing life-blood. But is it true, Salerio?
Have all his ventures fail'd? What, not one hit?
From Tripolis, from Mexico and England,
From Lisbon, Barbary and India?
And not one vessel 'scape the dreadful touch
Of merchant-marring rocks?
SALERIO
Not one, my lord.
Besides, it should appear, that if he had
The present money to discharge the Jew,
He would not take it. Never did I know
A creature, that did bear the shape of man,
So keen and greedy to confound a man:
He plies the duke at morning and at night,
And doth impeach the freedom of the state,
If they deny him justice: twenty merchants,
The duke himself, and the magnificoes
Of greatest port, have all persuaded with him;

But none can drive him from the envious plea
Of forfeiture, of justice and his bond.

JESSICA

When I was with him I have heard him swear
To Tubal and to Chus, his countrymen,
That he would rather have Antonio's flesh
Than twenty times the value of the sum
That he did owe him: and I know, my lord,
If law, authority and power deny not,
It will go hard with poor Antonio.

PORTIA

Is it your dear friend that is thus in trouble?

BASSANIO

The dearest friend to me, the kindest man,
The best-condition'd and unwearied spirit
In doing courtesies, and one in whom
The ancient Roman honour more appears
Than any that draws breath in Italy.

PORTIA

What sum owes he the Jew?

BASSANIO

For me three thousand ducats.

PORTIA

What, no more?
Pay him six thousand, and deface the bond;
Double six thousand, and then treble that,
Before a friend of this description
Shall lose a hair through Bassanio's fault.
First go with me to church and call me wife,
And then away to Venice to your friend;
For never shall you lie by Portia's side
With an unquiet soul. You shall have gold
To pay the petty debt twenty times over:
When it is paid, bring your true friend along.
My maid Nerissa and myself meantime
Will live as maids and widows. Come, away!
For you shall hence upon your wedding-day:
Bid your friends welcome, show a merry cheer:

Since you are dear bought, I will love you dear.
But let me hear the letter of your friend.

BASSANIO

[Reads] Sweet Bassanio, my ships have all miscarried, my creditors grow cruel, my estate is very low, my bond to the Jew is forfeit; and since in paying it, it is impossible I should live, all debts are cleared between you and I, if I might but see you at my death. Notwithstanding, use your pleasure: if your love do not persuade you to come, let not my letter.

PORTIA

O love, dispatch all business, and be gone!

BASSANIO

Since I have your good leave to go away,
I will make haste: but, till I come again,
No bed shall e'er be guilty of my stay,
No rest be interposer 'twixt us twain.

Exeunt

SCENE III. Venice. A street.

Enter SHYLOCK, SALARINO, ANTONIO, and Gaoler

SHYLOCK

Gaoler, look to him: tell not me of mercy;
This is the fool that lent out money gratis:
Gaoler, look to him.

ANTONIO

Hear me yet, good Shylock.

SHYLOCK

I'll have my bond; speak not against my bond:
I have sworn an oath that I will have my bond.
Thou call'dst me dog before thou hadst a cause;
But, since I am a dog, beware my fangs:
The duke shall grant me justice. I do wonder,
Thou naughty gaoler, that thou art so fond
To come abroad with him at his request.

ANTONIO

I pray thee, hear me speak.

SHYLOCK

I'll have my bond; I will not hear thee speak:
I'll have my bond; and therefore speak no more.
I'll not be made a soft and dull-eyed fool,
To shake the head, relent, and sigh, and yield
To Christian intercessors. Follow not;
I'll have no speaking: I will have my bond.
Exit
SALARINO
It is the most impenetrable cur
That ever kept with men.
ANTONIO
Let him alone:
I'll follow him no more with bootless prayers.
He seeks my life; his reason well I know:
I oft deliver'd from his forfeitures
Many that have at times made moan to me;
Therefore he hates me.
SALARINO
I am sure the duke
Will never grant this forfeiture to hold.
ANTONIO
The duke cannot deny the course of law:
For the commodity that strangers have
With us in Venice, if it be denied,
Will much impeach the justice of his state;
Since that the trade and profit of the city
Consisteth of all nations. Therefore, go:
These griefs and losses have so bated me,
That I shall hardly spare a pound of flesh
To-morrow to my bloody creditor.
Well, gaoler, on. Pray God, Bassanio come
To see me pay his debt, and then I care not!
Exeunt
SCENE IV. Belmont. A room in PORTIA'S house.
Enter PORTIA, NERISSA, LORENZO, JESSICA, and BALTHASAR
LORENZO
Madam, although I speak it in your presence,

You have a noble and a true conceit
Of godlike amity; which appears most strongly
In bearing thus the absence of your lord.
But if you knew to whom you show this honour,
How true a gentleman you send relief,
How dear a lover of my lord your husband,
I know you would be prouder of the work
Than customary bounty can enforce you.

PORTIA

I never did repent for doing good,
Nor shall not now: for in companions
That do converse and waste the time together,
Whose souls do bear an equal yoke Of love,
There must be needs a like proportion
Of lineaments, of manners and of spirit;
Which makes me think that this Antonio,
Being the bosom lover of my lord,
Must needs be like my lord. If it be so,
How little is the cost I have bestow'd
In purchasing the semblance of my soul
From out the state of hellish misery!
This comes too near the praising of myself;
Therefore no more of it: hear other things.
Lorenzo, I commit into your hands
The husbandry and manage of my house
Until my lord's return: for mine own part,
I have toward heaven breathed a secret vow
To live in prayer and contemplation,
Only attended by Nerissa here,
Until her husband and my lord's return:
There is a monastery two miles off;
And there will we abide. I do desire you
Not to deny this imposition;
The which my love and some necessity
Now lays upon you.

LORENZO

Madam, with all my heart;
I shall obey you in all fair commands.

PORTIA

My people do already know my mind,
And will acknowledge you and Jessica
In place of Lord Bassanio and myself.
And so farewell, till we shall meet again.

LORENZO

Fair thoughts and happy hours attend on you!

JESSICA

I wish your ladyship all heart's content.

PORTIA

I thank you for your wish, and am well pleased
To wish it back on you: fare you well Jessica.

Exeunt JESSICA and LORENZO

Now, Balthasar,
As I have ever found thee honest-true,
So let me find thee still. Take this same letter,
And use thou all the endeavour of a man
In speed to Padua: see thou render this
Into my cousin's hand, Doctor Bellario;
And, look, what notes and garments he doth give thee,
Bring them, I pray thee, with imagined speed
Unto the tranect, to the common ferry
Which trades to Venice. Waste no time in words,
But get thee gone: I shall be there before thee.

BALTHASAR

Madam, I go with all convenient speed.

Exit

PORTIA

Come on, Nerissa; I have work in hand
That you yet know not of: we'll see our husbands
Before they think of us.

NERISSA

Shall they see us?

PORTIA

They shall, Nerissa; but in such a habit,
That they shall think we are accomplished
With that we lack. I'll hold thee any wager,
When we are both accoutred like young men,

I'll prove the prettier fellow of the two,
And wear my dagger with the braver grace,
And speak between the change of man and boy
With a reed voice, and turn two mincing steps
Into a manly stride, and speak of frays
Like a fine bragging youth, and tell quaint lies,
How honourable ladies sought my love,
Which I denying, they fell sick and died;
I could not do withal; then I'll repent,
And wish for all that, that I had not killed them;
And twenty of these puny lies I'll tell,
That men shall swear I have discontinued school
Above a twelvemonth. I have within my mind
A thousand raw tricks of these bragging Jacks,
Which I will practise.

NERISSA

Why, shall we turn to men?

PORTIA

Fie, what a question's that,
If thou wert near a lewd interpreter!
But come, I'll tell thee all my whole device
When I am in my coach, which stays for us
At the park gate; and therefore haste away,
For we must measure twenty miles to-day.

Exeunt

SCENE V. The same. A garden.

Enter LAUNCELOT and JESSICA

LAUNCELOT

Yes, truly; for, look you, the sins of the father are to be laid upon the children: therefore, I promise ye, I fear you. I was always plain with you, and so now I speak my agitation of the matter: therefore be of good cheer, for truly I think you are damned. There is but one hope in it that can do you any good; and that is but a kind of bastard hope neither.

JESSICA

And what hope is that, I pray thee?

LAUNCELOT
Marry, you may partly hope that your father got you not, that you are not the Jew's daughter.
JESSICA
That were a kind of bastard hope, indeed: so the sins of my mother should be visited upon me.
LAUNCELOT
Truly then I fear you are damned both by father and mother: thus when I shun Scylla, your father, I fall into Charybdis, your mother: well, you are gone both ways.
JESSICA
I shall be saved by my husband; he hath made me a Christian.
LAUNCELOT
Truly, the more to blame he: we were Christians enow before; e'en as many as could well live, one by another. This making Christians will raise the price of hogs: if we grow all to be pork-eaters, we shall not shortly have a rasher on the coals for money.
Enter LORENZO
JESSICA
I'll tell my husband, Launcelot, what you say: here he comes.
LORENZO
I shall grow jealous of you shortly, Launcelot, if you thus get my wife into corners.
JESSICA
Nay, you need not fear us, Lorenzo: Launcelot and I are out. He tells me flatly, there is no mercy for me in heaven, because I am a Jew's daughter: and he says, you are no good member of the commonwealth, for in converting Jews to Christians, you raisē the price of pork.
LORENZO
I shall answer that better to the commonwealth than you can the getting up of the negro's belly: the Moor is with child by you, Launcelot.

LAUNCELOT
It is much that the Moor should be more than reason: but if she be less than an honest woman, she is indeed more than I took her for.
LORENZO
How every fool can play upon the word! I think the best grace of wit will shortly turn into silence, and discourse grow commendable in none only but parrots. Go in, sirrah; bid them prepare for dinner.
LAUNCELOT
That is done, sir; they have all stomachs.
LORENZO
Goodly Lord, what a wit-snapper are you! then bid them prepare dinner.
LAUNCELOT
That is done too, sir; only 'cover' is the word.
LORENZO
Will you cover then, sir?
LAUNCELOT
Not so, sir, neither; I know my duty.
LORENZO
Yet more quarrelling with occasion! Wilt thou show the whole wealth of thy wit in an instant? I pray tree, understand a plain man in his plain meaning: go to thy fellows; bid them cover the table, serve in the meat, and we will come in to dinner.
LAUNCELOT
For the table, sir, it shall be served in; for the meat, sir, it shall be covered; for your coming in to dinner, sir, why, let it be as humours and conceits shall govern.
Exit
LORENZO
O dear discretion, how his words are suited!
The fool hath planted in his memory
An army of good words; and I do know
A many fools, that stand in better place,
Garnish'd like him, that for a tricksy word

Defy the matter. How cheerest thou, Jessica?
And now, good sweet, say thy opinion,
How dost thou like the Lord Bassanio's wife?

JESSICA

Past all expressing. It is very meet
The Lord Bassanio live an upright life;
For, having such a blessing in his lady,
He finds the joys of heaven here on earth;
And if on earth he do not mean it, then
In reason he should never come to heaven
Why, if two gods should play some heavenly match
And on the wager lay two earthly women,
And Portia one, there must be something else
Pawn'd with the other, for the poor rude world
Hath not her fellow.

LORENZO

Even such a husband
Hast thou of me as she is for a wife.

JESSICA

Nay, but ask my opinion too of that.

LORENZO

I will anon: first, let us go to dinner.

JESSICA

Nay, let me praise you while I have a stomach.

LORENZO

No, pray thee, let it serve for table-talk;
' Then, howso'er thou speak'st, 'mong other things
I shall digest it.

JESSICA

Well, I'll set you forth.

Exeunt

ACT IV

SCENE I. Venice. A court of justice.

Enter the DUKE, the Magnificoes, ANTONIO, BASSANIO, GRATIANO, SALERIO, and others

DUKE

What, is Antonio here?

ANTONIO
Ready, so please your grace.
DUKE
I am sorry for thee: thou art come to answer
A stony adversary, an inhuman wretch
uncapable of pity, void and empty
From any dram of mercy.
ANTONIO
I have heard
Your grace hath ta'en great pains to qualify
His rigorous course; but since he stands obdurate
And that no lawful means can carry me
Out of his envy's reach, I do oppose
My patience to his fury, and am arm'd
To suffer, with a quietness of spirit,
The very tyranny and rage of his.
DUKE
Go one, and call the Jew into the court.
SALERIO
He is ready at the door: he comes, my lord.
Enter SHYLOCK
DUKE
Make room, and let him stand before our face.
Shylock, the world thinks, and I think so too,
That thou but lead'st this fashion of thy malice
To the last hour of act; and then 'tis thought
Thou'lt show thy mercy and remorse more strange
Than is thy strange apparent cruelty;
And where thou now exact'st the penalty,
Which is a pound of this poor merchant's flesh,
Thou wilt not only loose the forfeiture,
But, touch'd with human gentleness and love,
Forgive a moiety of the principal;
Glancing an eye of pity on his losses,
That have of late so huddled on his back,
Enow to press a royal merchant down
And pluck commiseration of his state
From brassy bosoms and rough hearts of flint,

From stubborn Turks and Tartars, never train'd
To offices of tender courtesy.
We all expect a gentle answer, Jew.

SHYLOCK

I have possess'd your grace of what I purpose;
And by our holy Sabbath have I sworn
To have the due and forfeit of my bond:
If you deny it, let the danger light
Upon your charter and your city's freedom.
You'll ask me, why I rather choose to have
A weight of carrion flesh than to receive
Three thousand ducats: I'll not answer that:
But, say, it is my humour: is it answer'd?
What if my house be troubled with a rat
And I be pleased to give ten thousand ducats
To have it baned? What, are you answer'd yet?
Some men there are love not a gaping pig;
Some, that are mad if they behold a cat;
And others, when the bagpipe sings i' the nose,
Cannot contain their urine: for affection,
Mistress of passion, sways it to the mood
Of what it likes or loathes. Now, for your answer:
As there is no firm reason to be render'd,
Why he cannot abide a gaping pig;
Why he, a harmless necessary cat;
Why he, a woollen bagpipe; but of force
Must yield to such inevitable shame
As to offend, himself being offended;
So can I give no reason, nor I will not,
More than a lodged hate and a certain loathing
I bear Antonio, that I follow thus
A losing suit against him. Are you answer'd?

BASSANIO

This is no answer, thou unfeeling man,
To excuse the current of thy cruelty.

SHYLOCK

I am not bound to please thee with my answers.

BASSANIO
Do all men kill the things they do not love?
SHYLOCK
Hates any man the thing he would not kill?
BASSANIO
Every offence is not a hate at first.
SHYLOCK
What, wouldst thou have a serpent sting thee twice?
ANTONIO
I pray you, think you question with the Jew:
You may as well go stand upon the beach
And bid the main flood bate his usual height;
You may as well use question with the wolf
Why he hath made the ewe bleat for the lamb;
You may as well forbid the mountain pines
To wag their high tops and to make no noise,
When they are fretten with the gusts of heaven;
You may as well do anything most hard,
As seek to soften that—than which what's harder?—
His Jewish heart: therefore, I do beseech you,
Make no more offers, use no farther means,
But with all brief and plain conveniency
Let me have judgment and the Jew his will.
BASSANIO
For thy three thousand ducats here is six.
SHYLOCK
What judgment shall I dread, doing
Were in six parts and every part a ducat,
I would not draw them; I would have my bond.
DUKE
How shalt thou hope for mercy, rendering none?
SHYLOCK
What judgment shall I dread, doing no wrong?
You have among you many a purchased slave,
Which, like your asses and your dogs and mules,
You use in abject and in slavish parts,
Because you bought them: shall I say to you,
Let them be free, marry them to your heirs?

Why sweat they under burthens? let their beds
Be made as soft as yours and let their palates
Be season'd with such viands? You will answer
'The slaves are ours:' so do I answer you:
The pound of flesh, which I demand of him,
Is dearly bought; 'tis mine and I will have it.
If you deny me, fie upon your law!
There is no force in the decrees of Venice.
I stand for judgment: answer; shall I have it?

DUKE

Upon my power I may dismiss this court,
Unless Bellario, a learned doctor,
Whom I have sent for to determine this,
Come here to-day.

SALERIO

My lord, here stays without
A messenger with letters from the doctor,
New come from Padua.

DUKE

Bring us the letter; call the messenger.

BASSANIO

Good cheer, Antonio! What, man, courage yet!
The Jew shall have my flesh, blood, bones and all,
Ere thou shalt lose for me one drop of blood.

ANTONIO

I am a tainted wether of the flock,
Meetest for death: the weakest kind of fruit
Drops earliest to the ground; and so let me
You cannot better be employ'd, Bassanio,
Than to live still and write mine epitaph.

Enter NERISSA, dressed like a lawyer's clerk

DUKE

Came you from Padua, from Bellario?

NERISSA

From both, my lord. Bellario greets your grace.

Presenting a letter

BASSANIO

Why dost thou whet thy knife so earnestly?

SHYLOCK
To cut the forfeiture from that bankrupt there.
GRATIANO
Not on thy sole, but on thy soul, harsh Jew,
Thou makest thy knife keen; but no metal can,
No, not the hangman's axe, bear half the keenness
Of thy sharp envy. Can no prayers pierce thee?
SHYLOCK
No, none that thou hast wit enough to make.
GRATIANO
O, be thou damn'd, inexecrable dog!
And for thy life let justice be accused.
Thou almost makest me waver in my faith
To hold opinion with Pythagoras,
That souls of animals infuse themselves
Into the trunks of men: thy currish spirit
Govern'd a wolf, who, hang'd for human slaughter,
Even from the gallows did his fell soul fleet,
And, whilst thou lay'st in thy unhallow'd dam,
Infused itself in thee; for thy desires
Are wolvish, bloody, starved and ravenous.
SHYLOCK
Till thou canst rail the seal from off my bond,
Thou but offend'st thy lungs to speak so loud:
Repair thy wit, good youth, or it will fall
To cureless ruin. I stand here for law.
DUKE
This letter from Bellario doth commend
A young and learned doctor to our court.
Where is he?
NERISSA
He attendeth here hard by,
To know your answer, whether you'll admit him.
DUKE
With all my heart. Some three or four of you
Go give him courteous conduct to this place.
Meantime the court shall hear Bellario's letter.
Clerk

[Reads]
Your grace shall understand that at the receipt of your letter I am very sick: but in the instant that your messenger came, in loving visitation was with me a young doctor of Rome; his name is Balthasar. I acquainted him with the cause in controversy between the Jew and Antonio the merchant: we turned o'er many books together: he is furnished with my opinion; which, bettered with his own learning, the greatness whereof I cannot enough commend, comes with him, at my importunity, to fill up your grace's request in my stead. I beseech you, let his lack of years be no impediment to let him lack a reverend estimation; for I never knew so young a body with so old a head. I leave him to your gracious acceptance, whose trial shall better publish his commendation.

DUKE

You hear the learn'd Bellario, what he writes:
And here, I take it, is the doctor come.

Enter PORTIA, dressed like a doctor of laws

Give me your hand. Come you from old Bellario?

PORTIA

I did, my lord.

DUKE

You are welcome: take your place.
Are you acquainted with the difference
That holds this present question in the court?

PORTIA

I am informed thoroughly of the cause.
Which is the merchant here, and which the Jew?

DUKE

Antonio and old Shylock, both stand forth.

PORTIA

Is your name Shylock?

SHYLOCK

Shylock is my name.

PORTIA

Of a strange nature is the suit you follow;
Yet in such rule that the Venetian law
Cannot impugn you as you do proceed.
You stand within his danger, do you not?

ANTONIO

Ay, so he says.

PORTIA

Do you confess the bond?

ANTONIO

I do.

PORTIA

Then must the Jew be merciful.

SHYLOCK

On what compulsion must I? tell me that.

PORTIA

The quality of mercy is not strain'd,
It droppeth as the gentle rain from heaven
Upon the place beneath: it is twice blest;
It blesseth him that gives and him that takes:
'Tis mightiest in the mightiest: it becomes
The throned monarch better than his crown;
His sceptre shows the force of temporal power,
The attribute to awe and majesty,
Wherein doth sit the dread and fear of kings;
But mercy is above this sceptred sway;
It is enthroned in the hearts of kings,
It is an attribute to God himself;
And earthly power doth then show likest God's
When mercy seasons justice. Therefore, Jew,
Though justice be thy plea, consider this,
That, in the course of justice, none of us
Should see salvation: we do pray for mercy;
And that same prayer doth teach us all to render
The deeds of mercy. I have spoke thus much
To mitigate the justice of thy plea;
Which if thou follow, this strict court of Venice
Must needs give sentence 'gainst the merchant there.

SHYLOCK

My deeds upon my head! I crave the law,
The penalty and forfeit of my bond.

PORTIA

Is he not able to discharge the money?

BASSANIO

Yes, here I tender it for him in the court;
Yea, twice the sum: if that will not suffice,
I will be bound to pay it ten times o'er,
On forfeit of my hands, my head, my heart:
If this will not suffice, it must appear
That malice bears down truth. And I beseech you,
Wrest once the law to your authority:
To do a great right, do a little wrong,
And curb this cruel devil of his will.

PORTIA

It must not be; there is no power in Venice
Can alter a decree established:
'Twill be recorded for a precedent,
And many an error by the same example
Will rush into the state: it cannot be.

SHYLOCK

A Daniel come to judgment! yea, a Daniel!
O wise young judge, how I do honour thee!

PORTIA

I pray you, let me look upon the bond.

SHYLOCK

Here 'tis, most reverend doctor, here it is.

PORTIA

Shylock, there's thrice thy money offer'd thee.

SHYLOCK

An oath, an oath, I have an oath in heaven:
Shall I lay perjury upon my soul?
No, not for Venice.

PORTIA

Why, this bond is forfeit;
And lawfully by this the Jew may claim
A pound of flesh, to be by him cut off

Nearest the merchant's heart. Be merciful:
Take thrice thy money; bid me tear the bond.

SHYLOCK

When it is paid according to the tenor.
It doth appear you are a worthy judge;
You know the law, your exposition
Hath been most sound: I charge you by the law,
Whereof you are a well-deserving pillar,
Proceed to judgment: by my soul I swear
There is no power in the tongue of man
To alter me: I stay here on my bond.

ANTONIO

Most heartily I do beseech the court
To give the judgment.

PORTIA

Why then, thus it is:
You must prepare your bosom for his knife.

SHYLOCK

O noble judge! O excellent young man!

JPORTIA

For the intent and purpose of the law
Hath full relation to the penalty,
Which here appeareth due upon the bond.

SHYLOCK

'Tis very true: O wise and upright judge!
How much more elder art thou than thy looks!

PORTIA

Therefore lay bare your bosom.

SHYLOCK

Ay, his breast:
So says the bond: doth it not, noble judge?
'Nearest his heart:' those are the very words.

PORTIA

It is so. Are there balance here to weigh
The flesh?

SHYLOCK

I have them ready.

PORTIA

Have by some surgeon, Shylock, on your charge,
To stop his wounds, lest he do bleed to death.
SHYLOCK
Is it so nominated in the bond?
PORTIA
It is not so express'd: but what of that?
'Twere good you do so much for charity.
SHYLOCK
I cannot find it; 'tis not in the bond.
PORTIA
You, merchant, have you any thing to say?
ANTONIO
But little: I am arm'd and well prepared.
Give me your hand, Bassanio: fare you well!
Grieve not that I am fallen to this for you;
For herein Fortune shows herself more kind
Than is her custom: it is still her use
To let the wretched man outlive his wealth,
To view with hollow eye and wrinkled brow
An age of poverty; from which lingering penance
Of such misery doth she cut me off.
Commend me to your honourable wife:
Tell her the process of Antonio's end;
Say how I loved you, speak me fair in death;
And, when the tale is told, bid her be judge
Whether Bassanio had not once a love.
Repent but you that you shall lose your friend,
And he repents not that he pays your debt;
For if the Jew do cut but deep enough,
I'll pay it presently with all my heart.
BASSANIO
Antonio, I am married to a wife
Which is as dear to me as life itself;
But life itself, my wife, and all the world,
Are not with me esteem'd above thy life:
I would lose all, ay, sacrifice them all
Here to this devil, to deliver you.
PORTIA

Your wife would give you little thanks for that,
If she were by, to hear you make the offer.

GRATIANO

I have a wife, whom, I protest, I love:
I would she were in heaven, so she could
Entreat some power to change this currish Jew.

NERISSA

'Tis well you offer it behind her back;
The wish would make else an unquiet house.

SHYLOCK

These be the Christian husbands. I have a daughter;
Would any of the stock of Barrabas
Had been her husband rather than a Christian!
Aside
We trifle time: I pray thee, pursue sentence.

PORTIA

A pound of that same merchant's flesh is thine:
The court awards it, and the law doth give it.

SHYLOCK

Most rightful judge!

PORTIA

And you must cut this flesh from off his breast:
The law allows it, and the court awards it.

SHYLOCK

Most learned judge! A sentence! Come, prepare!

PORTIA

Tarry a little; there is something else.
This bond doth give thee here no jot of blood;
The words expressly are 'a pound of flesh:'
Take then thy bond, take thou thy pound of flesh;
But, in the cutting it, if thou dost shed
One drop of Christian blood, thy lands and goods
Are, by the laws of Venice, confiscate
Unto the state of Venice.

GRATIANO

O upright judge! Mark, Jew: O learned judge!

SHYLOCK

Is that the law?

PORTIA
Thyself shalt see the act:
For, as thou urgest justice, be assured
Thou shalt have justice, more than thou desirest.
GRATIANO
O learned judge! Mark, Jew: a learned judge!
SHYLOCK
I take this offer, then; pay the bond thrice
And let the Christian go.
BASSANIO
Here is the money.
PORTIA
Soft!
The Jew shall have all justice; soft! no haste:
He shall have nothing but the penalty.
GRATIANO
O Jew! an upright judge, a learned judge!
PORTIA
Therefore prepare thee to cut off the flesh.
Shed thou no blood, nor cut thou less nor more
But just a pound of flesh: if thou cut'st more
Or less than a just pound, be it but so much
As makes it light or heavy in the substance,
Or the division of the twentieth part
Of one poor scruple, nay, if the scale do turn
But in the estimation of a hair,
Thou diest and all thy goods are confiscate.
GRATIANO
A second Daniel, a Daniel, Jew!
Now, infidel, I have you on the hip.
PORTIA
Why doth the Jew pause? take thy forfeiture.
SHYLOCK
Give me my principal, and let me go.
BASSANIO
I have it ready for thee; here it is.
PORTIA

He hath refused it in the open court:
He shall have merely justice and his bond.

GRATIANO

A Daniel, still say I, a second Daniel!
I thank thee, Jew, for teaching me that word.

SHYLOCK

Shall I not have barely my principal?

PORTIA

Thou shalt have nothing but the forfeiture,
To be so taken at thy peril, Jew.

SHYLOCK

Why, then the devil give him good of it!
I'll stay no longer question.

PORTIA

Tarry, Jew:
The law hath yet another hold on you.
It is enacted in the laws of Venice,
If it be proved against an alien
That by direct or indirect attempts
He seek the life of any citizen,
The party 'gainst the which he doth contrive
Shall seize one half his goods; the other half
Comes to the privy coffer of the state;
And the offender's life lies in the mercy
Of the duke only, 'gainst all other voice.
In which predicament, I say, thou stand'st;
For it appears, by manifest proceeding,
That indirectly and directly too
Thou hast contrived against the very life
Of the defendant; and thou hast incurr'd
The danger formerly by me rehearsed.
Down therefore and beg mercy of the duke.

GRATIANO

Beg that thou mayst have leave to hang thyself:
And yet, thy wealth being forfeit to the state,
Thou hast not left the value of a cord;
Therefore thou must be hang'd at the state's charge.

DUKE

That thou shalt see the difference of our spirits,
I pardon thee thy life before thou ask it:
For half thy wealth, it is Antonio's;
The other half comes to the general state,
Which humbleness may drive unto a fine.

PORTIA

Ay, for the state, not for Antonio.

SHYLOCK

Nay, take my life and all; pardon not that:
You take my house when you do take the prop
That doth sustain my house; you take my life
When you do take the means whereby I live.

PORTIA

What mercy can you render him, Antonio?

GRATIANO

A halter gratis; nothing else, for God's sake.

ANTONIO

So please my lord the duke and all the court
To quit the fine for one half of his goods,
I am content; so he will let me have
The other half in use, to render it,
Upon his death, unto the gentleman
That lately stole his daughter:
Two things provided more, that, for this favour,
He presently become a Christian;
The other, that he do record a gift,
Here in the court, of all he dies possess'd,
Unto his son Lorenzo and his daughter.

DUKE

He shall do this, or else I do recant
The pardon that I late pronounced here.

PORTIA

Art thou contented, Jew? what dost thou say?

SHYLOCK

I am content.

PORTIA

Clerk, draw a deed of gift.

SHYLOCK

I pray you, give me leave to go from hence;
I am not well: send the deed after me,
And I will sign it.

DUKE

Get thee gone, but do it.

GRATIANO

In christening shalt thou have two god-fathers:
Had I been judge, thou shouldst have had ten more,
To bring thee to the gallows, not the font.

Exit SHYLOCK

DUKE

Sir, I entreat you home with me to dinner.

PORTIA

I humbly do desire your grace of pardon:
I must away this night toward Padua,
And it is meet I presently set forth.

DUKE

I am sorry that your leisure serves you not.
Antonio, gratify this gentleman,
For, in my mind, you are much bound to him.

Exeunt Duke and his train

BASSANIO

Most worthy gentleman, I and my friend
Have by your wisdom been this day acquitted
Of grievous penalties; in lieu whereof,
Three thousand ducats, due unto the Jew,
We freely cope your courteous pains withal.

ANTONIO

And stand indebted, over and above,
In love and service to you evermore.

PORTIA

He is well paid that is well satisfied;
And I, delivering you, am satisfied
And therein do account myself well paid:
My mind was never yet more mercenary.
I pray you, know me when we meet again:
I wish you well, and so I take my leave.

BASSANIO

Dear sir, of force I must attempt you further:
Take some remembrance of us, as a tribute,
Not as a fee: grant me two things, I pray you,
Not to deny me, and to pardon me.

PORTIA

You press me far, and therefore I will yield.

To *ANTONIO*

Give me your gloves, I'll wear them for your sake;

To *BASSANIO*

And, for your love, I'll take this ring from you:
Do not draw back your hand; I'll take no more;
And you in love shall not deny me this.

BASSANIO

This ring, good sir, alas, it is a trifle!
I will not shame myself to give you this.

PORTIA

I will have nothing else but only this;
And now methinks I have a mind to it.

BASSANIO

There's more depends on this than on the value.
The dearest ring in Venice will I give you,
And find it out by proclamation:
Only for this, I pray you, pardon me.

PORTIA

I see, sir, you are liberal in offers
You taught me first to beg; and now methinks
You teach me how a beggar should be answer'd.

BASSANIO

Good sir, this ring was given me by my wife;
And when she put it on, she made me vow
That I should neither sell nor give nor lose it.

PORTIA

That 'scuse serves many men to save their gifts.
An if your wife be not a mad-woman,
And know how well I have deserved the ring,
She would not hold out enemy for ever,
For giving it to me. Well, peace be with you!

Exeunt Portia and Nerissa

ANTONIO

My Lord Bassanio, let him have the ring:
Let his deservings and my love withal
Be valued against your wife's commandment.

BASSANIO

Go, Gratiano, run and overtake him;
Give him the ring, and bring him, if thou canst,
Unto Antonio's house: away! make haste.

Exit Gratiano

Come, you and I will thither presently;
And in the morning early will we both
Fly toward Belmont: come, Antonio.

Exeunt

SCENE II. The same. A street.

Enter PORTIA and NERISSA

PORTIA

Inquire the Jew's house out, give him this deed
And let him sign it: we'll away to-night
And be a day before our husbands home:
This deed will be well welcome to Lorenzo.

Enter GRATIANO

GRATIANO

Fair sir, you are well o'erta'en
My Lord Bassanio upon more advice
Hath sent you here this ring, and doth entreat
Your company at dinner.

PORTIA

That cannot be:
His ring I do accept most thankfully:
And so, I pray you, tell him: furthermore,
I pray you, show my youth old Shylock's house.

GRATIANO

That will I do.

NERISSA

Sir, I would speak with you.

Aside to PORTIA

I'll see if I can get my husband's ring,
Which I did make him swear to keep for ever.

PORTIA

[Aside to NERISSA] Thou mayst, I warrant.
We shall have old swearing
That they did give the rings away to men;
But we'll outface them, and outswear them too.

Aloud

Away! make haste: thou knowist where I will tarry.

NERISSA

Come, good sir, will you show me to this house?

Exeunt

ACT V

SCENE I. Belmont. Avenue to PORTIA'S house.

Enter LORENZO and JESSICA

LORENZO

The moon shines bright: in such a night as this,
When the sweet wind did gently kiss the trees
And they did make no noise, in such a night
Troilus methinks mounted the Troyan walls
And sigh'd his soul toward the Grecian tents,
Where Cressid iay that night.

JESSICA

In such a night
Did Thisbe fearfully o'ertrip the dew
And saw the lion's shadow ere himself
And ran dismay'd away.

LORENZO

In such a night
Stood Dido with a willow in her hand
Upon the wild sea banks and waft her love
To come again to Carthage.

JESSICA

In such a night
Medea gather'd the enchanted herbs
That did renew old AEson.

LORENZO

In such a night
Did Jessica steal from the wealthy Jew

And with an unthrift love did run from Venice
As far as Belmont.

JESSICA

In such a night
Did young Lorenzo swear he loved her well,
Stealing her soul with many vows of faith
And ne'er a true one.

LORENZO

In such a night
Did pretty Jessica, like a little shrew,
Slander her love, and he forgave it her.

JESSICA

I would out-night you, did no body come;
But, hark, I hear the footing of a man.

Enter STEPHANO

LORENZO

Who comes so fast in silence of the night?

STEPHANO

A friend.

LORENZO

A friend! what friend? your name, I pray you, friend?

STEPHANO

Stephano is my name; and I bring word
My mistress will before the break of day
Be here at Belmont; she doth stray about
By holy crosses, where she kneels and prays
For happy wedlock hours.

LORENZO

Who comes with her?

STEPHANO

None but a holy hermit and her maid.
I pray you, is my master yet return'd?

LORENZO

He is not, nor we have not heard from him.
But go we in, I pray thee, Jessica,
And ceremoniously let us prepare
Some welcome for the mistress of the house.

Enter LAUNCELOT

LAUNCELOT
Sola, sola! wo ha, ho! sola, sola!
LORENZO
Who calls?
LAUNCELOT
Sola! did you see Master Lorenzo?
Master Lorenzo, sola, sola!
LORENZO
Leave hollaing, man: here.
LAUNCELOT
Sola! where? where?
LORENZO
Here.
LAUNCELOT
Tell him there's a post come from my master, with his horn full of good news: my master will be here ere morning.
Exit
LORENZO
Sweet soul, let's in, and there expect their coming.
And yet no matter: why should we go in?
My friend Stephano, signify, I pray you,
Within the house, your mistress is at hand;
And bring your music forth into the air.
Exit Stephano
How sweet the moonlight sleeps upon this bank!
Here will we sit and let the sounds of music
Creep in our ears: soft stillness and the night
Become the touches of sweet harmony.
Sit, Jessica. Look how the floor of heaven
Is thick inlaid with patines of bright gold:
There's not the smallest orb which thou behold'st
But in his motion like an angel sings,
Still quiring to the young-eyed cherubins;
Such harmony is in immortal souls;
But whilst this muddy vesture of decay
Doth grossly close it in, we cannot hear it.
Enter Musicians

Come, ho! and wake Diana with a hymn!
With sweetest touches pierce your mistress' ear,
And draw her home with music.

Music

JESSICA

I am never merry when I hear sweet music.

LORENZO

The reason is, your spirits are attentive:
For do but note a wild and wanton herd,
Or race of youthful and unhandled colts,
Fetching mad bounds, bellowing and neighing loud,
Which is the hot condition of their blood;
If they but hear perchance a trumpet sound,
Or any air of music touch their ears,
You shall perceive them make a mutual stand,
Their savage eyes turn'd to a modest gaze
By the sweet power of music: therefore the poet
Did feign that Orpheus drew trees, stones and floods;
Since nought so stockish, hard and full of rage,
But music for the time doth change his nature.
The man that hath no music in himself,
Nor is not moved with concord of sweet sounds,
Is fit for treasons, stratagems and spoils;
The motions of his spirit are dull as night
And his affections dark as Erebus:
Let no such man be trusted. Mark the music.

Enter PORTIA and NERISSA

PORTIA

That light we see is burning in my hall.
How far that little candle throws his beams!
So shines a good deed in a naughty world.

NERISSA

When the moon shone, we did not see the candle.

PORTIA

So doth the greater glory dim the less:
A substitute shines brightly as a king
Unto the king be by, and then his state

Empties itself, as doth an inland brook
Into the main of waters. Music! hark!
NERISSA
It is your music, madam, of the house.
PORTIA
Nothing is good, I see, without respect:
Methinks it sounds much sweeter than by day.
NERISSA
Silence bestows that virtue on it, madam.
PORTIA
The crow doth sing as sweetly as the lark,
When neither is attended, and I think
The nightingale, if she should sing by day,
When every goose is cackling, would be thought
No better a musician than the wren.
How many things by season season'd are
To their right praise and true perfection!
Peace, ho! the moon sleeps with Endymion
And would not be awaked.
Music ceases
LORENZO
That is the voice,
Or I am much deceived, of Portia.
PORTIA
He knows me as the blind man knows the cuckoo,
By the bad voice.
LORENZO
Dear lady, welcome home.
PORTIA
We have been praying for our husbands' healths,
Which speed, we hope, the better for our words.
Are they return'd?
LORENZO
Madam, they are not yet;
But there is come a messenger before,
To signify their coming.
PORTIA
Go in, Nerissa;

Give order to my servants that they take
No note at all of our being absent hence;
Nor you, Lorenzo; Jessica, nor you.
A tucket sounds
LORENZO
Your husband is at hand; I hear his trumpet:
We are no tell-tales, madam; fear you not.
PORTIA
This night methinks is but the daylight sick;
It looks a little paler: 'tis a day,
Such as the day is when the sun is hid.
Enter BASSANIO, ANTONIO, GRATIANO, and their followers
BASSANIO
We should hold day with the Antipodes,
If you would walk in absence of the sun.
PORTIA
Let me give light, but let me not be light;
For a light wife doth make a heavy husband,
And never be Bassanio so for me:
But God sort all! You are welcome home, my lord.
BASSANIO
I thank you, madam. Give welcome to my friend.
This is the man, this is Antonio,
To whom I am so infinitely bound.
PORTIA
You should in all sense be much bound to him.
For, as I hear, he was much bound for you.
ANTONIO
No more than I am well acquitted of.
PORTIA
Sir, you are very welcome to our house:
It must appear in other ways than words,
Therefore I scant this breathing courtesy.
GRATIANO
[To NERISSA] By yonder moon I swear you do me wrong;
In faith, I gave it to the judge's clerk:

Would he were gelt that had it, for my part,
Since you do take it, love, so much at heart.

PORTIA

A quarrel, ho, already! what's the matter?

GRATIANO

About a hoop of gold, a paltry ring
That she did give me, whose posy was
For all the world like cutler's poetry
Upon a knife, 'Love me, and leave me not.'

NERISSA

What talk you of the posy or the value?
You swore to me, when I did give it you,
That you would wear it till your hour of death
And that it should lie with you in your grave:
Though not for me, yet for your vehement oaths,
You should have been respective and have kept it.
Gave it a judge's clerk! no, God's my judge,
The clerk will ne'er wear hair on's face that had it.

GRATIANO

He will, an if he live to be a man.

NERISSA

Ay, if a woman live to be a man.

GRATIANO

Now, by this hand, I gave it to a youth,
A kind of boy, a little scrubbed boy,
No higher than thyself; the judge's clerk,
A prating boy, that begg'd it as a fee:
I could not for my heart deny it him.

PORTIA

You were to blame, I must be plain with you,
To part so slightly with your wife's first gift:
A thing stuck on with oaths upon your finger
And so riveted with faith unto your flesh.
I gave my love a ring and made him swear
Never to part with it; and here he stands;
I dare be sworn for him he would not leave it
Nor pluck it from his finger, for the wealth
That the world masters. Now, in faith, Gratiano,

You give your wife too unkind a cause of grief:
An 'twere to me, I should be mad at it.

BASSANIO

[Aside] Why, I were best to cut my left hand off
And swear I lost the ring defending it.

GRATIANO

My Lord Bassanio gave his ring away
Unto the judge that begg'd it and indeed
Deserved it too; and then the boy, his clerk,
That took some pains in writing, he begg'd mine;
And neither man nor master would take aught
But the two rings.

PORTIA

What ring gave you my lord?
Not that, I hope, which you received of me.

BASSANIO

If I could add a lie unto a fault,
I would deny it; but you see my finger
Hath not the ring upon it; it is gone.

PORTIA

Even so void is your false heart of truth.
By heaven, I will ne'er come in your bed
Until I see the ring.

NERISSA

Nor I in yours
Till I again see mine.

BASSANIO

Sweet Portia,
If you did know to whom I gave the ring,
If you did know for whom I gave the ring
And would conceive for what I gave the ring
And how unwillingly I left the ring,
When nought would be accepted but the ring,
You would abate the strength of your displeasure.

PORTIA

If you had known the virtue of the ring,
Or half her worthiness that gave the ring,
Or your own honour to contain the ring,

You would not then have parted with the ring.
What man is there so much unreasonable,
If you had pleased to have defended it
With any terms of zeal, wanted the modesty
To urge the thing held as a ceremony?
Nerissa teaches me what to believe:
I'll die for't but some woman had the ring.

BASSANIO

No, by my honour, madam, by my soul,
No woman had it, but a civil doctor,
Which did refuse three thousand ducats of me
And begg'd the ring; the which I did deny him
And suffer'd him to go displeased away;
Even he that did uphold the very life
Of my dear friend. What should I say, sweet lady?
I was enforced to send it after him;
I was beset with shame and courtesy;
My honour would not let ingratitude
So much besmear it. Pardon me, good lady;
For, by these blessed candles of the night,
Had you been there, I think you would have begg'd
The ring of me to give the worthy doctor.

PORTIA

Let not that doctor e'er come near my house:
Since he hath got the jewel that I loved,
And that which you did swear to keep for me,
I will become as liberal as you;
I'll not deny him any thing I have,
No, not my body nor my husband's bed:
Know him I shall, I am well sure of it:
Lie not a night from home; watch me like Argus:
If you do not, if I be left alone,
Now, by mine honour, which is yet mine own,
I'll have that doctor for my bedfellow.

NERISSA

And I his clerk; therefore be well advised
How you do leave me to mine own protection.

GRATIANO

Well, do you so; let not me take him, then;
For if I do, I'll mar the young clerk's pen.

ANTONIO

I am the unhappy subject of these quarrels.

PORTIA

Sir, grieve not you; you are welcome notwithstanding.

BASSANIO

Portia, forgive me this enforced wrong;
And, in the hearing of these many friends,
I swear to thee, even by thine own fair eyes,
Wherein I see myself—

PORTIA

Mark you but that!
In both my eyes he doubly sees himself;
In each eye, one: swear by your double self,
And there's an oath of credit.

BASSANIO

Nay, but hear me:
Pardon this fault, and by my soul I swear
I never more will break an oath with thee.

ANTONIO

I once did lend my body for his wealth;
Which, but for him that had your husband's ring,
Had quite miscarried: I dare be bound again,
My soul upon the forfeit, that your lord
Will never more break faith advisedly.

PORTIA

Then you shall be his surety. Give him this
And bid him keep it better than the other.

ANTONIO

Here, Lord Bassanio; swear to keep this ring.

BASSANIO

By heaven, it is the same I gave the doctor!

PORTIA

I had it of him: pardon me, Bassanio;
For, by this ring, the doctor lay with me.

NERISSA

And pardon me, my gentle Gratiano;

For that same scrubbed boy, the doctor's clerk,
In lieu of this last night did lie with me.
GRATIANO
Why, this is like the mending of highways
In summer, where the ways are fair enough:
What, are we cuckolds ere we have deserved it?
PORTIA
Speak not so grossly. You are all amazed:
Here is a letter; read it at your leisure;
It comes from Padua, from Bellario:
There you shall find that Portia was the doctor,
Nerissa there her clerk: Lorenzo here
Shall witness I set forth as soon as you
And even but now return'd; I have not yet
Enter'd my house. Antonio, you are welcome;
And I have better news in store for you
Than you expect: unseal this letter soon;
There you shall find three of your argosies
Are richly come to harbour suddenly:
You shall not know by what strange accident
I chanced on this letter.
ANTONIO
I am dumb.
BASSANIO
Were you the doctor and I knew you not?
GRATIANO
Were you the clerk that is to make me cuckold?
NERISSA
Ay, but the clerk that never means to do it,
Unless he live until he be a man.
BASSANIO
Sweet doctor, you shall be my bed-fellow:
When I am absent, then lie with my wife.
ANTONIO
Sweet lady, you have given me life and living;
For here I read for certain that my ships
Are safely come to road.
PORTIA

How now, Lorenzo!
My clerk hath some good comforts too for you.
NERISSA
Ay, and I'll give them him without a fee.
There do I give to you and Jessica,
From the rich Jew, a special deed of gift,
After his death, of all he dies possess'd of.
LORENZO
Fair ladies, you drop manna in the way
Of starved people.
PORTIA
It is almost morning,
And yet I am sure you are not satisfied
Of these events at full. Let us go in;
And charge us there upon inter'gatories,
And we will answer all things faithfully.
GRATIANO
Let it be so: the first inter'gatory
That my Nerissa shall be sworn on is,
Whether till the next night she had rather stay,
Or go to bed now, being two hours to day:
But were the day come, I should wish it dark,
That I were couching with the doctor's clerk.
Well, while I live I'll fear no other thing
So sore as keeping safe Nerissa's ring.
Exeunt

Chapter 14

Summary and Analysis

SUMMARY AND ANALYSIS OF ACT 1

Act I, Scene One

Antonio, a merchant, is in a melancholic state of mind and unable to find a reason for his depression. His friends Salerio and Solanio attempt to cheer him up by telling him that he is only worried about his ships returning safely to port. Antonio, however, denies that he is worried about his ships and remains depressed. His two friends leave after Bassanio, Graziano and Lorenzo arrive. Graziano and Lorenzo remark that Antonio does not look well before exiting, leaving Bassanio alone with Antonio.

Bassanio informs Antonio that he has been prodigal with his money and that he currently has accumulated substantial debts. Bassanio reveals that he has come up with a plan to pay off his obligations by marrying Portia, a wealthy heiress in Belmont. However, in order to woo Portia, Bassanio needs to borrow enough money so that he can act like a true nobleman. Antonio tells him that all his money is invested in ships at sea, but offers to borrow money for him.

Act I, Scene Two

Portia, the wealthy heiress, discusses her many suitors with her noblewoman Nerissa. She points out the faults that each of them has, often stereotyping each suitor according to the country from which he has arrived. Nerissa, a gentlewoman who works for Portia, asks her if she remembers a soldier who stayed at Belmont several years before. Portia recalls the man, and says, "Yes, yes, it was Bassanio" (1.2.97). Portia's servingman then arrives with news that four of her suitors are leaving, but another, the Prince of Morocco, has arrived.

Act I, Scene Three

Bassanio in engaged in conversation with Shylock, a Jew who makes his living as a moneylender. Bassanio has asked him for a loan of three thousand ducats, a very large sum at the time, for a period of three months. He further tells Shylock that Antonio is to "be bound," meaning that Antonio will be responsible for repaying the loan.

Shylock knows Antonio's reputation well, and agrees to consider the contract. He asks Bassanio if he may speak with Antonio first, and Bassanio invites Shylock to dinner. Shylock responds that he will never eat with a Christian.

Antonio arrives at that moment and Bassanio takes him aside. Shylock addresses the audience and informs them that he despises Antonio. He bears an old grudge against Antonio which is not explained, but Shylock is further upset that Antonio lends out money without charging interest, thereby lowering the amount he is able to charge for lending out his own money. Shylock turns to Antonio and tells him why interest is allowed in the Hebrew faith by quoting a biblical passage in which Jacob receives all the striped lambs from his father-in-law. Antonio asks him if the passage was inserted into the bible to defend interest charges. He states, "Was this inserted to make interest good, / Or is your gold and silver ewes and rams?" (1.3.90-91). Shylock replies that, "I cannot tell. I make it breed as fast" (1.3.92).

Antonio is upset that Shylock is considering charging him interest on the loan, and asks Shylock to loan the money without any interest. Shylock tells him that, "I would be friends with you, and have your love" (1.3.133). He offers to seal the bond, "in a merry sport" (1.3.141) without charging interest, but as collateral for the loan demands a pound of Antonio's flesh. Antonio thinks Shylock is only joking about the pound of flesh, and is happy to seal the contract. He remarks that, "The Hebrew will turn Christian; he grows kind" (1.3.174).

Analysis

The Merchant of Venice, like so many of Shakespeare's plays, opens with a depressed and melancholy character. The depression of Antonio at the beginning, for which he can give no explanation, is much like Antipholus of Syracuse in The Comedy of Errors. Portia, the wealthy Belmont heiress, is likewise a depressed and unhappy character in the opening scenes. The reasons for their melancholy, although never directly expressed, are due to their self-absorption. And as with Antipholus in The Comedy of Errors, it is only by taking a huge risk (or both) that they will be able to overcome their depression. For Portia, this risk taking can be seen in her love for Bassanio, which will require her to risk her entire inheritance in order for her to win him. For Antonio, the risk is even greater; namely a pound of flesh, representing his very life.

Bassanio represents the gambler who cannot lose. He is the sort of character that will risk everything, and having lost everything, will risk what he does not have. Thus Bassanio tells us, "In my schooldays, when I had lost one shaft, / I shot his fellow in the selfsame flight / The selfsame way, with more advised watch, / To find the other forth; and by adventuring both, / I oft found both" (1.1.140-144). He has often been compared to Jason in the Quest for the Golden Fleece, namely a risk-taker.

Portia as a character is an odd mixture of various traits. She is first presented as the ruler of Belmont, clearly in charge of both herself and those around her. However, we soon discover that she is not in charge, indeed it is "the will of a living daughter curbed by the will of a dead father" (1.2.21). Portia's reliance on the wishes of her dead father therefore contradicts the image of her as Belmont's ruler. Indeed, like many of the women in Shakespeare's plays, she will be unable to alter the plot around her as long as she is a woman. It is only later in the play, by dressing as Balthasar, a man, that she will finally be able to really command events and manipulate the play.

It is necessary to focus on the conflict between the Christians and the Jews throughout this play. Although the twentieth century has altered the way western civilization portrays the Jew in The Merchant of Venice, the compelling character of Shylock still disturbs and entices his audience. Shylock has historically been portrayed as a comic character, and in Shakespeare's day would have dressed quite differently from the other characters in order to distinguish himself from the Christians. The image of Shylock changed rapidly over the years, first making him a villain in the 1700s, a man to be pitied in 1814, and finally a tragic character in 1879.

Although Shylock is accused of representing much of what the Christians hate, it is through his conflict with Antonio in particular that Shakespeare pokes holes in the accusations of the Christian men. The most common error is to assume that the merchant referred to in the title is in fact Shylock himself. This is not the case, since Shylock is only a moneylender. Indeed, the merchant indicated is Antonio. This confusion surrounding Antonio and Shylock is purposeful, for it shows the audience how the Christians are in many ways as awful as the Jews they mock. It also sets the stage for misinterpretation. For example, Shylock states, "Antonio is a good man" (1.3.11), referring to the fact that Antonio is "good" for the money which Bassanio wishes to borrow. Bassanio takes this statement at face value, and agrees that Antonio is a nice man.

The seriousness of the Christian misunderstanding can be seen when Shylock makes the bond with Antonio:

"This kindness will I show.
Go with me to a notary, seal me there
Your single bond, and, in a merry sport,
If you repay me not on such a day,
In such place, such sum or sums as are
Expressed in the condition, let the forfeit
Be nominated for an equal pound
Of your fair flesh to be cut off and taken
In what part of your body pleaseth me.

Now Antonio repeats the same mistake made by Bassanio, thinking that Shylock is being "kind" when he agrees to loan the money without interest. Antonio states "The Hebrew will turn Christian; he grows kind" (1.3.174). Antonio is so convinced that he will be able to repay his debts that Shylock's request for a pound of his flesh as collateral strikes him as a joke, and therefore is not taken at all seriously.

Shylock's willingness to waive the interest payment brings to light an entirely new set of conflicts within the play. Shakespeare draws on Francis Bacon's statement, "It is against nature, for money to beget money," when he portrays the Christians as unselfish givers of all they have. Shylock defends his taking of interest by quoting the passage where Jacob is given the striped lambs. Antonio immediately rejects this as nonsense, asking, "Was this inserted to make interest good, / Or is your gold and silver ewes and rams?" (1.3.90-91). Shylock replies that, "I cannot tell. I make it breed as fast" (1.3.92).

This scene further focuses our attention on the use of sheep imagery in connection to money and breeding. Here Shakespeare plays on the words "use", "usury", and "ewes", all of which will be punned throughout the play. All the sheep imagery is on Shylock's side throughout, for he is fleecing the Christians, breeding the ewes. He therefore mentions Jacob as his defence for taking interest, and we can note later that Shylock's wife is named Leah, the same name that Jacob's first wife had. Shylock is also able to make his money breed like sheep through the charging of interest. On the other hand, the Christians have Jason and the Golden Fleece. This image is used in connection with Bassanio, the risk-taker, who risks everything to gain everything. The same image will figure later with Antonio, who is represented as a wether, a castrated sheep. Thus the concept is reinforced that Antonio does not make his money breed because he refuses to charge interest.

Summary and Analysis of Act 2

Act II, Scene One

The Prince of Morocco meets with Portia and tells her that he is often considered very handsome on account of his black skin. She tells him that unfortunately she does not have the right to choose the man who will marry her. Instead, her father created three caskets from among which each suitor must choose. Portia warns the Prince that if he chooses the wrong casket, he must swear to never propose marriage to a woman afterwards. The Prince of Morocco agrees to this condition and joins Portia for dinner before attempting to choose.

Act II, Scene Two

Lancelot, referred to as a clown, is the servant to Shylock. He tells the audience that he is thinking about running away from his master, whom he describes as a devil. However, he cannot make up his mind about whether to run away or not because his conscience makes him guilty when he thinks about leaving Shylock.

Lancelot's father, and old man named Gobbo, arrives with a basket. He is nearly completely blind and cannot see Lancelot clearly. Gobbo asks his son which way leads to the Jew's house, meaning Shylock's house. He mentions that he is searching for his son Lancelot. Lancelot decides to have some fun with his father, and so he pretends to know a "Master Lancelot" (a term for a gentleman's son, not a servant). He informs Gobbo that "Master Lancelot" is deceased.

Gobbo is clearly upset by this, and Lancelot kneels down in front of him and asks his father for his blessing. Gobbo at first does not believe that Lancelot is really his son, but then he feels his head and recognizes him.

Lancelot tells his father that he is wasting away serving Shylock and that he will turn into a Jew himself if he stays there much longer. Gobbo has brought a present for Shylock, but Lancelot instead convinces his father to give it to Bassanio, whom Lancelot hopes to have as his new master. Bassanio, coming onto stage at that moment, accepts the gift of doves and tells Lancelot that he may leave Shylock and join his service. He then orders one of the men to get Lancelot a new uniform to wear, and sends Lancelot away.

Graziano arrives and tells Bassanio that he wants to join him on the trip to Belmont, where Bassanio plans to go and woo Portia. Bassanio feels that Graziano is too loud and rude and asks him if he will be able to act more appropriately. Graziano says that he can, and that he will "put on a sobre habit" (2.2.171). Bassanio then agrees to take him to Belmont.

Act II, Scene Three

Jessica, the daughter of Shylock, meets with Lancelot and tells him that she will miss him after he leaves to go work for Bassanio. She hands him a letter to take to Lorenzo, who is supposed to be a guest of Bassanio's that night. After Lancelot leaves, Jessica remarks,

> *"Alack, what heinous sin is it in me*
> *To be ashamed to be my father's child!*
> *But though I am a daughter to his blood,*
> *I am not to his manners. O Lorenzo,*
> *If thou keep promise I shall end this strife,*
> *Become a Christian and thy loving wife.*

Jessica thus informs the audience that she is in love with Lorenzo, a Christian. She intends to meet him soon and run away from her father's house in order to marry Lorenzo.

Act II, Scene Four

Lorenzo, Graziano, Salerio and Solanio are preparing for a masque that night. Lancelot arrives with the letter from Jessica and hands it to Lorenzo. Lorenzo reads it and tells Lancelot to inform Jessica that he will not fail her. Lancelot leaves to bring the news to Jessica, and also to invite Shylock to Bassanio's house for dinner.

After the other two men leave, Lorenzo shows Graziano the letter from Jessica. He tells his friend that he and Jessica plan to steal away from her father's house that night, along with a great deal of her father's gold and jewels.

Act II, Scene Five

Shylock informs Lancelot that he will have to judge for himself whether Bassanio is a better master. He then calls Jessica, hands her the keys to the house, and tells her that he must leave for dinner that evening. Lancelot tells Shylock that there will likely be a masque that night. At this news, Shylock orders Jessica to lock up the house and not look out the windows. He says, "Let not the sound of shallow fopp'ry enter / My sobre house" (2.5.34-35).

As Shylock gets ready to depart, Lancelot privately tells Jessica that Lorenzo will come for her that night. She is grateful for the message, and after Shylock leaves she comments that, "I have a father, you a daughter lost" (2.5.55).

Act II, Scene Six

Salerio and Graziano are part of the masquers partying through the street of Venice. They stop and wait for Lorenzo, who has asked them to meet him at a certain spot. Lorenzo arrives and thanks them for their patience. He then calls out to Jessica, who appears in the window of Shylock's house dressed as a man. She throws out a casket to Lorenzo filled with much of her father's gold and jewels. Jessica then goes back inside and steals even more ducats (golden coins) before joining the men on the street.

Everyone departs except for Bassanio, who unexpectedly meets Antonio. Antonio tells him to get to the ship heading for Belmont, because the wind has started blowing the right way and the ship is ready to depart.

Act II, Scene Seven

The Prince of Morocco is brought into a room containing three caskets, gold, silver and lead. Portia tells him to make his choice. The Prince reads the inscriptions on all the caskets. Gold reads: "Who chooseth me shall gain what many men desire" (2.7.5). The silver casket has, "Who chooseth me shall get as much as he deserves" (2.7.7). Finally, the dull lead casket bears the inscription, "Who chooseth me must give and hazard all he hath" (2.7.9).

Portia tells the Prince that the correct casket, or the one that will allow him to marry her, contains a miniature picture of her likeness. The Prince looks over all the inscriptions a second time, and decides that lead is too threatening and not worth risking anything for. He also spurns the silver, which he feels is too base a metal to hold such a beautiful woman as Portia. The Prince therefore chooses gold.

Portia hands him the key, and he opens the casket to reveal a golden skull. The skull holds a written scroll that poetically indicates that he chose superficially. The Prince departs after a hasty farewell. Portia watches him go, and remarks, "A gentle riddance. Draw the curtains, go. / Let all of his complexion choose me so" (2.7.78-79).

Act II, Scene Eight

Salerio and Solanio meet in the street and discuss the hasty departure of Bassanio and Graziano for Belmont. They further tell the audience that Shylock returned home and discovered his daughter had run away with Lorenzo. Shylock then woke up the Duke of Venice and tried to stop Bassanio's ship, which had already set sail. Antonio assured Shylock that Jessica was not on board the ship, but rather had been seen in a gondola with Lorenzo. However, Shylock continues to blame Antonio for the loss of his daughter and his money.

Solanio informs Salerio that Shylock was later seen in the streets crying,

BLOCKQUOTE"My daughter! O, my ducats! O, my daughter!

Fled with a Christian! O, my Christian ducats!
Justice! The law! My ducats and my daughter!
A sealed bag, two sealed bags of ducats,"

Solanio is worried about Antonio, whom he says had better repay his bond with Shylock on time, because Shylock is furious about losing his daughter and his money and blames Antonio for it. Salerio indicates that a Frenchman mentioned a Venetian vessel had sunk in the English Channel the day before. Both men hope that it is not Antonio's ship.

Act II, Scene Nine

The Prince of Aragon arrives in Belmont and decides to choose from among the three caskets. Portia takes him into the room and makes him recite the oath never to reveal which casket he chooses, and further to promise never to marry should he choose the incorrect casket. The Prince of Aragon agrees and starts to read the inscriptions.

He rejects lead because of the ominous warning, and thinks that gold refers to the foolish populace. Instead he chooses silver which indicates he will receive what he deserves. The Prince takes the key and opens the casket to reveal a "blinking idiot" (2.9.53). The scroll indicates that those who are self-loving deserve to be called idiots, and would not make good husbands for Portia. The Prince is upset by his choice, but is forced to leave.

Portia is happy that the Prince has chosen the wrong casket. Her messenger comes into the room at that moment and informs her that a young Venetian has just arrived. Portia goes to see who it is, while Nerissa secretly wishes that it might be Bassanio.

Analysis

The virtue of marriage is very important for Shakespeare, who often ends his comedies with multiple marriages to signify a happy solution to many of the problems the characters have faced. Marriage is thus a way of achieving inclusion for Shakespeare, and it is notable that the characters which remain unmarried are often isolated and removed from the society, specifically Antonio and Shylock within this play. Marriage also represents a way to overcome difficulties; for Bassanio it will remove his debt, for Portia it will free her from her father's will and for Jessica is will allow her to escape her father.

Given this view of marriage, the choice of the caskets presents a horrifying risk for many of the participants, namely the threat that if they choose wrong casket they must swear to never propose marriage to a woman afterwards. In a sense, the failure to marry is as good as being castrated. In fact, Shakespeare creates this very analogy throughout The Merchant of Venice and ties it to the ability to make money breed. Thus in the first act Shylock mentions that he makes his money breed as fast as ewes and lambs. Antonio will further this metaphor in the final act, when he remarks that he is like a wether, or a castrated lamb, and thus unable to breed. For the suitors to Portia, then, swearing to never wed puts them on the same level as Antonio. By agreeing to not marry, they themselves become castrated.

Lancelot the clown is one of the more interesting characters. His treatment of his father is awful, considering that his father is mostly blind and has brought a present to his son. The entire scene mimics the biblical story of Jacob and Esau, though. The bible tells how Jacob tricked his father into giving him the inheritance by wearing wool so his father would think he was Esau. Lancelot does the same thing, by bending down and making his father "know" him by feeling his head.

Shylock's character starts to emerge very strongly within this act. We see him now not only as a moneylender demanding interest, but also as a villain. He shows a marked aversion to fun, demanding that Jessica lock the door and close the windows when he finds out there will be a masque that night. However, contrary to his statement in the first act, Shylock leaves his house to enjoy a dinner with Bassanio. Much of this act therefore develops the negative aspects of Shylock character.

However, the Christian faults are also exposed within this act. The faithlessness of Jessica has been an issue of discussion for many centuries, with the debate raging over whether she is justified in leaving her father. The crucial difficulty is that she does not merely run away, but she insists on stealing large amounts of her father's jewels and gold. Thus when Graziano remarks, "Now, by my hood, a gentile, and no Jew" (2.6.51), we can only see it as ironic. Ironic because she is stealing her father's money, so he is essentially implying Christians are thieves.

Jessica's actions also leave unanswered the question of why she is locked up in her father's home. The answer to this comes from an understanding of the relationship between money and breeding. Whereas in the beginning Antonio is impotent in the sense that his money does not breed, Shylock is not. Shylock further has the advantage of having a daughter.

Since the Jewish lineage is passed down via the maternal line, Jessica represents a way for Shylock's family line to continue. Thus, hoarding Jessica and his gold is Shylock's way of guaranteeing his successful breeding. In fact, Solanio makes this connection between daughter and money abundantly clear when he tells us that Shylock ran through the street of Venice crying:

> *"My daughter! O, my ducats! O, my daughter!*
> *Fled with a Christian! O, my Christian ducats!*
> *Justice! The law! My ducats and my daughter!*
> *A sealed bag, two sealed bags of ducats,"*

Thus for Shylock the simultaneous loss of his daughter and his money is in a sense the loss of his fertility.

Not only does her conversion to Christianity destroy Shylock's family line, it also makes him impotent in a metaphorical sense. Jessica takes two stones with her, which represent the "testicles" of Shylock, since stone was often used to mean testicle. Thus after her theft, Shylock joins Antonio in impotence, having lost his ability to breed. Indeed, the escape of Jessica marks the turning point of Shylock's fortunes, which will lead to his eventual destruction.

It is important that Jessica escapes not dressed as herself, but as a man. In fact, there is a never a scene on the Venetian streets in which a woman is present. The only way a woman can walk through the street of Venice is to dress as a man, a fact that will reinforced when Portia pretends to be Balthasar and dresses as a man before entering Venice. This is one of the primary differences between the worlds of Venice and Belmont.

The three caskets each bear inscriptions that tell us about the personalities of the characters who pick them. Gold reads: "Who chooseth me shall gain what many men desire" (2.7.5). The silver casket has, "Who chooseth me shall get as much as he deserves" (2.7.7). Finally, the dull lead casket bears the inscription, "Who chooseth me must give and hazard all he hath" (2.7.9). The Prince of Morocco first chooses gold and gets a death skull. The Prince of Aragon receives the picture of an idiot. This is symbolic, for he is an old man and hence is an idiot for thinking himself deserving of a young woman.

One of the most debated lines is when Portia sends the Prince of Morocco away by saying, "A gentle riddance. Draw the curtains, go. / Let all of his complexion choose me so" (2.7.78-79). This provincial comment stands in contrast with her upbringing and nobility. However, what soon becomes clear is that Portia is a very narrow character in her sense of friends. She chooses Bassanio over the more cosmopolitan suitors because he represents her Christian and Venetian world. Bassanio wins her because of the same thing, namely he alone of the suitors possesses the local characteristics necessary to interpret which casket to choose.

Unlike Portia and Bassanio, Jessica never has to be chosen by a casket. Instead, she tosses her casket out of the window for Lorenzo to catch. Thus her relationship, unlike that of Portia and Bassanio, has no test to make sure it is a good relationship. This lack of a test will create problems later, foreshadowed by Shakespeare when Lorenzo and Jessica compare themselves to many famous failed romances.

The Merchant of Venice is largely a play about interpretation. The suitors to Portia are condemned to sterility because they misread the caskets. Shylock's interpretation of the contract in 1.3 takes the "pound of flesh" seriously and literally, whereas Antonio thinks Shylock is being "kind." Later in the final scene, the outcome of the play - whether it becomes a comedic ending or a tragic one, will rest on Portia's interpretation of the law. Thus the play creates its drama and its plot through the constant interpretation of events and words. This crucial aspect is frequently used by Shakespeare in his remaining comedies, and it forms a crucial part of the plot in Much Ado About Nothing.

SUMMARY AND ANALYSIS OF ACT 3

Act III, Scene One

Solanio and Salerio discuss the rumor that Antonio has lost yet a second ship. Shylock enters and complains that both

Solanio and Salerio had something to do with his daughter's flight. They do not deny it, but instead ask Shylock if he has heard about Antonio's losses.

Shylock tells them that Antonio should "look to his bond" and make sure he repays the money, or else Shylock is planning on taking his pound of flesh. Shylock is furious with Antonio, whom he blames for the loss of Jessica, and also bears an older grudge against the man. He then delivers his famous soliloquy, "Hath not a Jew eyes? Hath not a Jew hands, organs, dimensions, senses, affections, passions..." (3.1.49-50). The speech concludes with Shylock saying that he will be revenged for all the times he has been treated badly by Christians.

One of Antonio's servants arrives and bids Solanio and Salerio to go to Antonio's house. They leave, and Tubal, another Jew, arrives to speak with Shylock. Tubal has been in Genoa, where he tried to locate Jessica. He tells Shylock that Jessica had been in the city, and had spent over eighty ducats while there. She had also traded a turquoise ring for a monkey, a ring which Shylock regrets losing because he had received it from his wife Leah. However, Tubal also brings Shylock news that Antonio has lost yet a third ship, and is almost certain to go bankrupt in the near future. Shylock is excited by this news, since he has decided that he would rather exact revenge on Antonio than receive his three thousand ducats back.

Act III, Scene Two

Portia tells Bassanio that she wants him to wait a month or two before choosing from the caskets so that she may be guaranteed his company for a while longer. Bassanio tells her that he is desperate to choose, and feels like he is being tortured the longer he waits. Portia finally agrees to take him into the room with the caskets.

Portia orders music to be played for Bassanio, and one of her servants starts to sing a song in which the rhymes all rhyme with lead. Bassanio speaks directly to the audience and tells them that too many things are gilded and coated with ornaments. He therefore decides to do away with gold, comparing it to Midas' greed. The silver casket he also ignores, saying it resembles money and is therefore too common. He thus chooses the lead casket and finds Portia's picture inside.

Bassanio is overjoyed by the picture and remarks that it is a beautiful "counterfeit". He then takes the scroll and reads it: "You that choose not by the view / Chance as fair and choose as true" (3.2.131-132). Bassanio goes over to Portia with the note, and she offers him everything she owns, including herself. Portia then hands Bassanio a ring as a token of her love and commitment and tells him never to lose it. He promises, telling her that if he ever stops wearing the ring it will be because he is dead.

Graziano then informs them that he would like to be married as well. He tells Bassanio and Portia that he and Nerissa (the chambermaid to Portia) are in love. Bassanio is thrilled for his friend and agrees to let them get married as well.

Jessica, Lorenzo and Salerio arrive at Belmont. Bassanio is happy to see all of them, but Salerio then hands him a letter from Antonio. Bassanio turns pale at the news that Antonio has lost his fortune and his ships, and he asks Salerio if it is true that all of Antonio's ventures have failed. Salerio tells him it is true, and that Shylock is so excited about getting his pound of flesh that even if Antonio could repay him he would likely refuse it.

Portia asks what amount of money Antonio owes to Shylock, and then orders Bassanio to return to Venice and offer Shylock six thousand ducats to destroy the contract. She informs Bassanio and Graziano that she and Nerissa will live like widows in their absence. They all agree to get married first and then go straight to Venice to rescue Antonio.

Act III, Scene Three

Shylock has come to watch Antonio be taken away by a jailer. Antonio pleads with Shylock to listen to him, but Shylock says, "I have sworn an oath that I will have my bond," (3.3.4) and refuses to listen to any of the pleas for mercy. After Shylock departs, Antonio tells Solanio that Shylock hates him because he used to loan money to men who were in debt to Shylock, thus preventing Shylock from collecting the forfeiture. Antonio is prepared to pay his "bloody creditor" the next day in court, but prays that Bassanio will arrive in time to watch him die.

Act III, Scene Four

Portia and Nerissa, worried about their new husbands, tell Lorenzo that they are going to stay at a local monastery for a few days in order to pray. After Lorenzo and Jessica leave, Portia sends her servant Balthasar to her cousin Doctor Bellario with instructions that Balthasar should bring anything Bellario gives him to Venice. Portia then informs Nerissa that they are going to dress up as men and go to Venice in order to help their husbands.

Act III, Scene Five

Lancelot and Jessica are in an argument over whether she can be saved by God since she was born a Jew. Lancelot tells her that since both her parents are Jews, she is damned. She protests that she can be saved once she becomes a Christian because her husband Lorenzo is a Christian. Lancelot then makes a joke, and says that Lorenzo is a bad man because by converting all the Jews he is raising the price of pork (since Jews do not eat pork, but Christians do). Lorenzo then arrives and orders Lancelot to go inside and prepare the table for dinner. He and Jessica praise Portia for being such a wonderful hostess before entering the house to get their dinner.

Analysis

By far the most interpreted and critiqued section of this act is Shylock's famous speech:

"Hath not a Jew eyes? Hath not a Jew hands, organs, dimensions, senses, affections, passions; fed with the same food, hurt with the same weapons, subject to the same diseases, healed by the same means, warmed and cooked by the same winter and summer as a Christian is? If you prick us do we not bleed? If you tickle us do we not laugh? If you poison us do we not die? And if you wrong us shall we not revenge? If we are like you in the rest, we will resemble you in that. If a Jew wrong a Christian, what is his humility? Revenge. If a Christian wrong a Jew, what should his sufferance be by Christian example? Why, revenge. The villainy you teach me I will execute, and it shall go hard but I will better the instruction."

This passage has been interpreted in many ways, from comedic to villainous to tragic. In the twentieth century, it has almost always taken on a tragic character as a result of WWII. Shylock speaks the lines to defend his resolution to take a pound of Antonio's flesh. However, the passage is difficult to interpret because of Shylock's position in the society. As a Jew, he could not have been on the street screaming for revenge, since this would only lead to more persecution. Thus, one interpretation has taken the lines to be comic, in the sense of using comedy as a mask to hide fear. Like a child who makes jokes out of insecurity, Shylock tries to defend his right to exact the pound of flesh.

Bassanio's choosing from the caskets has also generated controversy. Portia first begs Bassanio to wait at least a month, hoping to spend time with him before he chooses among the caskets. When he refuses to wait, she plays music for him. Some scholars have noted that each of the rhymes of the song rhyme with lead, thus providing a subconscious hint. What is interesting is that Bassanio differs from the other suitors in not reading the inscriptions. Thus he is forced to choose with his eyes alone, saying, "Therefore, thou gaudy gold, / hard food for Midas, I will none of thee. / Nor none of thee, thou pale and common drudge / Tween man and man" (3.2.100-103). He refers to the fact that gold denotes greed, and thus is worthless as it was for Midas who could not even eat his food because it turned to gold on him. Silver represents money, or coins, passing between men and therefore Bassanio rejects it as well. The lead casket symbolizes his penchant for risk-taking, and indeed the scroll reads as much, "must hazard all he has." Bassanio is an insider, a risk-taker who likes the threat that lead poses, and a man who espouses the Christian ideal of "the last shall be first."

The fact that Bassanio is able to choose the casket without reading the inscription is in some sense born out by the scroll. The scroll says, "You that choose not by the view / Chance as fair and choose as true" (3.2.131-132). However, there is a converse to Bassanio's risk-taking, namely Portia. Portia takes her own risk each time suitor chooses, and is forced to give Bassanio all that she has. "Myself and what is mine is now to you and what is yours converted" (3.2.166). She does not have a choice in this matter, since it is ordained by her dead father's will.

Portia further gives Bassanio a ring, making him promise to wear it forever. This is an inversion of the marriage ceremony, and is her way of testing Bassanio's fidelity and love. In Shakespeare's time it was more often the women whc were accused of infidelity, tricking their husbands. Portia cleverly reverses this by making Bassanio swear to keep the faith with her.

The imagery of sheep emerges again in this act, this time in a Christian setting rather than a Jewish one. Graziano says, "We are the Jasons; we have won the fleece" (3.2.240). This Christian take on the sheep imagery is interesting because it is so different from Shylock's interpretation. Rather than make money breed, the Christians prefer to risk everything in search of gaining everything.

Bassanio requires this interpretation, he is after all a gentleman, and therefore considers monetary issues to be beneath him. This is in opposition even to Antonio, who still regards money as a necessity. Bassanio prefers instead to rely on his breeding for success. He tells Portia, "I freely told you all the wealth I had / Ran in my veins: I was a gentleman;" (3.2.253-254).

There has been a great deal of scholarly interest in the relationship between Bassanio and Antonio. Antonio's comments and undeniable willingness to support Bassanio have led many to conclude that there is a homoerotic undercurrent to their relationship. Indeed, Antonio's desire at the end is not to keep his life but rather that, "Pray God Bassanio come / To see me pay his debt, and then I care not"

(3.3.35-36). Although it may stretch the plot to argue for a homosexual relationship between the two men, what cannot be disregarded is the way in which Portia carefully removes Antonio from the plot at the end. This will be seen later in the play, where she is the one to free him from the contract, and is later the person to inform him about his ships. Thus any relationship between Antonio and Bassanio is trumped by the marriage with Portia, who will further draw Bassanio to her by playing a ring trick on him (see acts four and five).

The fact that women never explicitly appear in Venice is reinforced in this act as well. Portia and Nerissa must first pretend to go to a monastery in order to escape from Belmont, where Lorenzo and Jessica are staying. Portia also contrives to dress them as men in order to go to Venice. She further uses her kinship with Doctor Bellario to give her credibility and allow her to control the actions in the upcoming scenes. However, what can never be denied is the fact that Portia still relies on a man for her credibility, and requires a man's dress in order to alter events in the play.

SUMMARY AND ANALYSIS OF ACT 4

Act IV, Scene One

Antonio is brought before the Duke and the magnificoes of Venice to stand trial for failing to pay off his obligation to Shylock. The Duke is upset about the penalty, a pound of Antonio's flesh, but cannot find any lawful way of freeing Antonio from his bond. Shylock enters the court and the Duke tells him that all of the men gathered there expect him to pardon Antonio and forgive the debt.

Shylock replies that he has already sworn by his Sabbath that he will take his pound of flesh from Antonio. He is unable to provide a good reason for wanting to punish Antonio in this manner, other than to say, "So can I give no reason, nor I will not, / More than a lodged hate and a certain loathing / I bear Antonio" (4.1.58-60).

Bassanio then comes forward and offers Shylock the six thousand ducats as repayment for the loan. Shylock tells him that even if there were six times as much money offered to him, he would not take it. The Duke asks Shylock, "How shalt thou hope for mercy, rend'ring none?" (4.1.87). Shylock responds that he is doing nothing wrong, and compares his contract with Antonio to the Christian slave trade. He tells the Duke that he does not demand that the Christians should free their slaves, and therefore the Christians should not demand that he free Antonio.

The Duke threatens to dismiss the court without settling the suit brought by Shylock if Doctor Bellario fails to arrive. Salerio tells him that a messenger has just come from Bellario, and Nerissa enters dressed as a man and informs the Duke that Bellario has sent a letter to him. Shylock whets his knife on his shoe, confident that he will receive his pound of flesh.

The letter from Bellario recommends a young and educated doctor to arbitrate the case. The Duke asks where the young doctor is, and Nerissa tells him that he is waiting outside to be admitted into the court. The Duke orders him to be brought in, and Portia enters dressed as a man, pretending to be a doctor named Balthasar.

Portia tells the Duke that she has thoroughly studied the case and then asks, "Which is the merchant here, and which the Jew?" (4.1.169). Antonio and Shylock both step forward, and Portia asks Antonio if he confesses to signing the contract. He does, and Portia then says that Shylock therefore must be merciful. She delivers a short speech on mercy, but Shylock ignores it and demands the contract be fulfilled. Portia then asks if no one has been able to repay the amount, but since Shylock has refused the money there is nothing she can do to make him take it. She comments that she must therefore side with Shylock.

Shylock, impressed that Portia is supporting his case, says, "A Daniel come to judgment, yea, a Daniel!" (4.1.218). Portia rules that Shylock has the right to claim a pound of flesh from next to Antonio's heart according to the bond. Antonio's bosom is laid bare and Shylock gets ready to cut. Portia asks him if he has a surgeon ready to stop the bleeding once he has taken his pound of flesh. Shylock says, "I cannot find it. 'Tis not in the bond" (4.1.257).

Just as Shylock is about to start cutting again, Portia says that the bond does not give him permission to shed Antonio's blood. The laws of Venice are such that if any Venetian's blood is shed, all the goods and lands of the perpetrator may be confiscated by the state. Shylock realises that he cannot cut the flesh without drawing blood, and instead agrees to take the money instead. However, Portia is not willing to back down and instead only gives him the pound of flesh, further saying that if he takes a tiny bit more or less he will be put to death himself. Shylock, unable to comply with this stipulation, decides to withdraw his case.

Portia tells Shylock to remain in the court. She says that Venice has a further law which says that if any foreigner tries to kill a Venetian, the foreigner will have half of his property go to the Venetian against whom he plotted, and the state will receive the other half. In addition, the life of the foreigner will be in the hands of the Duke, who may decide to do whatever he wants to. Shylock is forced to kneel on the ground before the court, but the Duke pardons his life before he can beg for mercy.

Shylock instead asks the Duke to kill him, saying, "Nay, take my life and all, pardon not that. / You take my house when you do take the prop / That doth sustain my house; you take my life /When you do take the means whereby I live" (4.1.369-373). Antonio intervenes on Shylock's behalf, and asks the Duke to allow Shylock to keep half of his wealth. He further offers to take care of the half he was awarded as a form of inheritance for Jessica and Lorenzo. The only requirements Antonio puts on his offer are that Shylock must convert and become a Christian, and further that he must give everything he owns to Lorenzo upon his death.

Shylock, wretched and having lost everything he owns, tells the court that he is content to accept these conditions. The Duke leaves and tells Antonio to thank the young doctor who has saved his life. Bassanio and Graziano go to Portia and thank her profusely, and Bassanio offers the young doctor anything he wants. Portia decides to test her husband's trustworthiness, and asks him for the engagement ring, the ring which she made him vow never to part with. He refuses, and Portia and Nerissa leave. However, at Antonio's urging, Bassanio takes off the ring and gives it to Graziano, telling him to take it to Portia and invite her to dinner that night at Antonio's.

Act IV, Scene Two

Portia gives Nerissa the deed by which Shylock will pass his inheritance to Lorenzo. She tells Nerissa to take it to Shylock's house and make him sign it. At the moment Graziano catches up with the two women and gives the ring to Portia. She is surprised that Bassanio parted with it after all, and Nerissa decides to test Graziano in the same way. Nerissa takes the deed and asks Graziano to show her the way to Shylock's house.

Analysis

Shylock's reasons for wanting to kill Antonio come across as very arbitrary and obscure. He compares his desire to kill Antonio with "Some men there are love not a gaping pig, / Some that are mad if they behold a cat". He follows this with the statement, "So can I give no reason, nor I will not, / More than a lodged hate and a certain loathing / I bear Antonio". This inability on Shylocks's part to give a concrete answer as to why he wants to kill Antonio can only be explained by understanding the doubling between Shylock and Antonio.

This doubling of Shylock and Antonio takes place through the way they use money and family. Antonio starts the play unable to make his money breed because he takes no interest. He further has no wife or children and therefore emerges as an impotent character. Antonio reveals in Act Four what sort of person he represents: "I am a tainted wether of the flock". The "wether" is a castrated male sheep, thus directly stating the fact that Antonio is unable to breed. Shylock starts the play on the opposite extreme, able to make his money breed with interest and his family breed through Jessica. However, it is Antonio who convinces him to not take interest on this particular bond, and it is later Antonio whom Shylock accuses of allowing Jessica to escape. Thus for Shylock, Antonio represents the man who made him impotent as well. His hatred towards Antonio can thereby be explained. It is further irony that in this act Antonio makes Shylock convert to Christianity, thus removing even that distinction between the two men. In essence, the destroyed Shylock at the end of the play is very similar to the melancholy Antonio in the beginning.

Portia adds to this sense of doubling when she arrives in the court. She asks, "Which is the merchant here, and which the Jew?". Indeed, given the confusion so many people have with the title, it is often this very question which is asked. Scholars have tried to attribute her question to blind justice, arguing that Portia does not want to show any favourites. However, on an Elizabethan stage she would be able to recognize Shylock immediately from his distinctive dress.

The essence of doubling is reinforced even more with the double exclusion of the two men at the end of the play. Antonio, having received half of Shylock's wealth, essentially takes over for Shylock by using Shylock's money. Scholars have debated about the nature of the "merry bond" between Shylock and Antonio. Some have suggested Shylock meant to circumcise Antonio, others think he meant to make Antonio take over his place. The fact that Shylock accepts a Christian condition of taking no interest is supposedly offset by the fact that if Shylock wins, Antonio must act Jewish.

Another interesting interpretation deals with why Antonio must stand trial at all. In the Bible Paul said that Jewishness is an internal condition, not external. This implies that Shylock is Jewish not because he was born that way, but because he acts that way. Thus Antonio's mistreatment of Shylock violates this explanation of Jewishness by despising Shylock because of his external features. It is this sin for which Antonio is judged.

Throughout this play there is also the concept of the scapegoat. The scapegoat was used as a way of purging a town of its sins by heaping them onto the unfortunate animal instead. The town would drive one goat out of town and sacrifice another. Both men fit this description in The Merchant of Venice, with Shylock clearly driven out of society and Antonio representing the goat about to be sacrificed.

One of the great ironies of this play is where Shylock calls Portia, "A Daniel come to judgment, yea, a Daniel!" (4.1.218). Daniel was the biblical judge of Susanna, a woman accused of inchastity by the Elders. The story is famous because Daniel rules in Susanna's favour, thus rescuing her. In addition to freeing her, he then further convicts the Elders. Shylock's mistake is that he is premature in calling Portia a Daniel, because he is the one who represents the Elders, and Antonio signifies Susanna. This inversion comes only a few lines later, when Portia not only frees Antonio, but convicts Shylock of attempted murder.

The relationship between Antonio and Bassanio comes to the forefront in this section. Antonio can literally be seen as a lover of Bassanio, willing to die for him. This creates the conflict between Portia and Antonio, a conflict she is willing to test by demanding that Bassanio give her his ring. The fact that Bassanio parts with the ring for Antonio's sake, as does Graziano, implies that Bassanio chooses Antonio over Portia. This of course is unacceptable, as is seen in the next act where Portia severally chastises Bassanio for loving a man more than he loves her.

The rings have a further meaning though. They are given by Bassanio and Graziano as a token of respect and friendship to people they deem to be men. Thus the ultimate symbolism is that the rings are given to friends who are also their wives. This fusion of friendship and marriage is an unusual one and serves to strengthen the relationship between the couples.

SUMMARY AND ANALYSIS OF ACT 5

Act V, Scene One

Lorenzo and Jessica, still at Belmont, sit outside and enjoy the night. They compare the night to the stories of Troilus and Cressida, Pyramus and Thisbe, and Dido and Aeneus, and then extend the analogy to their own love affair. They are interrupted by Stefano, who tells them that Portia is returning home with Nerissa. Lancelot then arrives and informs Lorenzo that Bassanio will also be back by morning. Both Lorenzo and Jessica return to the house and listen to music.

Portia and Nerissa, dressed as themselves again, return home and enter the building. Lorenzo recognizes Portia's voice and comes to greet her. She orders the servants to pretend as if she had never left, and asks Lorenzo and Jessica to do the same. Soon thereafter Bassanio, Graziano and Antonio arrive.

Nerissa demands that Graziano show her the ring he gave away to Portia's "clerk" in Venice. They start to argue over it, with Graziano defending his action as a form of kindness for Antonio. Portia overhears them and pretends to "discover" what happened. She then demands that Bassanio show her his ring, which he of course cannot do. Portia and Nerissa then berate their husbands for giving away the rings, and even tell them that they would prefer to sleep with the doctor and his clerk rather than with their unfaithful husbands.

Antonio offers his assurance that neither Bassanio nor Graziano will ever give away their wives' gifts again. Portia thanks him and asks him to give Bassanio another ring to keep. Bassanio looks at the ring and recognizes it as being the same ring he gave away. Portia then tells him that the doctor came back to Belmont and slept with her. Bassanio is amazed and does not know how to respond.

Portia finally clears up the confusion by informing Bassanio that she and Nerissa were the doctor and the clerk. She further has good news for Antonio, namely a letter that indicates that three of his ships arrived in port safely. Nerissa then hands Lorenzo the deed from Shylock in which he inherits everything after Shylock dies. The play ends with Graziano promising to forever keep Nerissa's ring safe.

Analysis

One of the most ridiculous moments in this act involves Lorenzo and Jessica, who compare their love with the three disastrous love stories. They invoke Troilus and Cressida, Pyramus and Thisbe, and Dido and Aeneus as their models. This is ironic in the highest degree because all the invoked lovers are failures. For example, Pyramus and Thisbe commit suicide, and Dido kills herself when Aeneus leaves her. This hearkens back to the ease with which Jessica handed over the casket in the previous acts. Their love never underwent any form of test, either with the casket, or with the rings, which Jessica apparently trades for a monkey. Thus they in a sense condemn their love to failure like those of the failed lovers.

Much of this scene involves Portia and Nerissa teaching their husbands the value of the marriage. The gifts of the rings serve to represent the sanctity and holy promise of the marriage. Thus, for Bassanio and Graziano to give away the rings is a violation of their marriage contract, a sign that they love Antonio more than their wives. Since this cannot be allowed, Portia uses her ring trick to force Bassanio to give up Antonio. The joke that Portia creates is when she says, "I'll have that doctor for my bedfellow" (5.1.232), thus implying that Bassanio needs to realise the ring is given to him alone, and that giving it away violates the relationship implicit in their marriage contract. The twinning and oppositeness of Antonio and Shylock was remarked on earlier in the analysis. This same twinning and oppositeness exists between Belmont and Venice. Belmont represents music and leisure, Venice signifies money and laws.

However, as Belmont is of course built upon the money from Venice, it depends on gold and inheritance. This is seen most clearly when the deed from Shylock is handed to Lorenzo, which is similar to the way Portia derives her wealth in Belmont from a dead father's will. However, the luxury of Belmont is not necessarily considered positive. Venice produces merchants such as Antonio, whereas Belmont produces Lorenzo, a lazy beggar.

The three pairs of lovers represent the comic ending. But what should be a happy ending is violated and broken by Antonio and Shylock. Both men remain outsiders at the end of the play, alone and removed from the happy luxury of Belmont. Both outsiders also have been immasculated by the end. Shylock via the loss of his money and his daughter, Antonio by losing Bassanio to Portia. The lowest level of

Antonio's defeat is when Portia hands him his money and ships at the end, essentially telling him to return to Venice and forget about Bassanio.

Chapter 15

Study Questions

Q. Discuss the Dramatization of the Conflict of Christian and Jew in "The Merchant of Venice"

Through an ancient plight between Moses and Jesus, Christian believers have monopolized western society and pushed away Jewish believers. Shakespeare's Merchant of Venice directly dramatizes the fight of a Semitic society oppressed in the face of English culture. The characters of Shylock the Jew and Antonio the Christian are the two comparisons that Shakespeare writes into the storyline. Both Shylock and Antonio live in Venice, avenging one another for each other's business inside the Rialto. Through their conflict, Shakespeare dramatizes difference by using setting, language use and characterization.

Perceptive/ insightful comments on the character of Antonio.

The character of Antonio (who is Christian and the merchant) is humanized from the very moment he is introduced to the audience. Unlike Shylock, Antonio has the support and care of his friends who are inquisitive as to why he is emotionally unhappy. He appears to be a loving and caring companion, especially in his kindness toward helping his friend Bassanio:

Quotation is an integral part of the commentary.
"Within the eye of honour, be assur'd
My purse, my person, my extremest means
Lie all unlock'd to your occasions."
(Merchant of Venice: Act I, scene i, l.137-139).

Analysing language and showing insight.

Here, the first person pronoun "my" is repeated to emphasise how generous Antonio is. The verb "unlock'd" also suggests freedom and openness, ironically contrasting with Antonio's later arrest.

In contrast, Shylock's character and the fact that he is Jewish is not as important as that he is the money-lender. Shakespeare uses the token Jew to form a character who is money hungry at work, power hungry at home and anti-Christian in every way possible. These words have a negative connotation used by Shakespeare to suggest that not only is Shylock a bad person, but also an evil one. While Shylock weighs up the idea of taking Antonio's credit on application from Bassanio, he comments in a derogatory manner of the irony of Antonio's situation:

> *"How like the fawning publican he looks!*
> *I hate him for he is a Christian...*
> *I will feed fat the ancient grudge I bear him..."*
> *(Merchant of Venice: Act I, scene iii, l.36-42).*

Shylock's simile focuses on Antonio's obsequious nature. The alliteration of "feed fat" draws attention to Shylock's intense desire for revenge and he will later feed his desire for blood and flesh.

Using this technique of maintaining positive, caring connotations for Christianity and negative, evil connotations for Semitism, Shakespeare guides the audience to a decision on the obvious: Christians are good, Jews are bad. At this point, however, it is notable to comment that in the time the play was written Shakespeare would have known no other Jews other than those called "conversios" who had converted to Christianity. This is due to Jews being effectively banned from England in 1290. This illustrated the attitude of the society that Shakespeare lived and grew up believing: a society of anti-Semitics.

Without this decision between Christian and Jew being made, the overall plot would fail to portray the clash between the merchant and the money-lender. So it is central to the play that Shakespeare uses the Christian and Jew relationship in introducing the emotion of hate between the two religions for no other reason than to "stew the pot" and increase tension:

Again, ideas supported and quotation integrated into argument.

"Call me misbeliever, cut-throat dog
And spet upon my Jewish gabardine..."
(Merchant of Venice: Act I, scene iii, l.106-107).

With this volatile cocktail of emotion, Shakespeare uses this opportunity to add another complexity to the emotion of the play. The Jew's own daughter elopes to marry a Christian - worse in fact; the Christian is Antonio's Christian-friend. Consequently, Shylock becomes overwhelmed by his emotions and calls for Antonio's flesh in payment of the bond. This advances the author's strategy to which we may draw similarities to a game of chess. It provides a dramatic floor in which to elevate the argument between the merchant and the money-lender and bring it in to the court and the face the law:

"The Duke cannot deny the course of the law:
For the commodity that stranger have
With us in Venice, if it be denied,
Will much impeach the justice of the state..."
(Merchant of Venice: Act III, scene iv, l.26-29).

The setting of the court heightens the dramatic conflict of the characters. Venice was renowned as a place of rigorous justice. The opposing values of Antonio and Shylock can be explored in a formal setting, where mercy comes up against revenge.

Throughout the play Shakespeare is able to manipulate the hate between Christian and Jew as a socio-religious flaw of the human mind. Creating intense three-dimensional arguments, the author explores a fundamental element of the Elizabethan English psyche. He takes this opinion of the Jewish belief, and uses it to portray a spiteful tale of a Christian merchant and a Jewish money-lender within the context of a comedy. The play appears to be simply coincidental in its religious battles, but in heavy analysis, it is clear that Shakespeare uses this grounding in The Merchant of Venice as a strategy to reflect England and its extreme Christian ethnocentrism.

Q. Describe the Shakespeare's Plea for Human Values in the Merchant of Venice?

Of the many unforgettable characters who poured out of the vast breadth of Shakespeare's imagination, one of the most fascinating is Shylock, the Jew. Though he appears in only five out of twenty scenes in *The Merchant of Venice,* Shylock has attracted the major share of interest in the drama's long history on the stage and in critical literature. One's first association with *The Merchant of Venice* is invariably Shylock. "Shylock" has become a term of disapproval, a link in the history of anti-Jewish stereotype, just as Shylock's "pound of flesh" has become a metaphor for cruel and relentless greed.

The experience of this stereotype still makes many uncomfortable with *The Merchant of Venice.* As a result, the trend has developed of reversing the apparent tendency of the drama: Shylock is portrayed not as a hateful character, but as one who commands our sympathies. Many critics and scholars have devoted themselves earnestly and voluminously to proving that Shakespeare did not create a Jewish villain.

All who love the work of Shakespeare would wish that Shylock was not a villain, that Shakespeare had not drawn an anti-Jewish portrait. But if we are to read the play honestly, we must admit that he did. Not only does Shylock have many villainous qualities, but the average reader must also get the notion that Shylock is a typical Jew, and that this is what Jews are like. Shylock is referred to as "the Jew" over sixty times, and as a Jew he is repeatedly associated in one form or another with the devil. But having said this, we must immediately add that the very fact that there are so many interpretations of Shylock indicates that some ambiguity—perhaps deliberate, as is my contention—is written into the texture of the drama itself.

Shakespeare's portrait of the Jew could not possibly derive from first-hand contact with Jews or with Jewish life. There had been almost no Jews in England for over three hundred years and no Jewish community life even of the most rudimentary form. Shakespeare knew no Jews, but he knew well the stereotype of the Jew as a nefarious, bloodthirsty monster.

William the Conqueror, for his own benefit, brought the Jews to England. The wealth and power of the nobility was based on land, but in a rising money economy the nobility often needed ready cash. They forced numbers of Jews to lend to themselves as well as to the peasants so that these latter could pay their dues to the nobility. Since the nobility did not use the money for productive gain, ultimately they could not make good on their debts.

As long as the nobility were economically solvent, the Jewish position was excellent. But when they gravely overextended themselves, the position of the Jews began to deteriorate. Fearing the loss of their pawned lands, the nobility turned the wrath of the oppressed peasantry from themselves and against the Jews, often using as instrument the teachings and rulings of the church.

A reign of terror was generated against the Jews which led gradually to their humiliation and impoverishment, expropriation of their wealth, and their final expulsion in 1290 after brutal riots had been let loose against them. To justify the ferocity with which Jews were attacked, excuses just as ferocious had to be made. The image of the Satanic Jew flourished in literature, ballads and plays, and was used both as a justification of the terrible treatment of the Jews and as encouragement to the masses to attack them.

Thus arose the stereotype of the Jew that Shakespeare knew. But why the Jew, as the poet Pope put it, that Shakespeare drew? The image of the villain Jew was absolutely necessary to the central theme of *The Merchant of Venice*: the ideal of unconditional love.

Shakespeare lived in the midst of an economic revolution that was changing Europe from an agrarian to a commercial economy, from a feudal aristocracy to a commercial, democratic, middle-class society. He sometimes defended the old values against the new, particularly when he sensed tendencies in the new that he felt were destructive of human values. There is abundant evidence that Shakespeare feared the motive of material gain so important in the rapidly expanding development of commercial capitalism, lest it subvert the values of loyalty for its own sake, friendship and custom-forged and time-honoured allegiances, all based on the structure of medieval feudalism.

In the agrarian economy of the Middle Ages when the lending of money was not for gain but only out of need, the church, in biblical tradition, enjoined: *mutuum datum inde sperantes*—give freely hoping for nothing (in return). By contrast, commercial values enjoined: never do anything or give anything unless you can take or get something in return. Antonio represents the old philosophy; Shylock, the new. Whereas Antonio and Bassanio give friends favours without even asking for reasons and expect nothing in return, certainly not more than they gave, Shylock always asks for a return with gain.

Did Shakespeare foresee that day when the urgent new commercial values would so suffuse human relationships that nothing would be done for love or friendship or the sake of giving alone, but only for the sake of gain; when a person would do something generous without any apparent motive of self-gain and people would ask, "What's his angle?"; when even the most important human relationships such as those between husband and wife, parent and child, would be judged in terms of commercial analogy—not "What am I giving to these relationships" but "What am I getting out of them"?

In the very first scene in which we meet Shylock, he uses the word "good"—*He is a good man*—not to mean virtuous, but "well-off," capable of paying back a debt. The criterion of virtue becomes not character but wealth. To Shakespeare's discerning soul, here lay tendencies destructive of all human values and humanity itself. Because they are at a premium in a society whose mainspring is struggle for profit, the getting and grasping motives are nurtured, whereas loving, giving motives remain uncultivated and atrophy. The motive of deeds for the sake of love alone disappears; only greed, selfishness, hostility and hate remain.

All of this negative tendency Shakespeare summed up in the word *usury*, that is, the lending of money for gain, giving not for love but for gain. Now, though there were no Jewish usurers in England in Shakespeare's time, the Jew symbolized usury, and Shakespeare could most forcefully express the evils he was attacking in the figure of a Jew.

But the point is that Shakespeare did not stop here. For his aim was not to attack Jews but to attack the greed and materialism of the Christians all about him. It was the "Jew" who could best be used to ring the contrast with "Christian" and to ask, "Which is which?" The word "Jew" was synonymous with evil. The word "Christian" meant good. The gold casket, on the inside of which was a skull and crossbones, symbolizes the choice of gold as the goal of life; this leads only to death. But there is another meaning to the casket. Just as one cannot judge what is inside a casket by its outer material, so all that glistens, like the name "Christian," is not gold.

When Shylock's daughter Jessica is in the very act of stealing her father's money, the so-called Christian, Gratiano, says admiringly that she is a Gentile and not a Jew. Even Lancelot Gobbo, the clown of the play, parodies this Christian concern for gain when he complains that too many Jewish converts to Christianity would raise the price of pork. Shakespeare makes the audience uncomfortable with its hypocritical stereotypes which allow it so easily to project its own guilt for greed onto the Jew.

Shakespeare goes even further, and this is the source of the deliberate ambiguity in the character of Shylock which makes a "tragic," sympathetic portrayal possible. His theme is unconditional love: love even when the object of love is not deserving, compassion just because human beings are frail. To communicate this message, Shylock must also have sympathetic, "good" qualities.

Shylock had to be a Jew and a villain to symbolize tendencies that Shakespeare deplored. He could be a comic figure because greed is sometimes ludicrous, but he could not be a monster. And so, though Shakespeare was an Elizabethan and of his time, he transcended his time and avoided the serotype of the Jew as a monster. Shylock says: *I am a Jew. Hath not a Jew eyes? Hath not a Jew hands, organs, dimensions, senses, affections, passions?...If you prick us, do we not bleed? If you tickle us, do we not laugh? If you poison us, do we not die? And if you wrong us, shall we not revenge? If we are like you in the rest, we will resemble you in that.* (III.i)

Shylock is both villain and comic, but he is also sympathetic. For Shakespeare has one more point to make. Moral weakness is found not alone in "the Jew" but in all men. Since all men have foibles, are weak, commit sins, are sometimes greedy and hateful, as they are all sometimes noble, there cannot be any simple rule for justice. Justice is necessary that society be ordered and endure. But a love that does not depend on merit is a *sine qua non* of the moral man.

Q. "Modern Humanitarianism has run riot on Shylock." Discuss.

"The Merchant of Venice" is concerned with two issues that were of importance in the Elizabethan Age: Jewry and Usury. It is generally assumed that the Elizabethan attitude to Jewry was hostile and that the execution of Roderigo Lopez in 1594 was characteristic of the Christian rejection of all 'Jews, Turks, Infidels and Heretics', who were considered to be "misbelievers". But this could also be a false assumption, for although the Jews were forced to convert to Christianity to live in England, once they did they were generally left alone. Marlowe in "The Jew of Malta" portrays a Machiavellian Jew, but one who is 'rarely mean' in his villainy. Usury was a contemporary and important issue during Shakespeare's time. Shylock is the negative and stereotype picture of the usurer that most of the Elizabethans had- one who was seen as a 'greedy dog', 'a leech'.

The interpretation of Shylock's character is difficult and also to some extent ambiguous. He was earlier portrayed as a comic character but later on could be interpreted as a malevolent villain. But if Shylock is taken as a comic character the whole power of the play is lost. He would almost become a ridiculous villain. It could also be that Shakespeare created Shylock as a match for Marlowe's Jew- one that was terrible, imposing but also human.

Shylock is one of the main characters of the play but this also depends on the way that his character is played. He has mostly been portrayed as a comic character but when he is the tragic protagonist he 'usurps the centre of the stage.' Shylock "represents the killjoy against whom the pleasure-loving characters unite." He represents a "a-social miserliness" and thus his villainy is somewhat mitigated and brought within the scope of humanist debate. Shylock exists as a visible complication to the smooth running of Bassanio's friendship with Antonio and his courtship of Portia. One can almost say that is the character that makes the plot possible.

As John Palmer has said, Shylock is "An imaginative realization of what it means to wear the Star of David." Shylock is a Jew in a Gentile Society, an alien who is never accepted. He is proud of his race, his religion but he is up against a Venetian society that is insufferable to the outsider. Even his daughter attacks all that he holds dear. She marries a Christian and takes away his money- his family pride, the only "props" in his life. He is humiliated and scorned at by the Christians. One feels sympathy for such a man, who is "more sinned against than sinning."

During the trial scene it is even less easy to make a moral decision, a comfortable discrimination between the gentle Christian and rapacious Jew. The reader's and the audience's sympathies are directed towards Shylock who earlier had pleaded his humanity: "Hath not a Jew eyes? Hath not a Jew hands, organs, dimensions, senses, affections, passions?" Our compassion is due to Shylock's plight but also because of the unease that we experience at the behaviour of the Christians: "A Daniel...! Mark Jew!"

Here the Christian cruelty is on par with that of the Jew. However in the 20th C we are more sensitive and conscious about political correctness.

The issue of racism has further complicated Shylock's character. Shylock's role attracts greater sympathy.

One feels that the Venetian Christians have denied Shylock's humanity and we are all the time reminded of the Anti-Semitism of the Nazi's and of the Genocide that took place during the holocaust.

We are more concerned with alien rights than the Elizabethans were. These modern attitudes then in the words of Edwin Booth, tend "to lift (Shylock) out of the darkness of his native element of revengeful selfishness into the light of the venerable Hebrew, the Martyr, the Avenger."

Shylock can be seen as a product of centuries of racial persecution. Thus Shylock 's character has oscillated between the malignant caricature and the dignified tragic hero.

Is Shylock a representation of the Jewish hatred for Christians or is he motivated due to his personal hatred for Antonio? When Shylock says,

"I hate him for he is a Christian: But more for...He lends out money gratis..." one realises that his hatred is based on money and he is not the religious martyr that he portrays himself to be. He takes a gamble when he lends the money and makes Antonio sign the "merry" bond. He has no way of knowing that all of Antonio's fortune will sink and that he will be able to take the forfeit. His hatred for Antonio and the rest is apparent throughout.

Shylock is the representative of the money code, the greed and the hoarding that is contrasted to the Christian code of honour. But does he embody the evil side of the power of money? Or is he just a scapegoat who embodies the qualities embedded in the Venetians? As mentioned earlier, Shylock's character raises a lot of questions. He may have been victimized due to the Christian hypocrisy.

It could be that he is a villain who is allowed to express the sort of treatment that has made him what he is and he justifies his route to villainy. We, with our modern considerations for alien rights, could be turning a plea for the right to revenge into a plea for equal treatment. His cause might win our sympathy but the ferociousness of the means loses it.

However the humanity of Shylock as seen here is an unconscious byproduct of thé Shakespeare's dramatic genius. It is an example of the interplay between technical craft and creative imagination. It is an example of a character so dynamic that it takes over from the writer and assumes dimensions of an independent entity. He evokes an interest that is beyond the scope of the play. Shylock for us is not just a Jew; he stands for all the people that are discriminated against, people who suffer injustice due to their colour, religion and even caste. And this is the universality of Shakespeare; he created a character not for his time but for all times. But Shakespeare also set a dramatic problem when he established 'the villain as hero' as Shylock does 'steal the show' and overshadows the formal hero. We have to be aware of the 'intellectual ' and 'emotional limits' that Shakespeare might have faced when dealing with these issues during his time. One's view of Shylock influences the interpretation of the other major characters and also determines that of the whole play. And it is true that, as E.W. Godwin said, "at Shylock's exit the play is virtually over."

Shylock evokes multiple reactions in the reader and the audience. When we view the Christian smugness and hypocrisy we see a modern parallel to the treatment of the American Negro. But one is also repulsed by his treatment of his daughter and his mercenary attitude. If we wish to do full justice to the character of Shylock as well as to Shakespeare's dramatic genius in creating such a character we have to explore the Elizabethan aspects of the play and not view it only with our present concern for racial discrimination and economic conflict.

Q. Whether the Merchant of Venice is an anti Jewish play or not? Discuss

Two recent studies of Shakespeare and early modern attitudes towards Jews come to remarkably different conclusions on the question of whether or not *The Merchant of Venice* is an anti-Jewish play. James Shapiro's richly historical *Shakespeare and the Jews* offers fascinating evidence about the scope and complexity of anti-Jewish attitudes embedded in the "cultural moment" of Shakespeare's play, but he shies away from directly accusing either playwright or play of promoting or trading on anti-semitism, claiming that such terms are "anachronistic... inventions of nineteenth-century racial theory" and thus, "fundamentally ill-suited for gauging what transpired three hundred years earlier". The objection is important; modern discourses about race are significantly different from their early modern religious forbears. However, this does not render questions like "Is the play intentionally anti-Jewish" irrelevant. Does the play invite us to share Antonio's attitudes toward Jews? Does it mean us to regard Shylock (and so revile Shylock) as a "typical" Jew? Shapiro shows us a "cultural moment" of late Elizabethan anxiety about national and religious identities, anxieties that very often surfaced as reactionary xenophobia and both anti-Jewish and anti-Catholic paranoia. We might reasonably and profitably ask whether or not the play exploits these anxieties and phobias, and if so how? Does the play endorse the anti-Jewish attitudes that according to Shapiro helped shape a nation's anxious search for Englishness?

Martin Yaffe's *Shylock and the Jewish Question* throws itself headfirst into the counter-intuitive claim that the play is intentionally and even obviously pro-Jewish, that the play invites us to revile Shylock, not as a typical Jew, but as a "bad Jew." Yaffe's argument assumes, without offering any historical evidence, that both playwright and audience would have regarded Shylock as a Jew who has abandoned traditional Jewish moral teaching and assimilated himself to the mercenary ways of Venetian capitalism. He is bloodthirsty and merciless because he is a materialist usurer, even a precurser of the modern secular liberal, not because he is a Jew. Of course I agree with Yaffe that stereotypes of Jews as merciless, bloodthirsty, and carnal-minded are all rooted in flagrant misconceptions of traditional Hebrew and Jewish teachings, but I simply cannot bring myself to imagine that either Shakespeare or his audience was free of such misconceptions. Shapiro's book offers more than enough evidence to the contrary.

Shylock as a "Bad Jew"

Though I think Yaffe's overall thesis unsound, even obtuse, its perspective sometimes prompts more interesting, even more accurate, readings of key passages in the play than traditional perspectives have. Yaffe's reading of Shylock's "I am a Jew" speech, for example, is in at least one important respect more historically correct than the one Shapiro's concluding remarks imply (Shapiro 228). Shapiro echoes the time-honoured reading of this speech as a moving appeal to universalist humanism; but we too easily forget how it might have sounded to a Renaissance Christian humanist:

I am a Jew. Hath not a Jew eyes? Hath not a Jew hands, organs, dimensions, senses, affections, passions; fed with the same food, hurt with the same weapons, subject to the same diseases, healed by the same means, warmed and cooled by the same winter and summer, as a Christian is? If you prick us, do we not bleed? If you tickle us, do we not laugh? If you poison us, do we not die? And if you wrong us, shall we not revenge? If we are like you in the rest, we will resemble you in that. If a Jew wrong a Christian, what is his humility? Revenge. If a Christian wrong a Jew, what should his sufferance be by Christian example? Why, revenge. The villainy you teach me, I will execute, and it shall go hard but I will better the instruction.

Shylock claims that Christians and Jews are not much different from each other, that they share an underlying carnal humanity. In Yaffe's words, "Shylock argues that Jews and Christians are alike in a low but undeniable respect: having eyes, hands, organs, dimensions, senses, affections, passions, and so forth, their behaviour is equally subject to the overriding needs and susceptibilities of the human body. Conditioned alike, they may therefore be expected to act alike". Shylock preaches a *kind* of humanism, but it is a far cry from the neoplatonic Christian humanism of, say Giovanni Pico della Mirandola, who taught that humanity is not so much a matter of shared physiology, but of shared godlikeness — "the intimate of the gods, the king of the lower beings,... the marriage song of the world, on David's testimony but a little lower than the angels". Shylock's humanism is more like the modern secular humanism implicit in the excuse, "after all I'm only human." On this score, Yaffe is precisely right; an audience that warms to Portia's mercy speech would regard Shylock's carnal humanism—revenge for revenge—as something very low indeed.

What Yaffe does not notice, for it hardly supports his argument, is that Shakespeare's audience would also have recognized in this speech the "carnal" mind they believed typical of all Jews. The carnal attitude Yaffe would attribute to Shylock's (and Venice's) "newly prominent" commercialism, a contemporary audience would have regarded as a Jewish attitude. Indeed, one of the play's chief themes is that commercialism, especially the emergent practice of favouring merchant law over common law and equity, and the general cultural slide towards the idolatries of the marketplace, all threaten traditional values much in the way Jews had long been regarded as a threat to Christianity. The play uses the Jew and the Merchant as complementary figures of each other; exaggerated mercantilism is made to look Jewish and the mythic bloodthirsty Jew is refigured as a business machiavel.

Yaffe also makes a very good point about Shylock's being bad at Bible interpretation. Yaffe regards Shylock as a "bad Jew," which in his book means an assimilated Jew. Shylock has "departed from the ways of his forbears" and become a money-grubbing Venetian financier. Although he still calls himself a Jew, he long ago stopped following the ancient laws of the Torah; indeed he cannot even read Torah profitably because he tends to read the scriptures "rather as a sourcebook for the creative businessman". An allegedly telling example of Shylock's perverse assimilationist hermeneutics is his attempt, in Act 1, scene 3 to read the story of Jacob and Laban from Genesis 30-31 as a biblical endorsement of usury. Yaffe correctly observes that traditional rabbinic commentary explicitly agrees with Antonio's (supposedly the Christian) reading of the Jacob and Laban episode — that Jacob used no guile or sharp practices in his dealings with Laban, but simply followed the Lord's commandments and allowed circumstances to be "sway'd and fashion'd by the hand of heaven". Shylock's reading is not, then, a traditional Jewish interpretation of Jacob's thriving, but a money-grubbing Venice-assimilated apostate's self-interested perversion of the story.

I agree, of course, that Shylock's reading of Genesis is not a typically rabbinic or even Jewish reading, but I think Yaffe is wrong about Elizabethean Protestant audiences. They probably would have regarded Shylock's self-serving hermeneutics as typically Jewish, and the play clearly invites us to think so. The typical Elizabethan Protestant would have offered quite a different account of Shylock's, or any Jew's, hermeneutic myopia — the widely held conviction that Jews simply cannot read the scriptures properly. In particular, it was believed they stubbornly read the Bible's promises in *carnal* senses rather than the *spiritual* senses which the Holy Spirit intended. Shakespeare's audience would probably have seen Shylock's carnal and self-serving reading of Genesis as typical of all Jews, since they generally believed that all Jews since Christ's advent had willfully given up their place in God's Church, God's Israel, and had become stubborn misbelievers, unable to read their own scriptures profitably. In short, all Jews were believed to have "departed from the ways of [their] forbears". To Elizabethan Christians, that was virtually the definition of a Jew.

Early Modern Protestant Versions of the Jew

I find Yaffe's misreadings of the "I am a Jew" speech and Shylock's hermeneutic myopia especially interesting because they pay attention to features of the play other critics ignore. Yaffe misreads these features because he has little sense of the powerfully ambivalent role played by the figure of the Jew in the Elizabethan Protestant imagination. When English Protestants read their Bibles, they read the patriarchs and prophets not just as figures of themselves; they thought of Moses, David, Ezekiel, and Daniel as co-religionists, members of God's Church. The ancient Israelites, taught Luther, Calvin, and the Geneva Bible annotations, were God's pre-advent Church.[4] The "Old Testament" Israelites, especially the patriarchs and heroes, were widely regarded as proto-Christian members of the true Church, elect from the beginning. But the post-advent Jews represented the worst form of stubborn and graceless apostasy. Except for the Pauline assurance that many of them would turn Christian at the last moment of history, these Jews stood for everything a Christian was not—selfish, impious, carnal-minded, stubborn, vindictive, merciless, envious, bloodthirsty, narrow-minded, and devoted to this world rather than to the world to come.

Examples of these attitudes towards Israelite and Jew can be found almost everywhere in early modern religious discourse, but they are especially prevalent in reformation commentaries on the Book of Daniel. The book of Daniel and contemporary commentaries upon it are important here because Shakespeare's play so loudly and complexly invokes the stories and teachings of the ancient Hebrew prophet. In the trial scene, Shylock expresses his delight at young Doctor Balthasar's (Portia's) summary judgment in his favour by dubbing him "a Daniel come to judgment, yea, a Daniel" (*Merchant* 4.1.218).

As Shapiro observes, "editors of the play uniformly note that the characters are alluding to the apocryphal story of Susannah and the elders" and that "the explanations go no further" than this Lewalski also observed, in 1962, that the name Portia borrows for her disguise as a young law clerk, Balthasar, was the name assigned to Daniel by Ashpenaz, King Nebuchadnezzar's "chief of the Eunuches" when Daniel and three other children of Israel's royal household were taken from Israel to live in captivity in Babylon. Thus, though Shylock probably alludes to the story from the book of Susanna when he praises Portia as "a Daniel come to judgment, yea, a Daniel," his allusion is already undercut and displaced by Portia's assumption of Daniel's Babylonian name as part of her disguise as judge. Her gesture alludes, not to the apocryphal Book of Susanna, but to what Christians considered the canonical book of Daniel. Only there is the prophet referred to by his Babylonian name. Portia, then, stands for one sort of Daniel, and Shylock invokes quite another; Graziano, probably unwittingly, calls attention to the differences between the two.

In what remains of this paper I will try to show in detail how Portia's Daniel represents the Daniel who was crucial to the Reformation notion of the converted, or *Christian* Jew as opposed to the blind and stubborn Jew, that Shylock betrays himself as precisely such a blind and stubborn Jew who effectively misrecognizes Daniel even as he invokes him, and that the play invites its audience therefore to revile Shylock as a typical Jew — myopic hermeneut, stubborn misbeliever, graceless and merciless dog — for whom forced conversion is too good a treatment. The play implies that Portia, disguised as Balthasar/Daniel, plays the role of a *true* Jew, that is, the Jew who recognizes Jesus as Messiah. It also implies that stubborn, misbelieving Jews like Shylock are not, properly speaking, Jews at all, but more truly like Nebuchadnezzar and the Babylonians, the pagan idolaters who are the bad guys in the book of Daniel. Shakespeare does invite us to revile Shylock as a "bad Jew," but not in the way Yaffe maintains; to an Elizabethan audience all Jews except those who, like Daniel, acknowledge Christ as Messiah, are "bad Jews."

Daniel as Christian Jew, the "True Jew"

Calvin wrote commentaries on nearly every book of the Bible, but his commentary on Daniel, one of the Bible's shorter books, requires two large volumes in the Calvin Translation Society series. Andrew Willet's *Hexapla in Danielem* also runs to two large volumes, much longer than his more well-known *Hexapla in Genesin,* even though the book of Daniel is about one quarter the length of Genesis. The English version of the Geneva Bible prints copious annotations around each of Daniel's twelve chapters. Protestants in Europe and in England were obsessively fascinated with the prophetic book of Daniel. The "Argvment" that introduces the Geneva version of the book of Daniel indicates why: "The great providence of God, and his singular mercie toward his Church are most lively here set forthe." Of all the prophets God has sent for the comfort of "his Church," Ezekiel and Daniel were particularly "adorned with such graces of his holie spirite, that Daniél aboue all other had most special reuelations of suche things as shulde come to the Church, even from the time that thei were in captiuitie, to the last ende of the worlde, and to the general resurrection." By "the Church" here is meant God's chosen people from the time of Abraham to the apocalypse, treated as a single predestined people throughout history from the old covenant to the new. To early modern Protestants, Daniel is a crux, textual and historical, in the saga of God's true Church. This is because they believed that Daniel foretold, not darkly or allegorically, but plainly and self-consciously, the exact number of years that would pass before the advent of "the sonne of man," or Jesus Christ. Daniel foresaw the cessation of the ceremonies in the temple, implying that Christ's sacrifice on the cross rendered temple sacrifice redundant. "Moreover," says the Geneva introduction, Daniel

> sheweth Christes office and the cause of his death, which was by his sacrifice to take awaye sinnes, and to bring euerlasting life. And as from the beginning God euer exercised his people vnder the crosse, so he teacheth here, that after that Christ is offred, he wil stil leaue this exercise to his Church vntil the dead rise againe, and Christ gather his into his kingdome in the heauens.

Daniel tells the world of his vision of God's providential plan for the salvation of his Church, from the Babylonian captivity to the apocalypse. In other words, the prophet Daniel comprehended the Gospel centuries before the birth of Christ, and even met the pre-incarnate Christ as "the sonne of man" in a vision, and preached this gospel to a largely unresponsive Israel. He is thus a pivotal figure in the history of God's true Church, the first Jew to become a Christian. Those who reject or misread Daniel's prophecy, then, are apostate Jews, complacent in captivity, the forerunners of the Scribes and Pharisees.

Early Protestant commentaries on Daniel always point out that stubborn Jews refuse to regard Daniel as a prophet or his book as canonical. Andrew Willet, like most Protestant commentators, notes that "The Iewes doe derogate much from the authoritie of this booke, not counting it among the Propheticall writings" (Willet 7). He opines that Jews have denied Daniel the authority of a prophet because they stubbornly resent Christ and the gospel in general. This denial, Willet implies, has grown firmer throughout history. "Elder Iewes" respected the book much as they did the other non-Mosaic books and wrote commentaries on it, but "the later Rabbines doe denie the booke of Daniel to be authenticall, and therefore do seldome reade it," and the reason for this is "because Daniel doth so evidently point out the time of the Messiah his comming" (7). Jews in general, implies Willet, have abandoned their heritage in God's true Church, ignored his special prophets, and denied his Messiah. Calvin's comments on this Jewish perversity are typical; according to his reading of Daniel 9:11, Israel's apostasy is not so much a matter of disobeying the law as refusing to hear the gospel from God's prophet:

In revolting, he says, *so as not to hear*. By these words Daniel expresses the determined obstinacy of the people, implying this was not occasioned by either error or ignorance; nay even sloth was not the cause of Israel's wilful blindness and inattention to God's precepts, but was only the beginning of this act of rebellion.

Giovanni Diodati, the uncle of John Milton's best friend, Charles, wrote in his *Pious Annotations upon the Holy Bible* that Daniel predicts Christ's redemptive death as "more cleerly shewn to him, then to any other Prophet" and adds that another point of the prophecy is "foretelling also that Christs Kingdome should be exercised, in justly punishing the Jewish Nation for their incredulitie and rebellion." Protestant commentaries uniformly read Daniel as foretelling Christ's redemption of "the elect" Jews and the damnation of the stubborn Jews. On Daniel 12:1, Diodati comments, "God shall deliver his elect out of the general reprobation, and extermination of the Jewish nation." Daniel was read as a wholesale indictment, by one of their own prophets, of Jews who deny Christ, even to the point of justifying their "general reprobation and extermination."

The enormous and hugely popular *Annotations upon all the books of the Old and New Testament* summarizes "the Propheticall part" of Daniel this way:

Daniels wisedome doth clearly shine forth, in shewing when the mystery of Mans Redemption should be wrought; and Ceremonies, and legal Sacrifices should cease, and be abolished, to give way to the service of God in Spirit and Truth; namely when the *Messiah* was slain.... [It] also tells the time precisely when the *Messiah*, by his death, should purchase for his Church spiritual deliverance, and set up his Spiritual, and everlasting Kingdome, by causing and meriting Salvation and Eternal felicity to all both Jewes and gentiles which were of the Election of Grace. Foretelling likewise the finall and fatal judgment of God to be executed by the *Romans* upon the *Jewish* Nation, for denying the Holy One of Israel, and betraying the Lord of life to be killed by the *Romane* power.

Many Protestants believed that Christ's second coming would be immediately preceded by a mass conversion of Jews, but we are mistaken if we think they meant all Jews. Calvin, for example, taught that only those Jews "elect" from the beginning of the world would be saved. Commenting on Daniel 9:27, he says quite bluntly, "I have no hesitation in stating God's wish to cut off all hope of restoration from the Jews, whom we know to have been blinded by a foolish confidence, and to have supposed God's presence confined to a visible temple. As they were thus firmly persuaded of the impossibility of God's ever departing from them, they ought to be deprived of their false confidence, and no longer deceive themselves by such flattering hopes" (*Commentaries on Daniel* 2. 228-29). And on Daniel 9:26: "Two points, then, are to be noticed here; first, all hope is to be taken from the Jews, as they must be taught the necessity for their perishing; and secondly, a reason is ascribed for this, namely, the determination of the Almighty and his inviolable decree".

According to Calvin, any Jew who had heard the gospel according to Daniel and persisted in denying both Christ and his prophet must perish; God decrees it. Shakespeare's play shows us a Jew who hears the gospel according to Portia, speaking as Balthasar, a Daniel in disguise. He misrecognizes Daniel as a clever young judge rather than God's prophet; he refuses to hear the teaching of mercy and redemption and grace. He therefore deserves to perish. This is the anti-Jewish logic of the play.

Luther's English disciple, George Joye, compiled in 1544 *The Exposicio[n] of Daniell the Prophete.* There he repeats Melancthon's caution about how properly to read biblical prophecies like Daniel's: readers "muste loke whyche parte containeth the lawes, whyche preache the promises and the gospell" (A8v). Though we normally expect to find "lawes" in the so-called "Old Testament" and gospel promises in the New, the point here is that Daniel preaches literal gospel promises in his prophetic book and the pertinacious "Jewes" simply refuse to "get it."

As what can be sayde clerelier and evidentlyer agaynste the Jewes, then that Daniel affirmeth Chryste to muste have ben borne duryng yet the common weal of Moses? Wherefore that horrible destruccion of Jerusalem and ruyne of the whole lande of Juda now paste.M.CCCC.lxxiiii. yeres do testifye Chryst to be borne, & it refuteth their mad & cursed pertinaci. Here must we note the lessons of the true invocacion and worship of God. As when Daniel praieth he acknowlegeth to God onely his owne and their synnes for whom he prayeth, and asketh of God onelye delyveraunce in the fayth and confidence of his mercy, adding by expresse name. For the Lorde Christe hys sake, that is for Messias sake promised.

According to this reading Daniel preaches Christ and "his mercy," the end of sacrificial ritual, and the destruction of the temple centuries before "the one like the sonne of man" condescends to become incarnate as Jesus Christ. Much like Paul who bragged that his authority as apostle derived from the "risen" Christ rather than the earthly Jesus, Daniel is here understood as an apostle to Israel authorized by the pre-incarnate Christ, appearing to him in visions as "the sonne of man," or "the similitude of a man" or as "Michael" (Daniel

8:15, 10:13, 21; 12:1). Early modern Protestant commentaries regarded Daniel as literally, not figuratively, preaching the gospel (Daniel 10:1 note b); Calvin, for example, claims that Daniel received interpretations of his visions directly "from Christ's lips" Of Daniel 7:27, Calvin says, "almost all, except the Jews, have treated this prophecy as relating to the final day of Christ's advent."

All Christian interpreters agree in this.... As to the Jews, theirs is no explanation at all, for they are not only foolish and stupid, but even crazy. And since their object is the adulteration of sound doctrine, God also blinds them till they become utterly in the dark, and both trifling and childish; and if I were to stop to refute their crudities, I should never come to an end.

Fourteen hundred and seventy-four years of salvation history, says Melancthon, testify to the truth of Daniel's visionary gospel; it is a gospel that came straight from the heavenly Son of God. What's more, in Daniel 9:1-19, commentators understood Daniel's famous prayer for forgiveness on behalf of Israel as addressed to Christ in Christ's own "expresse name". The Geneva notes to Daniel 1:7 also insist that Daniel's prayer on behalf of an apostate Israel is consciously addressed to Christ, glossing "Lords sake" as "That is, for thy Christs sake in whom [thou] wilt accept all our praiers." If Daniel prayed in Christ's name for forgiveness of Israel's sins, then Jews who do not recognize Daniel as a prophet-apostle and his teachings as gospel promises are perverse, stupid, crazy, mad, and cursedly pertinacious; as such they deserve "extermination." This is what the book of Daniel signified to many early modern Protestants.

When, therefore, Portia assumes the name Balthasar for her disguise as Bellario's law clerk, and assumes the post as special judge in "this strict court of Venice" — that is, a special court where merchants may expect summary judgment on contract enforcement regardless of their "nation" — Shakespeare invokes the popular Daniel lore of the age. This Daniel lore is precisely the discourse through which Bible-reading Englishmen and women thought about Jews. Portia thus not only preempts Shylock's allusion to Daniel, she preemptively corrects it. He alludes to the clever young judge of the story in Susanna who turns the Elders' perjuries against themselves, but Portia as Balthasar already stands for the prophet Daniel as Protestants understood him from the canonical scriptures: one who preaches Christ crucified, risen and come again, a sufficient sacrifice for all sins; the end of temple worship in types and shadows; the vanity of legal righteousness, and the necessity of praying for forgiveness and mercy "for thy Christs sake," and in his name.

In effect, the English Protestant's Daniel implies an "Old Testament" indictment of stubborn Jews; if he could believe in Christ even before Jesus's advent, based simply on prophetic visions, then the post-advent Jews who do not believe have no excuse. Shylock misrecognizes the Daniel he invokes; he therefore misses the point of Daniel's prophecy. That, in the minds of Shakespeare's contemporaries, is what makes him a "bad Jew," that is, a non-Christian Jew.

Misrecognizing Portia

Portia stands at the hub of a web of misrecognitions that generate this play's ironic humour and much of its anti-Jewish energy. But Shylock is not the only one who misrecognizes Portia. So also do Antonio and the Duke. The Duke mistakes her disguised sex for beardless youth. Thinking she is young, the Duke expects a certain kind of legal bias he had hoped to avoid in sending for "learned Bellario." At first his fears look justified, but this apparently young Doctor turns out to be the only one capable of turning the case before this "strict court of Venice" from a civil merchant affair to a very traditional criminal matter based on laws that underwrite very old and bigoted notions of nation and citizenship. We are thus invited to read the Venetians' misrecognition as an index of their blindness, though it is blindness of another sort than Shylock's, for it is neither pertinacious nor willful; they are deceived, but Shylock refuses to see or listen to Portia's teaching about mercy.

Understanding how the Duke and the Venetians misrecognize Portia requires that we know something about how cases in merchant law were handled in sixteenth-century Venice, or at least the way Englishmen, anxious about legal innovations designed to enable emergent capitalist practices, feared they were handled. Walter Cohen reminds us that "To the English, and particularly to Londoners, Venice represented a more advanced stage of the commercial development they themselves were experiencing" (Cohen 75). B. J. Sokol, writing about allusions to and anxieties about "the Law Merchant" in the play, concludes "it is likely that in the Elizabethan imagination mercantile law would seem Italian. The legendary image of Venetian commerce clearly impressed Shakespeare and his audiences, and this is joined with a contemporary belief that the Venetian state firmly applied laws equally to all". Various characters in the play — Salerio Antonio, Shylock — formulate and re-formulate the legal stone that presumably blocks any possible comic resolution: Venice's strength as an international commercial centre depends upon its reputation for upholding merchant and financial contracts regardless of the contracting parties' nation. Antonio puts it this way:

> *The Duke cannot deny the course of law,*
> *For the commodity that strangers have*
> *With us in Venice, if it be denied,*
> *Will much impeach the justice of his state;*
> *Since that the trade and profit of the city*
> *Consisteth of all nations.*

In their legal philosophy, then, Antonio and the Duke are in the uncomfortable position of basic agreement with Shylock. This is why the Duke spends so much private effort trying to get Shylock to settle out of court, and why his first public statements in the trial scene once again press for settlement without trial.

Gasparo Contarini's *Commonwealth and Government of Venice* is full of pride for Venetian internationalism, an internationalism that evoked admiration, envy, and trepidation from English readers. When Lewes Lewkenor's translation was published in England in 1599, several English poets, including Edmund Spenser, contributed prefatory sonnets. Spenser regards "Fayre *Venice*, flower of the last worlds delight" as the third and last "*Babel*," after Babylon and Rome. Venice is "next to them in beauty... /But farre exceedes [them] in policie of right." Like the other two Babels, the poem suggests, Venice, too, will self-destruct, and its innovative internationalist policies will be partly to blame. Another poem, by I. Ashley, compares Venice to Narcissus, and predicts its ruin in its pride. All these prefatory poems say something about Venice's innovative politics, law, and mercantile power. They all profess admiration for Venice's progressive policies, but also suggest there is something too worldly, too proud, carnal, and vaguely idolatrous about this third Babel of a city.

Contarini's text offers detailed accounts of Venetian innovations in merchant law. He opens by boasting that visitors to Venice are amazed at the city's "wonderful concourse of strange and forraine people, yea of the farthest and remotest nations, as though the City of *Venice* onely were a common and general market to the whole world" (Contarini 1). To support the development of international commerce, Venice instituted a whole set of new civil magistrates called the "New Auditors" with specialized responsibilities, "divided according to the qualitie of the causes and of the persons". Cases about property were assigned to one auditor/judge while cases about "other contracts, or bargaines" to another. Likewise, cases between citizens were assigned separately from cases between strangers, "or one with another strangers and citizens together". Yet another new division of magistrates was called "Judges or Consuls of the marchauntes": "These doe in their Judgements use a speedier dispatch then any other of the civil magistrates: which was so ordayned, to the ende that marchauntes, whose affaires might otherwise receyve great detriment and hinderance, with lingering and delayes might not be deluded or entertayned with long expectation of their right".

I do not want to suggest that Shakespeare precisely modelled his trial scene on actual Venetian civil procedure. The end of the scene, where the civil court prosecutes and decides a criminal charge, argues otherwise. The point is that

Venice, as Spenser's poem suggests, had a reputation for a civil court system peculiarly solicitous of merchants' "right" to a speedy judgment on principles that favoured liberty of contract. When the Duke warns the court that "Upon my power I may dismiss this court/ Unless Bellario, a learnèd doctor/ Whom I have sent for to determine this,/ Come here today", we are witnessing the sort of specialized civil procedure Contarini outlines. The Duke does not sit as judge in this court because it was customary to invite a "forraine" judge from one of the mainland Italian cities to sit in judgment over cases involving foreigners. The Duke would invite a specialist in such contracts from among the lists of "New Auditors" for merchant cases; the trial is expected to take place without delay and issue in a summary judgment.

Because this is such standard procedure, Shakespeare's Duke is already quite certain what the result will be, and though as Duke he can intervene whenever he pleases, he is loath to do what Bassanio asks — "Wrest once the law to your authority./ To do a great right, do a little wrong" — even to save Antonio. Whether we see Bassanio directing this plea to Balthasar as the appointed judge in this case, or to the Duke in his special authority, Portia's response is allowed to stand:

It must not be. There is no power in Venice
Can alter a decree establishèd.
'Twill be recorded for a precedent,
And many an error by the same example
Will rush into the state. It cannot be.

The Duke can delay the case if he wishes under colour of legal procedure, but he is a strong proponent of the new procedures for merchant justice, procedures designed to benefit merchants like Antonio, and to promote commercial interests in general. He is sorry for Antonio (4.1.3) precisely because he doesn't see how he can help him without impeaching a civil court system that has enabled Venice's success, without tarnishing the reputation that is the ground of its commercial preeminence. The third Babel's glory is at risk here.

There is, as it turns out, another more traditional brand of law lurking in the wings, but if the Duke knows of it, he doesn't know how to apply it in this case. No one, not the Duke, not even Antonio, can think of a way to inject equity into "this strict court of Venice" without putting Venice's reputation at risk. The play suggests that blindly promoting merchant law over equity and common law may make a city rich and beautiful, but it may also unintentionally give rein to the merciless and idolatrous lusts of unchristian beasts like Shylock. Merchant law and unbridled commercialism may build another Babel, another capitol of paganism and apostasy, another Rome.

Perhaps this is why Shakespeare's Duke, when he sends for a foreign judge to serve as auditor in this case, applies to the "learned Bellario" of Padua. Paduans were not Venetians, so Bellario is technically a foreigner, but according to legend, Venice was originally settled and founded by Paduans fleeing barbarian invasion. Padua, then, was Venice's father city and its link to a more traditional mainland past. Bellario qualifies as one of the "new Auditors," but he also represents the old country and its more traditional systems of law. The Duke, having spent so much energy trying to get Shylock to settle out of court, selects Bellario hoping that he may know how to inject an older sense of equity into "this strict court of Venice."

If this is so, Dr. Balthasar's first appearance in court must disappoint the Duke. Neither old, nor Paduan, Balthasar is astonishingly young and Roman. In his letter Bellario anticipates the Duke's disappointment by reassuring him that Balthasar is a *puer senex*: "I never knew so young a body with so old a head" (4.1.159-60). This could be code for "don't be disappointed; he's not the progressive young lawyer he appears." So the Duke accepts Balthasar and formally installs him as judge: "Take your place". But no sooner is he in place than Balthasar fulfills all the Duke's worst fears about an innovative young judge in this case. Before he has heard a word of testimony, young Balthasar has his judgment ready:

Of a strange nature is the suit you follow,
Yet in such rule that the Venetian law
Cannot impugn you as you do proceed.

This is summary enforcement of contract of the speediest sort! According to merchant law, apparently, this case is open-and-shut.

No doubt Portia's grand speech on the "quality of mercy" sounds very much like thc sort of thing the Duke might have welcomed from the "old head" of Bellario. It seems the young Balthasar is familiar with the old notion that mercy should be above justice, but he doesn't let traditional notions interfere with his summary judgment in the merchant's favour:

I have spoke thus much
To mitigate the justice of thy plea;
Which if thou follow, this strict court of Venice
Must needs give sentence 'gainst the merchant there.

There is a special irony in the ways the courtroom scene plays with the terms *old, new,* and *young* that is far more interesting and playful than the familar critical allegoresis of "Old Testament law" and "New Testament grace" allows for. To Shakespeare's Venetians "old" law is law the way it was practised before the recent innovations that established merchant law as distinctively Venetian and republican. Old lawyers from Padua might remember how to practise "old" law. "New" law means support for international commerce, summary judgments for merchants, a presumption in favour of enforcing contracts regardless of the parties' "nations." Venice's old law is not blind to nationalities, social rank, and citizenship; it would force Shylock to "show mercy" or die. The new law that enables Venice's commercial success, however, favours strict literalist interpretation of contracts and does not allow arguments about equity and mercy to affect its judgments. To the English Protestant imagination, then, Venice's new merchant law looks suspiciously like the "old law" they associated with Jews. The Duke and Antonio are new law advocates, even though this time new law puts Antonio at Shylock's (nonexistent) mercy.

Shylock also likes this new law, nobody more than he. The new law offers some hope of ridding himself of the persecutorial Antonio. Antonio has been running a one-man crusade against Jewish usury (a.k.a. Shylock) for years, but under the new merchant law, if Shylock can once find a way to haul Antonio before a court, that court promises him a status Antonio and his friends have so far denied him. On the Rialto,

Antonio calls him a dog and uses him like "a stranger cur". He calls Shylock beast and devil with impunity. He does all he can to hinder Shylock's business, by fair means and foul. But in the "strict court of Venice," Shylock knows that all that anti-Jewish blather will not count. Graziano can call him a dog, claim that his soul once belonged to a wolf hanged for murder, but "Till [he] can rail the seal from off my bond," says Shylock, he only hurts his lungs to shout so loud. Shylock believes that the Venetian court, famous for its practice of innovative merchant law, will allow him the status of a man, a *homo economicus*—a juridical emancipation. So, "new law" in this "strict court of Venice" does not stand, as so many critics have thought, just for Christian grace and mercy. In the first instance it stands, like Shylock, for summary justice according to a literal reading of the contract.

Unlike the Duke, Shylock was probably glad to see a young judge in Bellario's place. The legal innovations that favour contracts over equity and strive for judicial blindness to nation and citizenship hold out the promise to Shylock of judicial liberation. Shylock hopes the new Venetian law will allow him to stand as Antonio's equal before the law. But what Shylock cannot see is how the play has already associated Venice with Babel, legal innovation with merciless machiavellian business practices, and how the play is on the verge of making Shylock, the stubborn Jew (and therefore the false Jew), into the mascot for this new Babel. In the remainder of the scene, Portia—Daniel disguised as Balthasar—will unmask Shylock as truly the Nebuchadnezzar of the piece.

Daniel in Babylon; Shylock in Venice; The Jew as Nebuchadnezzar

At first we might think that the play's allusion to Balthasar, Daniel in Babylon, draws attention to Shylock's position as a Jew in Venice. As we have seen, the English frequently thought of Venice as a latter-day Babel. Shylock makes his way, even prospers, in Venice much as Daniel did in Babylon (or Jacob in Laban's house, or Joseph in Egypt). Nebuchadnezzar's court rewarded sages and oneiromancers; Venice rewards merchants and financiers. Like Daniel, Shylock sets limits to his assimilation; he reminds the Venetians he is a Jew: "I will buy with you, sell with you, talk with you, walk with you, and so following, but I will not eat with you, drink with you, nor pray with you".

This is a tempting interpretation, especially when Shylock invokes the story of Jacob and Laban, another instance of God's chosen man patiently prospering under oppression. But the play refuses to endorse this line of interpretation, preferring instead to play Shylock as the typically blinkered, self-serving hermeneut that Elizabethan Protestants believed all stubborn Jews were. This is especially evident when Shylock unwittingly casts himself as a self-righteous Pharisee when he calls Antonio a "fawning publican" And we have seen how the play mocks his reading of the Jacob story as endorsing usury and miserliness. When Shylock reads the Bible all he hears is "thrift is blessing." The play explicitly rejects such a reading of scripture as blindly and stubbornly "Jewish." It endorses Antonio's Protestant reading that God's blessing is "a thing" not in one's own "power to bring to pass/ But swayed and fashioned by the hand of heaven".

The play rewards the prodigal Bassanio with Portia's blessings of wealth; the casket lesson recommends giving and hazarding rather than careful thrift; Antonio first loses everything, and then gets most of it back as if by heavenly intervention. As Lewalski has argued, the play leans far more to the "take no thought for the morrow" end of the ethical spectrum and tends to indict Shylock's "fast bind, fast find" attitude as unchristian, and therefore, immoral.

I have already argued that the play undercuts and corrects Shylock's invocation of Daniel by presenting Portia disguised as Balthasar. Shylock tries to call to mind the clever young judge of Susanna, but the play insists that we pay attention instead to the prophet Daniel who preached Christ to stubborn Jews and mercy to oppressive Babylonians. When we do pay such attention, when we watch the play with the familiar stories of Daniel in Babylon fresh in our minds, some curious and fascinating readings emerge. I will conclude by sketching out just a few.

In the trial scene Dr. Balthasar is a kind of *silenus* figure. On the outside, he looks like a progressive young judge zealous for merchant law and summary judgments favouring contracts; inside he is Portia, heiress of Belmont, daughter of old money and imbued with ancient notions of citizenship, nationalism and privilege. This resembles Daniel in Babylon. Outside, he is Balthasar, sage and trusted councilor at Nebuchadnezzar's court, but inside he remains a Jew who worships the one true God. Every so often, Nebuchadnezzar must be reminded that Daniel is a Jew and that his God is truly "God of gods and Lord of kings". This is the Daniel the play endorses, but with a Christian twist—we must read *Jew* here as "real" Jew, or Christian. The play's Daniel is a Christian; Shylock's Daniel is just a false Jew's stubborn misreading of the Bible.

Shylock appears completely ignorant of the biblical Daniel's various encounters with Babylonian law. In Daniel chapter 6, certain officials, jealous of Daniel's success at court, conspire to catch him up with a new law. They urge King Darius to declare a new law forbidding worship of any god besides Darius knowing that Daniel will transgress. Darius realises too late what he has done; he loved Daniel and "was much distressed" and "set his mind to deliver Daniel" from this strict new law, labouring "till the sun went down to rescue him," but the jealous satraps have the law on their side: "Know, O king, that it is a law of the Medes and the Persians that no interdict or ordinance which the king establishes can be changed" (Daniel 6). Daniel is thrown to the lions. This story resembles Antonio's situation before the Duke. The Duke has been zealous for merchant law in Venice because it grows the economy and makes Venice famous and wealthy, but now Antonio has been caught on the wrong side of this new law, and the Duke, like Darius, wracks his brain for a way to save his merchant friend. But the law is the law; it cannot be changed even by the Duke's own voice. Just as Daniel must be saved from the lions by a miracle, so Antonio must be saved from the beastly Shylock's claws by a miracle—Portia.

This story, like the one in Daniel 3, is a cautionary tale about how strict application of novel laws can produce injustice. *The Merchant of Venice* is another such cautionary tale. When Shylock invokes the law, he unwittingly invokes the other side's champion, and ironically casts himself in the role of Daniel's Babylonian persecutors who would try to use the new laws to catch Daniel "on the hip." Dr. Balthasar looks at first like a young devotee of merchant law, but turns out to be an old-style prosecutor of the alien statutes. Shylock is called "the Jew" in this case, but winds up looking like the envious Babylonian satraps. And the real Daniel turns the law back on the satraps who go to the lions (6:24) without God's protection, much as Portia turns the old alien statutes on Shylock.

According to this reading, Shylock is cast as a kind of false Jew, the Jew who stubbornly misreads both Torah (the Genesis story of Jacob) and the prophets, who is blind to the salvation story they everywhere imply. According to Paul, Jews who stubbornly crave the law and ceremonies, especially circumcision and kashrut, are like children who refuse to see the "true" meanings of both. Calvin's comments on this are typical:

It was not without cause that God distinguished between us and his ancient people, by training them like children by means of signs and figures, and training us more simply, without so much external show.... This was the state of the Jews under the law. But we are like adults who, being freed from tutory and curatory, have no need of puerile rudiments.

Christians, then, are Jews grown up, the full grown children of father Abraham. Jews who stubbornly remain Jews are, in a sense, not really Jews at all any more, no longer the sons of Abraham, but sons of the "bondwoman" who was "cast out". Grownup Jews are Christians like Daniel; Jews like

Shylock are willfully stunted, pertinaciously puerile, literal-minded, and selfish.

The play embraces this familiar anti-Jewish trope, especially by way of Portia in disguise. Beneath the Babylonian disguise and name is the true Jew, a Daniel who preaches a Christian mercy that the law and its zealots cannot comprehend. Shylock is exposed as stubbornly deaf—he cannot hear the gospel even when it is preached by a prophet. His Daniel is a rulemonger, but the biblical Daniel is a champion of mercy over the law. He mistakes the Babylonian for the Jew, the disguise for the real thing. The "real" Daniel turns out to be the Christians' champion.

Another episode from the book of Daniel reinforces this trope. In Daniel 4, King Nebuchadnezzar calls upon young Balthasar to interpret a dream that baffles his other sages. The interpretation Daniel offers is a prophecy: as punishment for his overweening pride and his failure to show mercy to the oppressed (particularly the Jews in exile) Nebuchadnezzar "shall be driven from among men" and shall dwell with "the beasts of the field," eating grass and becoming "wet with the dew of heaven." He will continue this bestial existence, says Daniel to the King, until "[you] break off your sins by practicing righteousness, and your iniquities by showing mercy to the oppressed" According to the story, all this comes to pass; a "voice from heaven" condemns the great king to be "driven out from among men" and live like a beast until his "reason" returns, until he acknowledges the God of Israel and shows mercy on the oppressed. This Daniel story directly challenges Shylock's caricature of Judaism as a legalistic religion—"I stand here for law." In this story, Daniel is the champion of mercy over law, and the villain is the self-righteous Nebuchadnezzar who has forgotten God, and has forgotten to be merciful to the oppressed. He is condemned to live like a beast until his reason returns.

If we apply this Daniel story to the play, once again we find Shylock in the role of the pagan anti-Jewish oppressor steeped in his own self-righteous pride. Portia is cast as the prophetic Daniel disguised as Balthasar. The Duke and everyone else think the self-righteous Shylock is truly a beast — a dog, and an "inhuman wretch," a "currish Jew" — but the merchant law under which he brings his strange suit allows him the status of a human plaintiff. No one but Portia (like Daniel) knows how to interpret the situation, how to strip Shylock (like Nebuchadnezzar) of his ersatz humanness and return him to his underlying bestial status. She manages this by encouraging him at every turn to overplay his role as a stereotypically stubborn Jew — literal-minded, self-righteous, legalistic, envious, and even bloodthirsty. Of course, he plays it perfectly, thus exposing himself as the opposite of the "true" Jew represented by the Christian Daniel. He is instead the false Jew, a beast. Once he is exposed as such a beast, he can simply be prosecuted as such.

The play, then, is anti-Jewish in ways more sophisticated than we have recognized. Shakespeare may very well eschew, even scorn, more pedestrian forms of anti-Jewish humour, but he lends his astonishing imaginative powers to support some very sophisticated and elaborate versions of Protestant anti-Jewish polemic. It exploits and even endorses anti-Jewish discourses woven ever so tightly into the fabric of Protestant Christianity and reformation readings of the Bible.

The play also mocks the Venetians and betrays what appear to be typically English ambivalences about the growth of internationalism in commerce and law, anxieties that live on, perhaps, in the europhobias we read about today. Antonio, Bassanio, and the Duke, however, learn their lessons; they will not so blindly endorse the innovations of merchant law again. The play makes Shylock the mascot of stubborn misbelief, hermeneutic myopia, and a mercilessly machiavellian approach to business. He is cast as more Venetian than the Venetians, more Babylonian than even Nebuchadnezzar (who repented), and therefore not truly a Jew at all, for the true Jews, the *verus Israel*, says the play, are the Christians.

Q. Explain the Conflicts of Law and Equity in The Merchant of Venice.

William Carlos Williams once said that "Shakespeare is the greatest university of them all". This is especially true with respect to the law: a dedicated scholar can discover a wealth of information on legal issues in Shakespeare's works. Measure for Measure and The Merchant of Venice are, of course, explicitly "legal" in content, but more than twenty of the plays have some form of trial scene. Virtually all of the plays are tangentially concerned with some aspect of the law; at the very least, Shakespeare uses complex legal jargon to elicit a laugh. When one of the title characters in The Merry Wives of Windsor tosses out a line like:

If the devil have [Falstaff] not in fee simple [absolute possession], with fine and recovery [as of an entailment], he will never, I think, in the way of waste [despoiling], attempt us again (IV.ii.197-99, emph. added) the law students who made up a large portion of his contemporary audience must have roared with laughter, even if few others got the joke.

It is therefore not surprising that the interdisciplinary study of law and Shakespeare has grown into a fully recognized field, with major law schools offering advanced degrees. Such interdisciplinary examination has opened for us a new vista of understanding. The Merchant of Venice "has spawned more commentary by lawyers than any other Shakespeare play" (Kornstein 66). One can easily find a discussion of every legal concept raised in the course of the play (White 111-46), a detailed legal dissection of the trial scene in Act IV (Keeton 132-50), and even an imaginary appellate strategy on behalf of Shylock (Kornstein 83-85).

The link between Shakespeare and the law is not new; even a casual perusal of the literature will show that scholars have long realised that the legal discourse can lead to a better understanding of Shakespeare's works. I submit, however, that the converse is also true: that the study of Shakespeare can lead to a deeper understanding of the fundamental nature of law. A play like The Merchant of Venice has a great deal to offer in the course of such a reading. The action of the play is concerned with contract law, but issues of standing, moiety, precedent, and conveyance are also raised. At the most fundamental level, though, the trial scene in Act IV illustrates the conflict between equity and the strict construction of the law.

Equity, in the legal sense, is "justice according to principles of fairness and not strictly according to formulated law". This definition, while easily understandable, presents us with a problematic – even dangerous - structure of opposition. Law and fairness are set at extreme ends of some continuum of justice, and are exclusive. The definition implies that one can have justice according to "fairness," or justice according to "formulated law." Yet if law is not inherently fair, if there is need for a concept of equity, how can the law be said to be fulfilling its purpose? And if "fairness" is not to be found within the confines of "formulated law," from whence does it come? This is not a new argument, of course; the conflict between law and equity was recognized even in medieval England.

From earliest childhood, we are indoctrinated with a sense of justice, of fairness, of right and wrong. Every schoolyard echoes with cries of "No fair cheating!" We seem to know instinctively that some things are fair, some things are not, and our moral outrage is awakened when injustice is perpetrated.

It is this indignation, this sense that principles of fairness have been violated, that arouse many to question the theories and practices upon which our system of law and justice have been built. Some would claim, for example, that rape is a crime no less egregious than that of murder, and thus call for the execution of convicted rapists. Yet no state allows such execution solely for conviction of rape. It has become a fundamental tenet of American law that the state may not take the life of a felon unless the crime involved the taking of a life; rape alone, while devastating the life of the victim, does not result in death without some intervening act. The search for equity – for fairness – within codified law has led to some bizarre and arcane practices in Western courts; when drunk drivers spend more time in prison than some murderers, this fact becomes painfully apparent.

Equity, in fact, has become so intertwined with law in the justice system that it is difficult to see the lines of demarcation. We must remember, however, that such was not always the case. When Shakespeare wrote The Merchant of Venice, there were actually separate courts in England for the administration of law and equity. One appealed to the Court of Common Law to seek redress under codified law, or to the Court of Equity to avail oneself of the judgment of men. The two spheres were kept strictly separate, and it was not until the reign of James I that courts of law began to consider principles of equity in the resolution of disputes.

In such a system, the terms of forfeiture of a bond, like the one sealed between Shylock and Antonio, fell under the purview of the Courts of Common Law. These courts, in the sixteenth century, relied upon strict construction; that is to say, a literal reading of applicable law and the instruments made to employ such law. A contract, like the one made between Shylock and Antonio, was "fully enforceable at law". This means that any penalty stipulated in the contract would be automatically awarded if the contract were not strictly upheld. A delay in repayment of even a single hour would result in any forfeiture that the debtor had agreed to pay. It is this notion of "fully enforceable" contract that leads Portia to proclaim initially that "lawfully by this [contract] the Jew may claim/A pound of flesh".

The dichotomy between law and equity, between strict construction and principles of fairness, is evident in Shylock's initial proclamations. The law is on his side, and he knows it. When he states, "I stand here for law" (IV.i.142), and "I crave the law" (IV.i.204), these terms are meant in binary opposition to equity. Shylock seeks a justice based upon vengeance, not "fairness." He comes armed with a contract strictly enforceable and clings tenaciously to the most literal interpretation possible. It is evident that Shylock intends to wield the law as a weapon against Antonio; when Portia pleads with him to have a doctor stand by to save Antonio's life, Shylock obstinately refuses on the grounds that "Tis not in the bond".

In contrast to Shylock's reliance upon strict construction, Portia urges the consideration of principles of equity. She delivers a passionate speech on the need for considerations of humanity in the administration of the law:

Though justice be thy plea, consider this,
That in the course of justice none of us
Should see salvation. We do pray for mercy,
And that same prayer doth teach us all to render
The deeds of mercy.

Mercy, or the imposition of basic principles of fairness upon the strict letter of the law, lies at the heart of equity; a modern philosopher might refer to such considerations as "situational ethics." Portia's famous speech on the qualities of mercy attributes this capacity in mankind to a higher, divinely inspired form of law:

The quality of mercy is not strained.
It droppeth as the gentle rain from heaven
Upon the place beneath. It is twice blest;
It blesseth him that gives and him that takes.
... It is an attribute to God himself;
And earthly power doth then show likest God's
When mercy seasons justice (IV.i.182-95).

Portia thus articulates the fundamental conflict between law and equity; while justice can be found in each separately, there is a better form of justice to be obtained when mercy and fairness become considerations in the administration of the law.

Shylock soon learns, of course, that strict construction is a double-edged sword. When her appeal to equity fails in the force of Shylock's lust for vengeance, Portia must retreat to the battlefield of law, and here the moneylender is undone. Shylock's defeat on a legal technicality makes for good drama, but the legalities are based on a false premise, and even here the effects of equity in consideration of law can be seen. Shylock is awarded his pound of flesh, but is enjoined from taking any accompanying blood; since he cannot take the one without spilling the other, he is forced to abjure his forfeiture. It is a tenet of the common law, however, that any granted right must also entail any incidental powers necessary to its exercise. One jurist has likened Portia's winning argument to a judge granting an easement but denying the right to leave footprints on the ground, since the subsidiary right is not expressly granted in the contract (White 142n1). It is inconceivable that any codification of law could possibly cover all contingencies; that the law is, or even can be, flexible at all is a function of the principle of equity.

Shylock's punishment, and the evolving response of audiences over the course of four centuries, may also point to a crucial aspect of equity: that fundamental ideals of fairness can change over time to meet societal needs. Shylock comes to court to seek redress for default of a loan; he leaves the trial bereft of all of his property, stripped of his lifelong faith, and very nearly sentenced to death. Contemporary audiences likely would have applauded such a resolution; even a century ago, the world that saw the trial of Alfred Dreyfus would have found Shylock's treatment at the hands of the law completely fitting. In the post-Holocaust world, however, we recoil with revulsion from any hint of anti-Semitism whatsoever. The punishment of Shylock offends a cultural sensibility that cannot be denied, and political correctness forces us to decry its insinuations even as we applaud its syntax.

The Merchant of Venice is, at its heart, a skillful examination of the tension between law and equity. In the 1980 BBC production, Shylock enters the courtroom carrying a balance, a bit of stage direction that does not appear in the play script (IV.i.15sd). Of course, the obvious inference is that he intends to use the scales to weigh out his forfeiture, a pound of Antonio's flesh. Yet the scales have long stood as a symbol of justice; Homer's Iliad may be the first use of this symbol (XXII.249, for example), or it may be even older. If we view the two scales as representing law on one side, and fairness on the other, the point at which they balance is equity. When strict adherence to the law outweighs basic principles of fairness, there can be no justice. Bassanio may have the most poignant statement on the nature of equity when he urges the court to temper justice with fairness; should the law contain no room for mercy, he claims:

It must appear
That malice bears down truth. And I beseech you,
Wrest once the law to your authority.
To do a great right, do a little wrong (IV.i.211-14).

Q. Describe The Power of Mercy in Merchant of Venice

The idea of mercy is important in *The Merchant of Venice* because it provides a focus for the contrast between Venetian Christian society and the alien invader, represented by Shylock. Mercy occupies a "central" position in the trial scene, where the power struggle between aristocratic Venetian society and the threatening force Shylock comes to a climax. My thesis is that the contrast between (and equation of) mercy and revenge in the trial scene reveals the true nature of Venetian society as insecure, hypocritical and vengeful.

Mercy is clearly of greatest importance to the Christians in this text. It is only mentioned in the trial scene by two characters—the Duke (3 times) and Portia, in her guise as the lawyer Balthazar, (10 times). Mercy is significantly never mentioned by Shylock, implying either that he does not believe in it, or that he sees a hidden motive behind the Christians' insistence that he should be merciful to Antonio. By looking at what mercy means to the Christians and how they use it in the trial scene, I will try to show how it acts as a mirror for their true value system.

Mercy can be defined as "kind and considerate treatment that you show to someone, especially when you forgive them or do not punish them." It is a Christian value associated with the New Testament, thus contrasting with Shylock's Old Testament religion and its image of a more stern and vengeful God. In the first half of the trial mercy and revenge are contrasted. The Duke appeals to Shylock to be merciful as if he shared their Christian values—

Shylock the world thinks, and I think so too,
That thou but leadest this fashion of thy malice
To the last hour of act, and then 'tis thought
Thou'll show thy mercy...

The implication is that demanding Antonio's death for forfeiting a bond is "strange apparent cruelty", unnatural and that "the world" (Venetian aristocratic society) agrees with him. Shylock demands his bond with no other justification than "a lodg'd hate, and a certain loathing / I bear Antonio". He tries to justify taking a pound of Antonio's flesh by appealing to the Venetian's sense of ownership, equating it to their slaves—"The pound of flesh which I demand of him / Is dearly bought, 'tis mine and I will have it" (IV.i.99-100). Shylock's use of strange language and images (lines 44-58) makes him appear uncivilized in contrast with the Christians' talk of gentleness and mercy.

Portia's speech on mercy brings in the aspect of power, painting a grandiose picture to tempt Shylock to believe he can share this power by being merciful (and thus accepting Christian values)—

It blesseth him that gives, and him that takes,
'Tis mightiest in the mightiest, it becomes
The throned monarch better than his crown.

Shylock's reply - "My deeds upon my head! I crave the law" - makes him appear totally without mercy, at least superficially. However, we know that Shylock has little reason to trust Christian Venetian society because he has been abused and reviled by Antonio and others. It seems more likely that by being merciful, he would be accepting their value system and be taking the first step towards assimilation within Christian society (after all, his daughter has already converted voluntarily). Antonio would have won in court and in society, and could feel justified in treating Shylock with even less respect than before. In other words, Shylock would lose power, and this, in essence, is how we can view the conflict between Shylock and Antonio,as a power struggle. Once Shylock is defeated by Portia's clever interpretation of the law, we see that he is now at the mercy of the court. It is here that mercy and revenge become equated. Portia tells Shylock that for threatening the life of Antonio, his goods are forfeit "And the offender's life lies in the mercy / Of the Duke only...." (IV.i.351-

352). She finishes by saying "Down therefore, and beg mercy of the duke." (IV.i.359) Both the Duke and Antonio appear to be merciful when they spare his life and some of his wealth, but in light of Shylock's tenous position in Venetian society, it would appear that they are trying to completely crush him, especially when he is required to become a Christian. Shylock feels he might as well be dead—

> *Nay, take my life and all, pardon not that,-*
> *You take my house, when you do take the prop*
> *That doth sustain my house: you take my life*
> *When you do take the means whereby I live.*

To the Christians, then, mercy has different meanings and uses in this trial scene. It is used to try to tempt Shylock to recognize Christian values as superior to his own, to tempt him with the delusion of power if he accepts them, and when he refuses, to crush him and take away all his economic, religious and racial power. This abuse of mercy also reveals Venetian society to be greedy for power, hypocritical in its use of Christian values for secular aims, and vengeful. Mercy, and its uses and misuses, is revealed as having a power far greater than is at first apparent.

Q Write an Essay on Shakespeare's View on Judaism and Christianity Represented in The Merchant of Venice

"The merchant of Venice" is a play written by William Shakespeare before the duration 1958 and most probably in 1596. The play is set in the Capital city of Venice in Italy. Two characters dominate the main issues of this play Shylock and Antonio, at first we are introduced to the protagonist Shylock. Shylock is a Jew his character is stereotypically as evil and manipulative. Shakespeare has done this as throughout history and even within the Elizabethan period Jews were loathed, feared and branded Christ killers. Which form the barriers between the Jews and Christians in the play. The second character is Antonio who is a Christian and is not seen as a victim of anti-semitism like Shylock but when contrasted he is presented to be superior. The themes and issues explored in this play by the two characters interrelate injustice, power and racism. In this essay I hope to show how Shakespeare's view on Judaism and Christianity is represented through the characters in the different scenes that I will be exploring.

In Act 1 Scene 3 introduces Shylock in a street where Bassanio seeks him to borrow money in Antonio's name to pursue his love. The loan is for three thousand ducats, three times the amount of the bond. In this scene we as audience learn where the barriers are very obvious and Shylocks hatred for Antonio and the Christians.

How like a fawning publican he looks,
I hate him for he is a Christian:
He hates our sacred nation, and he rails
(Act 1, scene 3)

This immediately depicts Shylock is displaying elements of belligerence in rejection to ever forgive the Christians. We also see that how Shylocks believes his religion is more important than Christians, this is expressed clearly through his blunt direct statement 'I hate him for he is a Christian'. Shylock also presents his religion as superior to that of the Christian religion by saying his religion is 'sacred', he induces strong powerful words to emphasise his beliefs. From the tone of Shylock's speech there is a strong implication that he believes his religion is scorned and underrated.

There is genuine evidence when Shylock makes a great speech that he is a victim of anti-semitism:

You call me misbeliever, cut-throat dog,
And spet upon my Jewish gabardine,
You'd call me dog: and for these courtesies
(Act 1 scene 3)

Shylock makes this to speech to let the audience know he hates Antonio for having hindered him in business and for having him humiliated in public by spitting on him and calling him names. Shylock remembers this vividly, and this is expressed clearly through the shockingly dramatic account he gives. At this point we are almost inclined to believe

Shakespeare is sympathising on the maltreatment of Jews as he makes us sympathise with the anger and humiliation Shylock feels.

Shylock evidently despises Antonio and has already thought of revenge before Antonio speaks.

If I ever catch him once upon the hip
I will feed fat the ancient grudge I bear him.
(Act 1, scene 3)

He hopes to carry out exact revenge on Antonio for his own humiliation and the prosecution that the Jews have long suffered at the hand of the Christians. At this stage of this scene we learn of the agreement of the bond.

If you repay me not such a day,
Express'd in the condition, let the forfeit
Be nominated for an pound
Of your fair flesh, to be cut off and taken
(Act 1, scene 3)

Shakespeare uses alliteration 'fair flesh' to emphasise the importance of Shylock's ideas of the terms of the bond, the seriousness is highlighted clearly through the sharpness and pace of his speech as well. Shylocks thorough and carefully laid out speech initiates the audience to have an almost negative view towards Shylock because of his inappropriate enthusiasm in this malicious plan. Shakespeare at this point has conformed Shylock into the stereotypically negative idea of Jews, perhaps it is his own prejudiced feelings of Jews that he has done so. Although Antonio does not like borrowing money from Shylock he will for the loyalty of his close friend Bassanio.

Antonio's character shows that he is a risk taker. This is shown when he accepts Shylocks high interest rate.

Why fear not man, I will not forfeit it,
This bond expires, I do expect return
Of thrice three times the value of this bond.
(Act 1, scene 3)

Antonio does this to receive the term of the bond in this manner because he is confident that he will be able to repay the bond.

Meanwhile the audience perceiver the character Antonio as a man very loyal to his friend and again Shakespeare's prejudiced feelings are highlighted. Always throughout history Jews have come out worst between battles with Christians and in this scene this is true, we are given the overall picture of Antonio as the Christian man being honest and loyal whilst Shylock the Jew is presented as a hatred filled evil man as habitually believed in that period. Antonio is also presented by Shakespeare as a very courageous man:

Come on, in this there can be no dismay
My ships come a month before the day.
(Act 1, scene 3)

Shakespeare has effectively drawn our attention closely when we hear of Shylocks hatred and his terms of the bond and Antonio's bravery, in reality this is where our anxiety builds within the play because the audience is left very unsure because despite Antonio's bravery many will wonder whether it will be sufficient enough help for him in the hands of this clearly spiteful Jew Shylock.

The next scene that I am going to explore is Act 3 Scene 1; in this Shakespeare presents two different characters in the street of Venice, Salarino and Salanio both Christians and friends of Antonio, at this point Shakespeare has created a purpose to a focal point in the play and the actual plot itself. Here we learn of the conversation between Salarino and Salanio as they discuss Antonio's loss. At this point the audience is left reeling because Shylock's evil plan has prevailed, as Antonio will now be unable to pay the bond. We are at this point able to believe Shakespeare has followed the conventional theory of how the Jewish man always succeeds and the good Christian man is left the victim. Solanio even so calls Antonio 'the honest Antonio', and repeatedly calls him 'good' so that Antonio status is enhanced even more positively, and the audience is able to side with him even more so. In contrast Shylocks character is darkened and made more malignant when Solanio suddenly becomes fearful as he spots Shylock approaching.

Solanio mutters a prayer and likens Shylock to the 'devil'. Again the idea that Christians have always feared the Jews and their supposed evils is shown here, and this could be an indication of Shakespeare's own beliefs. I am a Jew: hath not a Jew eyes? hath not a Jew hands, organs, dimensions, senses, affections, passion, fed with the same food, hurt with the same weapons, subject to the same diseases, healed by the same means, warmed and cooled by the same winter and summer (Act 3, scene 1)

However this can be said only to a certain extent as Shakespeare at the same time contradicts the foreboding view the audience has on Shylock when Shylock gives a powerful speech about the suffering he has faced at the hands of Christian because he is a Jew. We express sympathy with Shylock because he has suffered much discrimination.

Shylocks passionate speech is in a way designed to remind the audience that Shylock is no different form any other man but it is religion that makes him an outcast in society.

Shakespeare adds more sympathy when he we learn the only companionship ever to Shylock was his daughter Jessica. We learn of how his daughter betrays him for a Christian. The impressions of theses two Christian characters are tormentors of Shylock in this scene and mock at every opportunity.

At this point it could be said Shakespeare is intellectually aware of the sufferings Jews go through and that Jews are not inferior that they suffer the pains of life that many do but at the end of Shylock's speech the audience feels they have been left with an imperiously greedy man who is so bitter he can not let go of his grudge against those who have mistreated him. At the end of this scene we notice the presence of another character Tubal who is a fellow Jew.

To inform Shylock

The final scene, which I am going to explore, is Act 4 Scene 1. This scene is set in a Vatican court. During the trial scene Shylock is there to claim his bond. At this point Shakespeare has effectively portrayed Shylocks obsessive hatred has become apparent towards

Antonio as Shylock is determined to take his revenge. This is all due as he was treated badly by the Christians by cutting "a pound of flesh"

In conclusion Shakespeare's views can be said to be ambiguous, because at many points in the play he seems to follow the conventional ideas of Jews being evil, and the stereotypical ideas that Christians had at that period, give exampleâ€¦. when Shylock is said toâ€¦showing Shakespeare has used the conventional idea that Jews areâ€¦evilâ€¦ however there are many times when these views are contradicted, for Shakespeare certainly does evoke much pity from the audience towards Shylocks sufferings, and at some points he seems to ridicule and shame the Christians mistreatment of Jews but the constant stream of attack that we perceive against the Jews diffuse this idea, it could be better said that Shakespeare to some extent defends the Jews or that he is open-minded but much evidence in the play suggests that he is biased, and his views side with the Christians, who at the end have succeeded against Shylocks evil bond.

And these views and ideas are perceived mainly through the characters Antonio and Shylock, Antonio the 'hero' and Shylock the 'evil' one, and the play ends with good prevailing evil, in all Christianity prevailing Judaism, with Christianity seen as the stronger and superior of the two and this being Shakespeare's view. Overall at the same time we are left wondering if Shakespeare is only playing along with reconvention attitudes towards Jews. So as not to offend his audience and there are certain attempts he makes that Jews are not evil, that they suffer much too, referring back to Swan

Q. Discuss the character of Shylock in William Shakespeare's The Merchant of Venice.

Or

Q. The question frequently asked after reading The Merchant of Venice is: is Shylock a victim or a villain? Describe

The best way to investigate this question is to explore the text of the play to find out what Shakespeare wanted us to believe.

Life for the Jews in the Elizabethan period was often very hard. In England Jews were viewed with distaste, suspected of a number of heinous crimes such as child murder. They were also distrusted by Christians for the rejection of Christ as the Messiah and because they did not lend money gratis. Many Christians were financially beholden to the Jews.

Roderigo Lopez was a Jew of Portuguese decent, who fled to England in 1559 where he worked as a physician. His practice grew, and in time he was appointed physician to the Queen of England. But the Earl of Essex found what he believed to be evidence that Lopez had accepted a bribe from the King of Spain to poison Queen Elizabeth. It is true that Lopez had underhand dealings with Spanish spies, but it is to this day unproven if Lopez ever intended any harm towards the Queen. However, he was found guilty and in 1996 he was hung, drawn and quartered for a crime he probably was never going to commit. The Merchant of Venice was written two years later in 1596, and the treatment of Shylock is similar to that of Lopez. Shylock is shunned by the Christians and treated as an outcast. Possibly, Shakespeare wrote this play as the Lopez case was fresh in people's minds, and he knew that a play about a detested Jew would be of great interest.

In Italy, where The Merchant of Venice is set, the Jews were being greatly prejudiced against; they were being expelled from the country, they were made to wear demoralising items such as 'badges of shame' and Jewish synagogues were turned into Christian churches. They were made to wear cloaks, caps or badges which indicated that they were beneath the Christians, and they were condemned to live in just one part of the city, the Ghettos, which were often of bad condition. The only place they were allowed to commune with Christians was on the Rialto where they could do business. The Rialto is where we first meet Shylock.

Many people say that Shakespeare drew ambiguous characters, and that Shylock is neither a victim nor a villain.

In fact Shakespeare's characters are very fairly created, nobody is entirely evil, none entirely good, which makes for greater realism. Shakespeare seems to deliberately try to make it hard for the audience to decide if Shylock is a victim or a villain, as he does with all the characters. For example, Antonio appears to be the perfect Christian, but is un-Christian towards Shylock. Bassanio is more feckless, but he learns through his mistakes. When Shakespeare first brings Shylock onto the stage he shows us someone who, at first sight, appears to be a stereotypical Jewish character: vengeful and grasping. Shylock's assertion that Antonio is a 'good' man refers not to Antonio's moral standing, but to his financial standing, and Shylock later says of Antonio:

> *"How like a fawning publican he looks.*
> *I hate him for he is a Christian:*
> *But more, for that in low simplicity*
> *He lends out money gratis, and brings down*
> *The rate of usance here with us in Venice."*

This makes Shylock seem to be an unpleasant character who dislikes Antonio just because he is a Christian and has different moral views, but Shakespeare later shows us that Antonio's treatment of Shylock is just as bad, for he hates Shylock for exactly the same reason; that he is of a different religion: '...he hath disgrac'd me, and hinder'd me half a million," Shylock says of Antonio, "laugh'd at my losses,

mock'd at my gains, scorned my Nation, thwarted my bargains, cooled my friends, heated mine enemies, and what's his reason? I am a Jew."

When Shylock justifies usury by quoting from the Bible, Antonio also says Shylock is like a devil citing scripture for his own purpose, "An evil soul producing holy witness..." and "a villain with a smiling cheek. A goodly apple rotten at the heart'. Shylock reminds Antonio of the names he has called him in the past: a 'misbeliever' a 'cut-throat dog' and 'all for use of that which is mine own'. In other words Antonio hates Shylock for loaning him and others money. Shakespeare makes the injustice which Shylock feels clear later in the speech:

"What should I say to you? Should I not say,
Hath a dog money? Is it possible
A cur can lend three thousand ducats? or
Shall I bend low, and in a bondman's key
With bated breath, and whisp'ring humbleness
Say this: Fair sir, you spet on me on Wednesday last;
You spurn'd me such a day; another time
You call'd me dog: and for these courtesies
I'll lend you thus much moneys."

This speech shows that Shylock feels, rightly so, that Antonio's treatment of him is unjust; Antonio treats him very badly, but then expects him to lend him money.

Another factor which induces sympathy towards Shylock is the scene in which Shylock talks about the ring his partner Leah gave him, 'it was my turkis, I had it of Leah when I was a bachelor: I would not have given it for a wilderness of monkeys.' However, Bassanio the Christian gives away the ring Portia gave him without too much regret, and this shows that Shylock is definitely not lacking in emotion or love, and in comparison shows Bassanio in a poor light.

In the courtroom Bassanio also says to Antonio:

"...life itself, my wife, and all the world,
Are not with me esteem'd above thy life."

Shylock finds the Christian view on marriage shocking, as he feels that husbands should give all to their wives, and love them more than anybody else:

"These be the Christian husbands: I have a daughter,
Would any of the stock of Barrabas
Had been her husband, rather than a Christian."

This tells us that perhaps Shylock has higher morals than Bassanio, and indeed though the lead casket stated that Bassanio should 'give and hazard all he hath', Bassanio is putting his friend in front of his wife which is challenging the vows he has recently made.

One of the most important scenes in The Merchant of Venice is the court scene, as this reveals a lot about Shylock and the other key characters. The overwhelming feeling is that Shylock wants justice. He lives in a community of Christians, who shun him at every opportunity and treat him like a dog. Maybe Shylock does act villainously and inhumanely by demanding a pound of flesh, but that could be because he's been victimised for so many years. Shylock wants justice for justice sake, even though he knows all he will ever gain is his moral victory: "...if it will feed nothing else, it will feed my revenge...".

There seems to be great bitterness in this speech, as is understandable; Bassanio might say that Antonio is the best of men, but although Antonio treats Bassanio with kindness and friendship, he treats Shylock quite the opposite. Shylock goes on to say:

> *"The pound of flesh which I demand of him*
> *Is dearly bought, 'tis mine, and I will have it.*
> *If you deny me: fie upon your Law*
> *There is no force in the decrees of Venice;*
> *I stand for judgement, answer. Shall I have it?"*

So Shylock is after justice, a justice which has been denied him and his kind for a long time. When Portia enters the court disguised as Balthasar, one of the first things she says is, "Which is the Merchant here? and which is the Jew?" Shakespeare has put that comment in for a reason; he might be saying that neither is better than the other, and in the laws of equality they are both the same.

During the court scene Portia makes an important speech:

> *"The quality of mercy is not strain'd...*
> *It blesseth him that gives, and him that takes,*
> *'Tis mightiest in the mightiest...*
> *It is an attribute to God himself..."*

At face value, Portia is saying that Shylock should be merciful towards Antonio, and release him from the bond, but Shakespeare is also trying to put across a message that all mankind should be merciful and accept mercy, and that nobody is entirely good or evil but a combination of both.

In conclusion I feel that Shylock is more a victim than a villain, although he does have a lot of unpleasant qualities. However, he seems to be emotional and has a strong sense of morality, as is shown when he talks about Leah and his views on marriage. The audience feels sympathy for Shylock because it appears everybody is against him, even his own daughter. Nothing seems to go right for him. In Shylock,

Shakespeare has created a character who is a villain in appearance but a victim at heart.

Q. Discuss the theme of love in Shakespeare's The Merchant of Venice.

Or

Q. Discuss the major themes in The Merchant of Venice.

A key theme in the book is love. There are many loving relationships in this play and not all are the type that involves the love that a man has for a woman, or vice versa. Bassanio and Portia, Jessica and Lorenzo and Gratiano and Nerissa are all types of love that involve a man and a woman, which are of course relevant to today's society. When one looks deeply into these relationships, they would see parallels to the ones of today. For instance, the concept that all three marriages will probably not last, is a parallel to the number of divorces that are occurring today.

More and more divorces are happening and the increase from other years is shocking! One of the main reasons why this is happening is that more people are getting married too fast and leaving no time to realise that there are not meant for each other. This is the same in two - and possibly three - of the relationships. Gratiano and Nerrissa got married after knowing each other for only several hours and Bassiano and Portia got marri ed before they go to know each other (, but you can't fault Portia for this, for strict policies were ordered onto her). Jessica and Lorenzo's marriage might split for other reasons. The second relationship that is explored in The Merchant of Venice is the type of man to man.

Homosexuality is a type of love that happens in any period in time and is even more relevant today, as homosexuality has blossomed even more in the 1990's, creating a large issue. Antonio's "love" may not be the type that we are thinking about, but if this happened today we might see it as homosexuality. Many say that Shakespeare is a homosexual from evidence from his many plays. The third type is between a man and his money. Shakespeare's portrayal of Shylock is a cold-hearted man, who only has one true love, his money. He would sacrifice anything for money (even his own daughter). Once again this theme is good, because you will find people like this in every period of time.

The second theme is anti-Semitism. Although we are not sure of Shakespeare being an anti-Semite we might think that he is, through his depiction of Shylock as a cold-hearted Jew, that hates Christians and wants to kill them. This view is well represented by the following excerpt from literary criticism: "[Shakespeare] planned a Merchant of Venice to let the Jew dog have it,... The text itself preserves enough evidence of the author's fixed intent to exhibit his Shylock as an inhuman scoundrel, whose diabolical cunning is bent on gratifying a satanic lust for Christian flesh, the Jew, in fact, who was the ogre of Medieval story and the cur to be exacerbated by all honest men" (Charleton 7).

Anti-Semitism is a very talked about issue not only for the Jewish people, but also for many non-Jews. The Merchant of Venice has been banned from public school's shelves in Toronto, for its endorsement of anti-Semitism. Parents and school boards are afraid the uneducated, young teenagers who have no real fir st hand interaction with Jewish people will believe that Shylock is the model of a common Jew and start hating all Jews.

For a Jewish person learning this book, he or she can create a parallel to anti-Semitic situations in his or her life to the ones faced by Shylock in the play (i.e. the courtroom scene). So this is a good contemporary theme, because it affects both Jews and non-Jews.

Finally, the theme of an inter-marriage, explored by Jessica and Lorenzo, is also a contemporary one. This theme is more understood to a Jewish person (rather to a non-Jew) in today's society. More and more Jews are leaving their faith in order to marry a gentile. The loss of Jewish identity across the world is staggering and is a very frightening issue for rabbis and Jewish people who practice and believe in the faith. The reaction, in a sometimes-left out silent scene, of Shylock after he learns that Jessica has eloped with Lorenzo is fantastic. We see him crying, screaming and then ripping his clothes and falling to the ground. This is a symbol of the way a Jew mourns for a lost loved one. To him, Jessica is dead and unfortunately that is something that is happening in many more Jewish households and even more unfortunate, the reaction of Shylock is not present.

Is The Merchant of Venice a classic? That is an issue that will be discussed for many years to come. But the argument for it being a classic definitely has some truth and evidence for it. The many themes of the play that are still relevant to us today, proves, to an extent, that The Merchant of Venice is a classic play. And those themes will always be contemporary for better or for worse and the play will always be... a classic.

Q. How far is Portia successful in Outwitting Shylock in Act IV Scene I of The Merchant of Venice.

"Portia: Have by some surgeon, Shylock, on your charge
To stop his wound, lest he do bleed to death.
Shylock: Is it nominated in the bond?"
Act 4 Scene 1 lines 255-257

This is the time that Portia traps Shylock into a corner and saves the life of Antonio at the same instance. Portia builds up her defences as Shylock lets his down as he believes that he is going to gain his pound of flesh from Antonio's breast nearest the heart.

As soon as Portia enters the court room she applies herself to try to cunningly outwit Shylock. When she initially enters the court room she performs the relevant actions performed in the court and automatically turns to interact with Shylock. She highlights that the course of action and the hearing is that of an odd one but she also begins to gain Shylocks trust by stating that

"Portia... the Venetian law
Cannot impugn you as you do proceed."
Act 4 Scene 1 lines 176-177

This is the beginning of her already constructed action plan to bring Shylock down and to also remove as much of his cruel ways from him.

As Portia weaves her way into Shylock's trust she, at many points, reassures herself that the proceedings are going as she wants them to be. She asks Shylock on line 181 if he wishes to show mercy to Antonio, but he avidly says that he will show no compassion.

Portia then goes onto speak about why Shylock could show mercy and for what reason but with0out pressuring him into this act. He declines the offer. He states that he "Shylock:... I crave the law

The penalty and the forfeit of my bond."
Act 4 Scene 1 lines 204-205

Portia takes this into account and also makes sure that the clerk that should be writing the proceedings is recording the current events. This gives Portia a fall back and also allows her to later reinforce her point that the Jew showed no consideration for the victim and also that he expresses his want for his bond and forfeiture many times over.

As Portia continually gains the trust of the Jew by stating that his bond is and how lawfully he may claim his forfeit, she is still building Shylock up for the gradual fall of his confidence and eventual cut of his possessions. Shylocks eagerness at this point as he believes that he is going to be able to collect what he wants allows him to express feelings that later Portia will use against him. This eagerness plays to Portia's plan and allows her yet further entrapment Shylock.

At this point Portia's overall strategy is working as she hopes and this co-operation from Shylock to willingly stab himself in the back and then leave with nothing allows the strategy to work out properly and well.

At this instant Antonio makes an arousing speech to his friends, especially Bassanio. Even this speech doesn't hinder Shylock in his greed for his forfeiture and he eagerly waits ready to pounce.

This is the pivotal point in Portia's plan. She states to Shylock what he is allowed, pound of flesh cut from the breast nearest the heart. Then Portia suddenly turns Shylock's trust and reliance on the judge and his own personal greed for the forfeiture.

"Portia: This bond doth give thee here not a jot of blood."
Act 4 Scene 1 line 304

At this Shylock's whole ideal is shattered. If there is no blood then how can he collect his forfeiture? If he isn't able to spill a single drop then how will he transfer the pound of flesh to the scales? His whole dream in pieces before his eyes. Through Portia's planning she had trapped him by making sure that he had stated small, but highly important statements. These where to make him state that if there was not something in the bond then it was void and could not be added. He also gave up the offer of thrice the number of monies on Antonio's head. This all constructed to ensnare Shylock and stop his slanderous action.

Portia then goes on to add more pain to Shylock's already suffering psyche. She tells him that as he has turned down the offers of the monies on Antonio's head that he must now perform the forfeiture. This leaves Shylock scorn and he is unable to escape the closed gate that he led himself into.

This then goes on. Portia follows on from the earlier punishment to inform Shylock that if he doesn't perform the forfeiture then he will leave with nothing. Half of his possessions will go to the treasury of the state and the other half is given to that who he brings order against, Antonio. This leaves Shylock with nothing not even any self dignity, as instead of taking the half of Shylock's possessions that Antonio is entitled to he instead lays down some ground rules for Shylock to follow. He first must become a Christian and second must give a gift of half of his possessions to his son in law,

Lorenzo, and his daughter, Jessica. Now Shylock has not even his own religion to rely upon as he has to follow that of Christianity which is new unto him, but Antonio does show mercy, unlike Shylock did towards him, so much as to allow Shylock to keep the half of his possessions but to give it to the above stated.

Portia's cunning plot not only diffused Shylock and knocked the winds out of his sails, but also saved Antonio's life in the process. Not only is this a pivotal point in the book, but it is also a pivotal point in Shylock's now changed life.

Q. Discuss how Shakespeare successfully portrays the characters in The Merchant of Venice.

Or

Q. This is a play that in spite of the change of manners and prejudices still holds undisputed possession of the stage.Elucidate

Shakespeare's malignant has outlived Mr. Cumberland's benevolent Jew. In proportion as Shylock has ceased to be a popular bugbear, "baited with the rabble's curse," he becomes a half-favourite with the philosophical part of the audience, who are disposed to think that Jewish revenge is at least as good as Christian injuries. Shylock is a good hater; "a man no less sinned against than sinning." If he carries his revenge too far, yet he has strong grounds for "the lodged hate he bears Anthonio," which he explains with equal force of eloquence and reason. He seems the depositary of the vengeance of his race; and though the long habit of brooding over daily insults and injuries has crusted over his temper with inveterate misanthropy, and hardened him against the contempt of mankind, this adds but little to the triumphant pretensions of his enemies. There is a strong, quick, and deep sense of justice mixed up with the gall and bitterness of his resentment. The constant apprehension of being burnt alive, plundered, banished, reviled, and trampled on, might be supposed to sour the most forbearing nature, and to take something from that "milk of human kindness," with which his persecutors contemplated his indignities. The desire of revenge is almost inseparable from the sense of wrong; and we can hardly help sympathising with the proud spirit, hid beneath his "Jewish gaberdine," stung to madness by repeated undeserved provocations, and labouring to throw off the load of obloquy and oppression heaped upon him and all his tribe by one desperate act of "lawful" revenge, till the ferociousness of the means by which he is to execute his purpose, and the pertinacity with which he adheres to it, turn us against him; but even at last, when disappointed of the sanguinary revenge with which he had glutted his hopes, and exposed to beggary and contempt by the letter of the law on which he had insisted with so little remorse, we pity him, and think him hardly dealt with by his judges.

In all his answers and retorts upon his adversaries, he has the best not only of the argument but of the question, reasoning on their own principles and practice. They are so far from allowing of any measure of equal dealing, of common justice or humanity between themselves and the Jew, that even when they come to ask a favour of him, and Shylock reminds them that "on such a day they spit upon him, another spurned him, another called him dog, and for these curtesies request he'll lend them so much monies"—Anthonio, his old enemy, instead of any acknowledgment of the shrewdness and justice of his remonstrance, which would have been preposterous in a respect-able Catholic merchant in those times, threatens him with a repetition of the same treatment—

"I am as like to call thee so again,
To spit on thee again, to spurn thee too."

After this, the appeal to the Jew's mercy, as if there were any common principle of right and wrong 'between them, is the rankest hypocrisy, or the blindest prejudice; and the Jew's answer to one of Anthonio's friends, who asks him what his pound of forfeit flesh is good for, is irresistible—

"To bait fish withal; if it will feed nothing else, it will feed my revenge. He hath disgrac'd me, and hinder'd me of half a million, laughed at my losses, mock'd at my gains, scorn'd my nation, thwarted my bargains, cool'd my friends, heated mine enemies; and what's his reason? I am a Jew. Hath not a Jew eyes; hath not a Jew hands, organs, dimensions, senses, affections, passions; fed with the same food, hurt with the same weapons, subject to the same diseases, healed by the same means, warmed and cooled by the same winter and summer that a Christian is? If you prick us, do we not bleed? If you tickle us, do we not laugh? If you poison us, do we not die? And if you wrong us, shall we not revenge? If we are like you in the rest, we will resemble you in that. If a Jew wrong a Christian, what is his humility? revenge. If a Christian wrong a Jew, what should his sufferance be by Christian example? why revenge. The villainy you teach me I will execute, and it shall go hard but I will better the instruction."

The whole of the trial-scene, both before and after the entrance of Portia, is a master-piece of dramatic skill. The legal acuteness, the passionate declamations, the sound maxims of jurisprudence, the wit and irony interspersed in it, the fluctuations of hope and fear in the different persons, and the completeness and suddenness of the catastrophe, cannot be surpassed. Shylock, who is his own counsel, defends himself well, and is triumphant on all the general topics that are urged against him, and only fails through a legal flaw. Take the following as an instance:—

"Shylock. What judgment shall I dread, doing no wrong?
You have among you many a purchas'd slave,
Which like your asses, and your dogs, and mules,
You use in abject and in slavish part,
Because you bought them:—shall I say to you,
Let them be free, marry them to your heirs?
Why sweat they under burdens? let their beds
Be made as soft as yours, and let their palates
Be season'd with such viands? you will answer,
The slaves are ours:—so do I answer you:
The pound of flesh, which I demand of him,
Is dearly bought, is mine, and I will have it.
If you deny me, fie upon your law!
There is no force in the decrees of Venice;
I stand for judgment; answer; shall I have it?"

The keenness of his revenge awakes all his faculties; and he beats back all opposition to his purpose, whether grave or gay, whether of wit or argument, with an equal degree of earnestness and self-possession. His character is displayed as distinctly in other less prominent parts of the play, and we may collect from a few sentences the history of his life—his descent and origin, his thrift and domestic economy, his affection for his daughter, whom he loves next to his wealth, his courtship and his first present to Lear, his wife! "I would not have parted with it" (the ring which he first gave her) "for a wilderness of monkies!" What a fine Hebraism is implied in this expression!

Portia is not a very great favourite with us; neither are we in love with her maid, Nerissa. Portia has a certain degree of affectation and pedantry about her, which is very unusual in Shakespear's women, but which perhaps was a proper qualification for the office of a "civil doctor," which she undertakes and executes so successfully. The speech about Mercy is very well; but there are a thousand finer ones in Shakespear. We do not admire the scene of the caskets: and object entirely to the Black Prince, Morocchius. We should like Jessica better if she had not deceived and robbed her father, and Lorenzo, if he had not married a Jewess, though he thinks he has a right to wrong a Jew.

The dialogue between this newly-married couple by moonlight, beginning "On such a night," etc., is a collection of classical elegancies. Launcelot, the Jew's man, is an honest fellow. The dilemma in which he describes himself placed between his "conscience and the fiend," the one of which advises him to run away from his master's service and the other to stay in it, is exquisitely humourous.

Gratiano is a very admirable subordinate character. He is the jester of the piece: yet one speech of his, in his own defence, contains a whole volume of wisdom.

"Anthonio. I hold the world but as the world, Gratiano,
A stage, where every one must play his part;
And mine a sad one.
Gratiano. Let me play the fool;

With mirth and laughter let old wrinkles come;
And let my liver rather heat with wine,
Than my heart cool with mortifying groans.
Why should a man, whose blood is warm within,
Sit like his grandsire cut in alabaster?
Sleep when he wakes? and creep into the jaundice
By being peevish? I tell thee what, Anthonio—
I love thee, and it is my love that speaks;—
There are a sort of men, whose visages
Do cream and mantle like a standing pond:
And do a wilful stillness entertain,
With purpose to be drest in an opinion
Of wisdom, gravity, profound conceit;
As who should say, I am Sir Oracle,
And when I ope my lips, let no dog bark!
O, my Anthonio, I do know of these,
That therefore only are reputed wise,
For saying nothing; who, I am very sure,
If they should speak, would almost damn those ears
Which hearing them, would call their brothers, fools.
I'll tell thee more of this another time:
But fish not with this melancholy bait,
For this fool's gudgeon, this opinion."

Gratiano's speech on the philosophy of love, and the effect of habit in taking off the force of passion, is as full of spirit and good sense. The graceful winding up of this play in the fifth act, after the tragic business is despatched, is one of the happiest instances of Shakespear's knowledge of the principles of the drama.

We do not mean the pretended quarrel between Portia and Nerissa and their husbands about the rings, which is amusing enough, but the conversation just before and after the return of Portia to her own house, beginning "How sweet the moonlight sleeps upon this bank," and ending "Peace! how the moon sleeps with Endymion, and would not be awaked." There is a number of beautiful thoughts crowded into that short space, and linked together by the most natural transitions.

When we first went to see Mr. Kean in Shylock, we expected to see, what we had been used to see, a decrepit old man, bent with age and ugly with mental deformity, grinning with deadly malice, with the venom of his heart congealed in the expression of his countenance, sullen, morose, gloomy, inflexible, brooding over one idea, that of his hatred, and fixed on one unalterable purpose, that of his revenge. We were disappointed, because we had taken our idea from other actors, not from the play. There is no proof there that Shylock is old, but a single line, "Anthonio and old Shylock, both stand forth,"—which does not imply that he is infirm with age — and the circumstance that he has a daughter marriageable, which does not imply that he is old at all. It would be too much to say that his body should be made crooked and deformed to answer to his mind, which is bowed down and warped with prejudices and passion.

That he has but one idea, is not true; he has more ideas than any other person in the piece; and if he is intense and inveterate in the pursuit of his purpose, he shews the utmost elasticity, vigour, and presence of mind, in the means of attaining it. But so rooted was our habitual impression of the part from seeing it caricatured in the representation, that it was only from a careful perusal of the play itself that we saw our error. The stage is not in general the best place to study our author's characters in. It is too often filled with traditional commonplace conceptions of the part, handed down from sire to son, and suited to the taste of the great vulgar and the small.—" 'Tis an unweeded garden: things rank and gross do merely gender in it!" If a man of genius comes once in an age to clear away the rubbish, to make it fruitful and wholesome, they cry, " 'Tis a bad school: it may be like nature, it may be like Shakespear, but it is not like us." Admirable critics!

Q. Explain the Poetic Verse and Rhyme in The Merchant of Venice

William Shakespeare's The Merchant of Venice, is a comedy play about the love exploits of several Italian characters, told in an objective third-person point of view. The play is set in Venice, Italy during the Renaissance. The protagonist, Antonio, is a merchant of Venice who is affluent, well-respected, and sociable. The title supports the supposition that Antonio is the protagonist because it is termed The Merchant of Venice, indicating the story of the merchant. Antonio's best friend, Bassanio, is an impecunious romantic who borrows money on Antonio's credit to court the woman he loves. Since Bassanio is in a perpetual state of indebtedness he requires money to appear affluent enough to marry Portia, the beautiful maiden from Belmont. The central antagonist is Shylock, a Jewish money lender who gives Bassanio the desired funds on Antonio's credit, but on one unusual condition. Instead of his usual rate of interest if the debt is not repaid in three months, Shylock desires to take one pound of flesh off Antonio's body. Antonio's ships (his bond) are due to return before the contract expires so Antonio agrees to the contract which is legally signed under Venetian law.

Meanwhile, Shylock's daughter, Jessica, falls in love with a Christian and friend of Antonio named Lorenzo. Against her father's wishes Jessica elopes with Lorenzo and Bassanio and Portia are wed. However, misfortune hits Antonio as his ships are lost or destroyed at sea; and thus, his bond can not be fulfilled. Shylock takes Antonio to court to force him to pay the bond. In court, Shylock is despised by those present while Antonio is looked upon commendably. Portia and her lady-in-waiting, Nerissa disguise themselves as judge and clerk, respectively, and proceed to carry out the case. Shylock insists that he be allowed to take a pound of Antonio's flesh as the legal contract states and refuses to accept triple the amount owed to him. Portia then cleverly agrees to Shylock's demands, but instructs him that he may only take one pound of flesh and not spill even a drop of Antonio's blood or he will "diest, and all [his] goods are confiscate." Realizing the impossibility of his task, Shylock reluctantly concedes to become a Christian and give the deeds to his holdings to the state and Antonio because his task is unfeasible.

In the first Act Solanio, a friend of Antonio and Bassanio, makes an allusion to Roman mythology. "Now, by two-headed Janus, Nature hath framed strange fellows in her time." Solanio then makes an analogy, "[they] will laugh like parrots at a bagpiper," in an attempt to brighten up Antonio who is depressed over the condition of his ships. Also in the first Act, Antonio reveals his genuine friendship and devotion to Bassanio: "Within the eye of honour, be assured My purse, my person, my extremest means Lie all unlocked to your occasions." Antonio has declared and assured his best friend that his money, himself, and his most earnest efforts are available to Bassanio. Friendship is a key theme of The Merchant of Venice. Bassanio quickly uses Antonio's friendship to beget another loan from him after Antonio discloses his devotion to Bassanio. When Antonio is placed on trial though, Bassanio admits that "life itself, my wife, and all the world / Are not with me esteemed above thy [Antonio's] life. / I would lose all, ay, sacrifice them all / Here to this devil [Shylock] to deliver you." In this moment, Bassanio pronounces his persistent friendship with Antonio.

Several allusions to Greek mythology are present in The Merchant of Venice. When Bassanio tells Antonio of Portia's wealth, beauty and the attempts of her suitors, he uses an allusion. Referring to Jason of Greek mythology, Bassanio states: "Renowned suitors, and her sunny locks/ Hang on her temples like a golden fleece,/ Which makes her seat of Belmont Colchos' stand,/ And many Jasons come in quest of her." Later in Act III, Gratiano, another friend of Antonio and Bassanio, also alludes to the story of Jason after Bassanio has won the hand of Portia: "We are the Jasons, we have won the Fleece." An archetype and metaphor from Greek mythology can be found in the interaction of Launcelot, a clown and servant to Shylock, with Jessica in Act III after Portia and Bassanio are to be wed: "Thus when I shun Scylla, your father,/ I fall into Charybdis, your mother."

Each scene in the first and last Acts end in rhyme as do several intermediary scenes in the play. In the first and last act the following end-line rhymes are used: "Make/sake," "before/door," "dismay/day," and "thing/ ring." The rhymes add to the poetic verse of the characters' lines. Each of the three scrolls contained in Portia's boxes includes proverbial messages which are written in complete rhyme, usually rhyming the same word. The rhyme strengthens the importance of the scrolls and the action surrounding their use. After Bassanio opens the lead box and has been determined to be the true suitor for Portia in Act III, his acceptance pronouncement is delivered entirely in rhyming prose, stressing the significance of that event. It is important to note that only the protagonist, Antonio, has all of his lines written in verse. All other characters oscillate between verse and prose.

The main theme of The Merchant of Venice is love versus money. The conflict arises in the suitors of Portia, and in the character of Shylock. Each suitor is given the choice to discover the portrait of Portia from one of three boxes; gold, silver, and lead. The suitors prior to Bassanio, choose the boxes of precious metals, raising the issue of appearance versus reality, another theme of the play. However, they are unsuccessful because as the scroll informs: "You that choose by the view/ Chance as fair and choose as true." Thus, the superiority of reality over appearances is established. Furthermore, the motto of the gold casket blatantly states: "All that glisters is not gold." By choosing the least precious box, which inscription states that its chooser must "give and hazard all he hath," Bassanio chooses his love for Portia rather than her wealth.

Shylock is an avaricious outsider, distinguished from the other characters by his religion, profession, and hatred of the beloved Antonio. Shylock demonstrates his viciousness by utilizing symbolism to attack Antonio when his bond falls through: "Thou call'dst me dog before thou hadst a cause, But, since I am a dog, beware my fangs." Upon hearing the news of his daughter's marriage to a Christian he laments: "My daughter! O my ducats! O my daughter!...My ducats and my daughter." His equal concern for his money and his daughter demonstrate his distorted values and overemphasis on money.

Shylock's money is his life and his only protection so that he becomes obsessed by it. Portia, Bassanio, and Antonio only use money to achieve an end result. Bassanio uses borrowed money to travel to Belmont and win over Portia. Portia offers her wealth to Bassanio to help his best friend, Antonio, who freely lent his indebted friend more money. Thus, Portia, Bassanio, and Antonio do not allow their lives to revolve around money as Shylock does. During the trial in Act IV though, Shylock demonstrates that he has learned money is not everything: "If every ducat in six thousand ducats / Were in six parts, and every part a ducat, / I would not draw them, / I would have my bond." Shylock recognizes that forcing Antonio to suffer forfeiture of his flesh for the bond is more important than mere money.

Religious prejudice and stereotypes are present and perform important roles in the lives of the characters. Shylock, a Jewish moneylender who subsists on the practice of usury, is disdained and discriminated against by the dominantly numbered Christians in the play: "O, be thou damned, inexexcrable dog/... for thy desires / Are wolvish, bloody, starved, and ravenous." He is taunted with a pun by Gratiano: "Not if thy sole, but on thy soul, harsh Jew, / Thou mak'st thy knife keen." Shylock feels wronged by Antonio and by other Christians merely because "I [Shylock] am a Jew." In Act III, Shylock informs Salerio of his true reasons for desiring Antonio's flesh: "[because] it / will feed my revenge." His motives are revealed in this scene, as he attempts to prove his equality by hypothetically asking: "Hath not a Jew eyes? Hath not a Jew hands, / organs, dimensions, senses, affections, passions?" However, his questions fall upon indifferent ears. Shylock faces the external conflict of man versus society because he is a minority, and is overwhelmed witty Christians.

The climax of the play occurs in the fourth Act when Antonio is placed on trial. The previous acts had built up to the climax by establishing the contract and introducing Portia's quest for marriage, and Bassanio's success. In the fourth act, resolution is made of the contract which Antonio and Shylock had signed. Unexpectedly appearing at the trial, Portia arbitrates the disagreement. Her emergence allows Bassanio to repay his debt to Antonio by freeing Antonio of the bond due to Shylock. Portia and Nerissa had disguised themselves as men to achieve a favorable outcome to the trial. Their act of deception, is a motif that appears in The Odyssey and The Orestia Trilogy.

During the trial the theme of mercy versus revenge emerges. In the beginning of the trial Portia insists that "the Jew be merciful," but Shylock is insistent on the specifics of his contract and the promise of flesh. Clever Portia, however, declares that "This bond doth give thee here no jot of blood; / The words are expressly are 'a pound of flesh.'" When Shylock realises that his task is impossible he is taunted a second time by Gratiano, in an ironic tone: "A Daniel still say I, a second Daniel! / I thank thee, Jew, for teaching me that word." Portia then sentences Shylock to further humiliation; to surrender his assets and even convert to Christianity.

The final act of the play takes place in the moonlight of Belmont with musicians playing. Portia, Nerissa, and Jessica each reveal their double-identities as members of the court to Lorenzo and Bassanio. Lorenzo's use of poetic alliteration while talking to Jessica enriches the setting and supports the theme of harmony in the conclusion of the play: "How sweet the moonlight sleeps upon this bank! / Here will we sit and let the sounds of music / Creep in our ears. Soft stillness and the night / Become the touches of sweet harmony. / Sit Jessica."

William Shakespeare's The Merchant of Venice, contains poetic verse and rhyme that creates vivid and logical imagery. The powerful bond of friendship between Antonio, the protagonist, and Bassanio is revealed through their words. Shylock, the antagonist, is portrayed as a villainous Jew, dependent on usury and void of mercy. However, the clever Portia is able to out wit Shylock and obtain justice for the Christians.

Q. Compare the Marriage Plot and the Trial Plot in the Play

It is worthwhile to take a close look at the marriage and trial plots in The Merchant of Venice. The antagonists of the respective plots have similar goals; they seek access to power and privilege. However, the types of power they seek is very different. The methods they use of gaining power are also differ. Bassanio succeeds with his intent, but Shylock fails. Focusing on the before mentioned plots, one may draw some conclusions concerning the reasons of success and failure in this play.

Let us look at the marriage plot. Already in I,i Bassanio reveals his plans of wooing Portia. He describes his undertaking as a quest; "her sunny locks/ Hang on her temples like a golden fleece/ Which makes her seat of Belmont Colchos' strond,/ And many Jasons come in quest of her. We might notice how he describes Portia's looks in an almost petrarchan manner. He is describing a single feature of her (her hair), and thereby objectifying her.

More importantly, Bassanio's words tell us that he is aware of the economic gains that he can achieve through the bond of marriage. This makes us ask an essential question: What does Bassanio want to achieve through wooing Portia?

According to Frank Whigham in "Ideology and Class Conduct in The Merchant of Venice", he wants power through an assimilation into the elite. Bassanio has lost ventures before, but now he's venturing to be free from financial worries. He seeks to rid himself with the fear the Venetians share when it comes to loss of security and privilege through the loss of money. To this we might add that he also seeks love in marriage.

Since Bassanio spoke of his undertaking as a quest, it is natural to assume that there is a certain risk involved. So what does Bassanio risk? Obviously he is risking his friend's life. When Antonio signs the bond to help Bassanio, there is a certain risk that Antonio might die, how improbable it might seem to them at that point. He is also facing the risk of financial loss, should he fail in his quest. And if he fails in his quest, he is barred from the company of Portia and he is barred from access to the elite. But Bassanio does not fail. So what were the means to his success?

Again, according to Whigham, Bassanio succeeds because he is (consciously or subconsciously) aware of the language and outer credentials of style that Portia relates to. Bassanio shares Portia's assumptions and views of the world, and is therefore able to choose the right casket by using their shared credentials of style. By denouncing gold and silver Bassanio gains access to gold and silver (i.e. the wealth of Portia). By scorning choices based on style, he uses a certain mode of style to get what he wants. His rhetoric and his goals are not exactly in concord, but he gets what he wants; wealth and access to the elite.

If we look at the trial plot, it is quite clear that Shylock also wants power. But he does not want to be included into Christian society, he seeks power over it. His reasons, although obscure to the Venetians of the play, are not incomprehensible. Antonio has tried to ruin his business (I, iii, 39-40) and in view of the treatment he has been given of the Christians of the play (I, iii, 106-123), it is natural that he might find his position somewhat undeserving and even worthy of revenge.

Shylock's means of getting in power are different than Bassanio's. Shylock is trying to defeat the system by using the system. He does not want to be included in the Christian society, because he knows that would only restore him hierarchically and thereby render him powerless. He would again be the underdog. Shylock believes that he only risks the loss of three thousand ducats when he decides to have his revenge, but he ends up losing everything he has, even his religion.

In the trial scene, Shylock never tries to hide what he wants. He wants his pound of flesh, and thereby Antonio's life. One might argue that it is Shylock's honesty that becomes his downfall. In the end there is no doubt in anyone's mind that he, as an alien, did "seek the life of a citizen" (IV, i, 347), and that he therefore is liable to persecution.

Accordingly, we can claim that the trial plot and the marriage plot both can be seen as trials determining access to power. Shylock fails because he is unable to see the law as an ideological tool created by the elite.

He does not realise that the law is not literal and objective, it is created to protect its creators. The law, in this respect, becomes biased and dishonest. Bassanio, in his trial, uses decorum and style in order to get what he wants. He is being dishonest in his rhetoric when it comes to his desires for wealth, but by displaying the proper style, he gets what he wants.

Chapter 16

Critical Essays

THE MERCHANT FORMERLY KNOWN AS JEW REDEFINING THE RHETORIC OF MERCHANTRY IN SHAKESPEARE'S *MERCHANT OF VENICE*

In his one-man show *Shakespeare's Villains,* the actor Stephen Berkoff portrays Shylock as hunchbacked, rumpled, spitting out curses and delivering his famous "If You Prick Us" speech miming the stroking of a beard with Machiavellian gusto. Berkoff's Shylock is not the humanized character that has come to dominate post-Holocaust reproductions of the play. It is, as Berkoff himself declares, the representation of a myth. Berkoff's characterization, however, does not leave us with the question that so many others have tried to answer-is Shylock a representation of Shakespeare's anti-Semitism? His representation (accurately anti-Semitic as it is, as this essay will contend) provides a more interesting quandary.

If we grant that Shylock is a myth, two important questions result: from what cultural material is he constituted, and more significantly, what particular purpose did this character serve in the seventeenth-century English imaginary? In order to address these questions, the play must be critically re-examined in not only its historical context, but its economic one as well. While critics have long examined Shylock's humanitarian appeal, almost no critical attention has been paid to how Shylock functions as a site wherein anxieties about the way capitalism and, in particular, usury affected national and religious identities. As economic historians such as Immanuel

Wallerstein and Fernand Braudel have shown in their histories of capitalism, early modern England, like the continent, was feeling the sometimes uncomfortable push and pull of a new economic order at this time-one where the merchant was no longer conflated with the Jew, and one where Portia's question, "which is the Merchant here? And which the Jew?" took on an ontological significance beyond Portia's seemingly innocent query.

The Jew and the "English Jew" in the Early Modern Period

In the English imaginary of the pre-readmission period, the expelled Jew was a Jew frozen in time: no matter what the particular economic circumstances of Jewish life in Europe (or, for that matter the roles of those few Jews living in England prior to 1656) the English perception of the Jews was overdetermined by England's experience with Jewish money-lending in the medieval period. Thomas Wilson concretizes this association in his *Discourse upon Usury*, written in 1572, almost three hundred years after the expulsion. Vilifying usury, Wilson reminds his reader of its most hated practitioners and their banishment from the realm-a punishment he suggests for Christian practitioners of his day:

> What is the matter that Jewes were so universallye hated wheresoever they come? For soothe, usurie is one of the chief causes, for they cobble all men that deale with them, and undoe them in the end. And for thys causes they were hated in England, and so banished wortheleye, with whome I woulde wyshe all these Englishemen were sent that lende their money or their goods whatsoever for gayne, for I take them to be no better then Jewes.

As Joshua Trachtenburg notes, not only was the term "usury" synonymous with Jew in the Middle Ages and later, but the appellation of merchant connoted Jewishness in the English vernacular during this period (188-189).

English fear of the Jews arose primarily from paranoia around proto-capitalist activities such as usury with which Jews were intimately associated. Understanding usury as the "labor pains of capitalism" Jacques Le Goff describes the epistemological trauma that accompanied capitalist activities during the medieval period:

The sudden eruption and spread of the monetary economy threatened old Christian values. Capitalism, a new economic system, was ready to take shape. If it did not require new technology to get started, it at least made wholesale use of practices that had always been condemned by the church.

The fact that money-lending was perhaps the most visible symptom of this new economic relationship did nothing to help the perception of Jews either in the early modern period or in the Middle Ages. Money-lending depended upon a discredited perception of money's possibilities-one that focused on money's unnatural generation through the charging of interest-on its transvaluative capacities. Jewish economic activity in these areas enabled a conception of their identity that stressed a diabolic otherness: in the early modern imagination, the cabal was initially defined through Jewish economic activity.

Debates about the effects of the medieval English Jewish community and its economic activities on the English imaginary have ranged from Stephen Greenblatt's dismissive remark that "there was no Jewish question in Marlowe's England; there were scarcely any Jews" to an assertion of Shakespeare's irreducible Jewishness by some less reputable critics. Although the English "Jewish" question has been studied in great detail by historians of the period, literary critics had paid little attention to it until James Shapiro's work, *Shakespeare and the Jews*.

Shapiro exhaustively surveys the literary and historical analyses of the English Jewish question. His analysis affirms the existence of a Marrano Jewish community in early modern London and questions the reasons behind the relative lack of material on this subject in early modern English studies. Although his critique of historical omissions is important, what is most useful in Shapiro's book is his discussion of the Jewish presence in early modern England. Having proved a minor Marrano/Jewish presence in early modern London, Shapiro abandons the counting game and concludes that what is interesting is "not the raw numbers of Jews... as much as the kind of cultural preoccupation they became".

Shakespeare's representation of Shylock is a telling symptom of the unique perception of Jews that dominated the English consciousness at this time. Apart from the consistency with which the Jew is figured in the English consciousness (as economic parasite), what is distinctive about the English preoccupation with the Jews is its continuity, given that there was no visible Jewish presence in England during this time. While the Jewish question for other countries was a "living" issue-in the sense of there being active Jewish communities in many areas of Eastern-Europe at this time—English-Jewish stereotyping stemmed primarily from the English experience of the Middle Ages.

Thus, the English imaginary around the Jewish question was obscure and bogey-like: the characterization of Jews as economic parasites in their anti-English/Christian activities resulted from a kind of historical immaturity-a vision that depended upon the oft-recited tales about Jews that appeared in the nation's collective folk-lore. As John Russell Brown notes in his introduction to the *Merchant of Venice,* "In England at this time, the Jews were not a people to fear, but were rather a fabulous and monstrous bogey belonging to remote times and places." Thus, at a time when Jews were integrated into diverse professions in other countries, English writers persisted in their association of Jews with usury, "sharp dealing" and counterfeiting.

In his study, *European Jewry in the Age of Mercantilism,* Jonathan Israel notes the predilection in historiography of the early modern period to "treat the early modern period in Jewish history as basically just an extension of the Jewish Middle Ages." Repudiating such an interpretation, Israel claims "that there is much to commend the drawing of a firm dividing-line between the medieval and early modern epochs in the historical experience and consciousness of western Jewry". Shylock's characterization, then, is a profoundly inaccurate representation of Jews' economic and social location in communities outside of England and France at this time.

Jewish usurers, while still extant, were increasingly becoming a rarity. They were supplanted, instead, by a new class of Jewish professionals-doctors, notaries, and merchants-who together drastically changed Jewish customs and life in Eastern Europe and Germany.

THE MERCHANT AND THE JEW

While the Jew in the English imagination was a sort of bogey-man, embodied in the character of Shylock as bloodthirsty, vengeful and intractably anti-Christian, Shylock nevertheless functions as a palliative figure in the play. Precisely because of his intractable Jewishness, he allows the early modern audience to reassert a needed epistemological divide between the (disreputable) merchant-Jew and the new breed of heroic commodity adventurers that began to dominate the (Christian) mercantile landscape. The growth of early modern capitalism made the easy equivalence between merchant and Jew an epistemological impossibility. To assuage anxieties around merchantry's inherently Jewish taint, Shylock must become super-Jew-too Jewish for even the other Jews in the play. The title of Shakespeare's play is a truncated symptom of the confusion of terms in this period. As Martin Yaffe points out in his study, *Shylock and the Jewish Question,*

Shakespeare's title... has the peculiarity of distributing the announced description of the play's one protagonist among more than one of its city dwellers, perhaps even among all of them to some extent, whether citizen (like Antonio) or mere resident.

Yaffe sees this peculiar vagueness as stemming from the commonalties that exist between Shylock and Antonio with regard to profession. Yaffe observes that Shakespeare "homogenizes his characters to a remarkable extent, by indicating their common dependence on a given political setting". In contrast to Yaffe, I would suggest that it is just this anxiety-provoking homogeneity that the play alleviates by dramatically resurrecting the bogey-like medieval Jew against which the early modern merchant-adventurer (Antonio and his ilk) might be contrasted. The title is less an indicator of an enlightened recognition of the homogeneity of Christian and Jew than a reminder of the anxiety-provoking equivalence that it is the play's task to remedy. Although for a *medieval* English audience the "Merchant of Venice" was most likely "the Jew of Venice," by the late 1500's burgeoning companies of merchants made such an association increasingly problematic. Faced with a general public that viewed their financial dealings with considerable suspicion, the trading companies were at pains to avoid the taint of Jewishness that pervaded perceptions of their business practices, especially those that frequently employed usury as a means of accruing capital. In a sermon dedicated to the London Company of Merchants, Daniel Price expressed his dismay about anachronistic understandings of the merchant in the popular imagination:

That Aristotle detested them and their life, that the ancient laws did not admit any merchant to bear any office... that Cicero affirmeth their getting of money to be most odious, giving this reason... that they get their living by lying. I hope the merchants of our time deserve not to be so thought of. *Many of these merchants were Jews*, gentiles, heathens, infidels... I hope none such are to be found among you, for you are Christians.

While Shylock is a sufficiently unsavory character against which to contrast the kindlier, gentler merchant that Price describes, his character does not allay anxieties wrought by another aspect of early modern capitalist relationships. Unlike Christopher Marlowe's Barabas in *The Jew of Malta* who embodies the worst excesses of the speculative economy, Shylock does not represent a capitalist bogey as much as a medieval one.He does not work to undo the economic bases of Venetian society, but rather insists on medieval forms of valuation that were antiquated by this time. As such, Shylock at once seems to guarantee the literalism of contract-based relationships that seemed threatened by speculation while at the same time strengthening his characterization as an economic parasite *par excellence*-demanding Antonio's blood for currency. Shylossssssck here reflects an obsession with economic rationality and transparency that were singular features of the debate around the market and its effects on social relationships. In his book, *Worlds Apart: The Market and the Theatre in Anglo-American Thought,* Jean-Christophe Agnew explains the economic logic that informed the relocation of the market outside city boundaries:

By assigning an extraterritorial status to commodity transactions and by circumscribing those same transactions with a variety of ceremonial and festive practices, city leaders sought to turn the market's explosive aspect to creative and controlled account.... Here, as elsewhere, the point was to set clear bounds upon trade's mysterious capacity to bring incommensurable qualities meanings and values into equivalence through the purely fictive convention of the money form... (25)

In an ironic confirmation of this ethos of transparency and legitimacy of bonds, we see Antonio while chained to his jailkeeper defending Shylock's insistence on the letter of the law as the sole basis for reliable economic exchange:

> *The duke cannot deny the course of law:*
> *For the commodity that strangers have*
> *With us in Venice, it if be denied*
> *Will much impeach the justice of the state,*
> *Since that the trade and profit of the city*
> *Consisteth of all nations* (*III. iv.* 26-31).

By functioning (in one sense) as the erstwhile representative of the unbreakable sanctity of bonds, Shylock frames Antonio in an uncomfortable epistemology of economic relationships. For Antonio, transvaluation is the new norm: what was once sacrosanct because untransformable (bonds/ contracts) are, within his economic ethos, always a possible object of transformation. His speculative ethos is exemplified most clearly in his exchange with Bassanio where he seems at first glance to sacrifice all for simple friendship's sake. In his article, "The Ideology of the Merchant of Venice" Michael Ferber confirms Antonio's "complicity" with the proxemics of the speculative economy even in his dealings with Bassanio:

The play's general problem, the congruence of spiritual or moral values, may be adumbrated in its title. It is easy to imagine a play about the friendship of two men put to the text... in a plot where practical, worldly concerns are not at issue... They might both be soldiers of fortune like Bassanio, devoted comrades-at-arms now on leave in a bewildering sophisticated city... But Antonio... happens to be a merchant. (431)

According to Ferber, Antonio is a hero, but a hero encumbered by his identity. As a merchant, Antonio can not but occupies an immanently ambiguous position morally. As Ferber continues, "Shakespeare makes Antonio a hero, but the strain is evident; if anything [Antonio] seems to collaborate in it [his ruin], and among the reasons he does so is his full complicity in the way things are done in Venice, even by his enemy Shylock" (451).

The epistemological contrast between Antonio and Shylock is perhaps most evident in the latter's comments on the kinds of speculative trading ventures in which Antonio is engaged. Considering the economic riskiness of Antonio's ventures, Shylock remarks to Bassanio:

[M]y meaning in saying he is a good man, is to have you understand me that he is sufficient—yet his means are in supposition: he hath an argosy bound for Triples, another to the Indies, I understand moreover upon the Rialto, he hath a third at Mexico, a fourth for England, and other ventures he hath squandered abroad,—but ships are but boards, sailors but men, there be land-rats, water-rats, water-thieves, and land-thieves (I mean pirates), and then there is the peril of waters, winds, and rocks... (I. iii. 13-23).

Shylock's anachronism rests in his refusal to adopt the new ethic of transvaluation that Antonio embraces. While the latter becomes the representative of an economy based on speculation and risk, Shylock is stubbornly medieval in his insistence on the specific requirements of the bond, particularly the one between him and Antonio As a result, Shylock becomes monstrous to the audience of the play precisely because he refuses to engage in the new ethic of transvaluation that where bonds of flesh or friendship are effortlessly transformed into bonds of currency. While Antonio might easily be seen as a Christian Shylock at this point in the play, Shakespeare is at pains to rescue him from such an association. By rejecting usury, Antonio becomes a new kind of merchant adventurer barely supported by the exigencies of the market-Christian yet capitalist, adventurous yet honorable: an identity that, as the play demonstrates, cannot survive within the new market economy.

Shylock himself recognizes the danger that he as a Jew and broker of bonds poses to Antonio. Disingenuously, Shylock works to assuage the fears of Bassanio by acknowledging the inherent economic irrationality of the bond itself when understood in the context of transvaluation and speculation.

> *O father Abram, what these Christians are,*
> *Whose own hard dealings teaches them suspect*
> *The thoughts of others! Pray you tell me this,—*
> *If he should break this day what should I gain*
> *By the exaction of the forfeiture?*
> *A pound of man's flesh taken from a man,*
> *Is not so estimable, profitable neither*
> *As flesh of muttons, beefs, or goats,—I say,*
> *To buy his favour, I extend this friendship...*
> *(I. ii. 156-164)*

Shylock's protests to Bassanio, however, only confirm for the audience his unholy bloodlust. In his 1562 tract against usury, Thomas Wilson warns his readers against the suspicious meekness that characterizes the usurer's initial attitude towards his potential client. Likening a crusade against usurers to King Edgare's crusade against the wolves, Wilson writes:

Now yf your lordeship, with others, could procure by your good meanes that in your tyme there mighte bee never a usurers heade in England, I doe thinke you shoulde doe a greater good deede to thys lande, than ever was doone by the kyllinge of wolfes. For these bee the greedie cormoraunte wolfes in deede that ravyn up both beaste and man, who whyles they walk in sheepeskynne, doe covertlye devoure the flocke of England under coloure of their wealth and counterfeit honesty.

Although Shylock plays lip service to an ethic of transvaluation that he does not intend to honour, his role as usurer nevertheless inserts him within the kind of a relationship of speculation that his literalist economic bent would seem to disallow. Here we notice an important contradiction that further alienates Shylock from his early modern audience. Shylock appears to rely upon an economic epistemology of equivalency (where pounds of flesh can not be rendered currency) even though his role as usurer places him within just such a system of transvaluative exchange. Medieval in his insistence on his bond, Shylock nevertheless subsists within an economic order that even Antonio sees as founded in an unholy magic of economic relationships:

That Shylock should "choose" to do wrong reminds us, though, of the simultaneously most damning and yet socially and ideologically most reassuring charge to be leveled at usurers in Shakespeare's time, namely that usurers are heretics, willful choosers of the wrong course and, therefore, most deserving of unqualified reproach.

Drawing from Henry Smith's 1591 *Examination of Usury*, Thomas Moisan confirms the English association of usury with heresy: "[O]ne saith well... that our usurers are Heretics, because after manie admonitions yet they maintaine their errours, & persist in it obstinately as Papists do in Poperie"

- In distinguishing the "merchant of Venice" from the "Jew of Venice" the play proleptically positions Shylock as the Jewish magician of old, breeding money through the debts of Christians rather than the lambs of Jacob and Esau. As Lisa Jardine remarks in her essay "Alien Intelligence" the "barrenness of money was a fundamental tenet of early modern Christianity-so the vividly literal idea of 'making money' is fraught with difficulty". Although "making money" was commonplace in England at this time—so much so that even Elizabeth's parliament attempted to regulate the rates of interest that could be charged-anti-usury tracts nevertheless insist on its essentially alien and diabolical nature. And as Jews were almost always historically "remembered" in these tracts by their usurious lineage, they are necessarily tainted by the sense of cabalistic mystery that attended the representation of usury in these writings.

Wilson's *Discourse upon Usury* is an interesting document to examine for its subtle "jewing" of the merchant-usurer in its fictional recreation of a debate between a preacher, a doctor, a lawyer, and a merchant named appropriately, Gromel Gayner. The Preacher, Ockerfoe, is usury's most vigorous prosecutor in this discourse. His strategy against the merchant, predictably usury's most vigorous defender, is to insist that usury falls beyond the bonds of Christian behaviour, thus insinuating that its practitioners are not Christians. Given the Preacher's multiple mentions of Jewish usury (four to be exact, in a peroration of twenty pages) it is reasonable to assume that the Jew is posed as the existential "other" of the Christian-if, in other words, the Merchant is *not* a Christian, then he is made a Jew:

For you oughte to lende freely unto all men, riche and poore, lord and gentlemene, kyng and caysar so that God, being the lord of the ryche as well as of the poore, hath utterly and precisely forbidden all usurie amongst all men that are of the household of faith, except perhaps you will saye, that ryche men are no christians.(253)

Earlier, Ockenfoe also intimates that the Merchant's behavoir is unchristian:

Lawyer: ... [W]ho I pray you woulde lende but to have some benefite of his money? And is that any harme when bothe do gayne?

Merchant: Gods blessyng of your hart for so saying, for I did never lende money in my lyfe but for gayne, and whether my neyghbour gayned, or noe, I knowe not. I wyshed well unto hum, but by Saynt Marye, I woulde bee sure firset to doe well myselfe, whatsoever came of him.

Preacher: Herein you wanted charitie, and shewed yourselfe not to be a perfect Christian.

In a later passage, the Doctor amplifies the "jewing" of the lending Merchant:

The chauses that have moved wyse and godly men to deteste usury besides the plaine prohibiton are diverse and substancial, and therefore woorthy to bee considered most diligently. The Iewe, that hath used thys horrible sinne most above all others, and might lawfullye use the same, before Christs coming, upon any straunger, as appeareth plaine in Exodus, hath so robbed the Christians wheresoever hee came, that his evill lyvinge seene, hee is banished out of the most places in christendome, and worthely, for surely that common weale and country cannot longe stande in prosperous estate and welfare, where merchants and all others become usurers. And no better do I call them then Iewes, yea, worse than any infidel that willing lyve by the onely gayne of their money. (283)

The proxemics of the Merchant's economic survival mark him as other in this text in ways that are identical to the Jews of the Middle Ages: he is not the heroic merchant-adventurer whose commodities sail openly on the winds of chance, but rather a character embodying the hidden parasitism that is necessary for the market's effective functioning.

- Shylock's house is one such metonymic indicator of his economic parasitism. Not only were the homes of Jews physically different from their Christian counterparts (the homes of prominent Jews were built of stone rather than wood), but these residences were associated with the economic role of the Jews in England. Interestingly, Jewish homes were frequently located near royal residences so that resident Jews might obtain protection in times of riot from royal authorities

- Jewish homes were frequently perceived as the repositories of vast riches, a conception that led, especially in times of social unrest, to their destruction in the hope of recovering the presumed wealth inside. William of Newburgh, a thirteenth-century monk, chronicles the York riots of March 16-17 1190 in his *History of English Affairs* (1201):

  The zeal of the Christians against the Jews in England... broke out fiercely. It was not indeed sincere, that is, solely for the sake of the faith, but in rivalry for the luck of others or from envy of their good fortune.... [M]any of the province of York plotted against the Jews, not able to suffer their opulence, when they themselves were in need, and, without any scruple of Christian conscience, thirsting for the blood of infidels from greed or booty.... Some of these, having given up their estates to them [the Jews] for the money they had received, were now oppressed by great want; some, bound by their own sureties, were pressed by the exactions of the Treasury to satisfy the royal usurers. One stormy night no small part of the city became on fire either by chance, or as is believed, by arson perpetrated by the conspirators, so that the citizens were occupied with their own houses in fear of the fire spreading... And while the fire gloomily increased in strength, the robbers seized their booty and left the burning house, and by help of darkness retired unobserved and heavy laden [having, of course, murdered all the occupants of the house first]. (147)

  Although William of Newburgh chastises the rioters in this Chronicle, the invasion of Jewish homes and the destruction of their occupants-property and persons-was the dominant expression of English rage during the Middle Ages. These pogroms were cathartic for several reasons: they destroyed a visible symbol of Jewish prosperity (the stone house) while at the same time invading, and thus psychically cleansing a culturally fraught site of suspicion and fear. The question of what went on in Jewish homes was an overwhelming obsession to the English at this time and later-as is attested to by the various communal strictures against entering Jewish homes.

- The invasion of Shylock's house-by his daughter no less-is the wished-for dream of the English who still struggled with "the Jewish question" although freed from a living Jewish presence for centuries. Not only was the Jewish home a site of potential fear, but it was also understood to intermix economic and familial practice. The role of Jewish males as money-lenders could not be separated from their roles as *pater familias*. Luther's attack on the Jewish usurers in his "The Jews and Their Lies," for example, focuses on the idleness of the Jewish home as the clearest manifestation of exploitation: "they, pious crew, idle away their days at the fireside in laziness, feasting and display." Thus, Shylock's admonition to Jessica to "look to his house... For I did dream of money-bags tonight" places him (even in his own psyche) within this particular ideological trope of the English imaginary by rhetorically collapsing the home with his economic survival. Shylock's cry "my daughter and my ducats, my ducats and my daughter" confirms the connection and sets up the Jew's home as the appropriate site of Christian economic revenge. Jessica's robbery of the home's riches (her self-gilding) is an epistemic confirmation of the way in which the home, its inhabitants and economic positioning are all one to the English (and ostensibly to the Jew): "*Jes.* I will make fast the doors and gild myself/With some more ducats, and be with you straight" (II. vii. 49-50).
- The relational context of bond-making is also what finally distinguishes the merchant from the Jew in the play. Bonding continues as a trope throughout the play and causes us to question the supposed distinction between Shylock's bonding of Antonio and the Christians bonding of each other. For if Shylock is the

economic parasite *par excellence*—breeding money and insisting on blood—how do we understand the relationships between the other characters in the play-the Christians whose bonds with each other are also constitutively economic in character? Antonio's bond with Bassanio renders economic rationalization invisible. It is instead based in a quintessentially Christian ethos—one of faith rather than the cold logic of economic calculation. While Shylock calculates his bond (or purposely miscalculates, so that Antonio will be in his debt) Antonio seems to bind Bassanio to himself with the simple interest of faith and good will. Bassanio's parable of economic faith relies heavily on the framing of such relations in terms of child-like innocence and good will:

In my school-days when I had lost one shaft,
I shot his fellow of the self-same flight
The self-same way, with more advised watch
To find the other forth, and by adventuring both,
I oft found both: I urge this childhood proof
Because what follows is pure innocence.
I owe you much, and (like a willful youth)
That which I owe is lost, but if you please
To shoot another arrow that self way
Which you did shoot the first, I do not doubt,
(As I will watch the aim) or to find both,
Or bring your latter hazard back again.
And thankfully rest debtor for the first.
(I. i. 140-151)

Of course, Antonio's bond does not come without an "interest" payment of its own. In some sense, Bassanio's flesh (the arrow) is what Antonio claims at the end of the play, the exchange of which is signified by the former's willingness to part with Portia's ring on behalf of Antonio.

- The different kinds of bonds reach their points of contention and eventual (if uncomfortable) resolution in the trial scene. The bonds here are framed by the anxious association of merchant-capitalism and (Jewish) usury with which the play grapples. The literalist rhetoric of Shylock, for example, is an uncomfortable reminder of the rhetoric of English pro-usury pamphlets in the early modern period, the most noteworthy of which is perhaps Robert Filmer's defence of usury, entitled *Quaestio Quadlibetica or a Discourse whether it may be Lawful to take use for money.* Filmer here relies heavily on a literalist interpretation of the Biblical discussions of usury in ways that resemble Shylock's own parsing of the law of the bond. Dissecting each Biblical mention of usury for its exact prescription and attendant loopholes, Filmer's defence reads almost as a parody of itself, and when considered alongside the play-text, resonates uncomfortably with Shylock's prosecutorial ethic. Introducing the subject to his readers, Filmer emphasizes his careful study of the Biblical sources that have been (mis)interpreted as forbidding usurers by readers less perceptive than himself:

As soon as I had understand in the affaires of this World, I became sensible how grievous it was to lie under the heavy disease of paying Interest, Consideration or Use (term it how you will) for money: And finding it generally condemned by those whose judgments and learning I most esteem, I began to question with myself whether the sinne were not of that nature that I my self in paying did concur in the same offence with the taker.... Upon which occasion I began to search farther, and as for Scripture I confess the prohibitions in it seemed to me to have much of the Laws terms for no other than the common-wealth of the Jewes.

Ironically, Filmer's defence of Christian usury necessarily functions as a defence of Jewish usury as well primarily because he legitimates his arguments through a rigorously literalist reading of the Biblical proscriptions against usury. For Filmer, what the Bible does not explicitly disallow is allowed. Citing Nehemiah's rebuke of Jews who took interest from members of a community of heathens, Filmer glosses it as follows:

So then Nehemiah never naming usury, nor mentioning the law against it, but supposing the act of Nobles to be lawfull, but not expedient, doth incline my belief to think that this oppression was not properly called usury, although it had a covenant for gain... Any man would think that to rebuke and reclaim men from their sin the way had been to have named it in particular, or the Law by which it was prohibited: but *Nehemiah* does neither of these, he only tells them, it was not good what they did, and asks them if they ought not to walk in the fear of their God because of the reproach of the heathen their enemies, not because of a particular law against usury.

Since Deuteronomic law only prevents Jews from lending to each other, Filmer argues that it in no way prevents the Jews (or anyone else) from lending with interest to a stranger. And since Christians are not Jews, Filmer claims that Jewish laws do not apply to gentile communities:

To give some brief accompt to the reader of the substance of the scattered arguments in this Tracture, he must know; That my scope and intention is to show that Usury is not where in Scripture forbidden to Christians: but that it is as lawfull as any other contract or bargain, unless the Laws of the Land do prohibit or moderate it as point of state or policy)

In order to contend with anti-usury tracts such as Robert Fenton's popular *Treatise of Usurie* (1611), Filmer debunks the anti-usury argument by offering a radically different understanding of the Biblical prohibition. Filmer continues his analysis of the semantic confusion around usury by offering this understanding of God's prohibition:

I undertake to manifest, that the Definitions of Usury (wherein Dr Downam and Dr. Fenton mainly differ between themsel'es) are neither warrantable by the rules of art; nor justifiable by any proof or ground in Scripture, or by any testimony of antiquity either in Councils or Fathers...

And the lawes given by God about Usury are such as by the Coherence of the Texts, and the Conference of other places, do sheweth that those lawes did only intend a prohibition of taking Usury of such as borrowed in case of extreme necessity, and were so poor that they were in charity to be relieved.

Where lending to the grievously impoverished might be seen as usury, lending to those who are financially competent is certainly not and may be considered a legitimate application of the practice of interest. After all, argues Filmer, the lender must be guaranteed some surety, and be reimbursed for his temporary inability to "gain" from the stock of money that he has lent to his client.

While it would be unfair to say that Filmer would agree with Shylock's reasoning in the trial scene, Filmer's rhetoric of literalism is nevertheless echoed by Shylock in his insistence on the letter of the bond with Antonio, rather than the spirit. Like Filmer, Shylock willfully ignores the spirit of the bond: he refuses to commute Antonio's debt into anything but the pound of flesh stipulated. Filmer, likewise, blinds himself (and tries to blind his reader) to the spirit of the Christian ethic which views usury as immoral and unchristian in all cases. Like Shylock, Filmer points out the hypocritical ways in which the religious of his time have tried to disguise usury as charity. Discussing the "mountains of piety" that were raised to relieve the poor ruined by the usury of the Jews, Filmer points out that even the managers of this charitable store charged interest:

A *mountain of piety* is a stock of Money raised by the charity of good people, who observing the poor ruined by the Usury of Jewes, did voluntarily contribute good store at treasure, whereby they *upon security* might have money at low rate to relieve their wants, which because the mass is great, and the thing is pious and charitable in itself, is called a mountain of piety. But in respect the officers and other charges incident unto it cannot be had without some emoluement, therefore the borrower pays somewhat by the month for the lone of that he receives.

Thus, while Shylock is at once a resurrection of the medieval Jewish usurer of old in order to serve as a palliative contrast to the "Antonian" merchant, he is also a reminder of the debate about usurers that dominated the English landscape at this time. The English usurer, as represented in the works of Wilson and others, was constituted as monstrous in his own right—Wilson even goes so far to say that the English usurer is worse than the Jew:

I [Preacher in Wilson's *Discourse*] Shall say: they [English usurers] are worse than Jewes. For go wither you will throughout Christendom and deale with them[Jews] you shall have under tenne in the hundredth, yea, sometimes for six in their handes, whereas English usurers exceede all goddes mercye, and will take they care not how much, wythout respect had to the partye that borroweth what losse, daunger, hinderaunce soever the borrower susteyneth.

Wilson's argument draws considerable power from his comparison of the English usurer with the Jew.. To be worse than the Jews-in monetary or in any other matter-is to enter a realm from which moral rescue was almost impossible. And it was precisely this fear of being "Jewed" that animated both defences of merchants and Antonio's characterization.

- Set against the context of such debates, the relevant audience of Portia's "mercy" speech reaches far beyond the figure of Shylock. Yet the play is anxious to collapse these unsavory practices of English merchants and moneylenders within the figure of Shylock. He is made to contain, however uncomfortably, the usurious and unpopular facets of the English merchant, even if this resolution is subject to some leakage given the cultural context of continued English usury. Like the purging of Jews that occurred in the English Middle Ages, the play attempts to purge the usurious and hence (Jewish) aura that tainted the merchant-class at this time. Rather than the subject of a purge, then, the Jew is the agent of one-leaching out the bad blood from the semiotics surrounding merchantry and capitalism at this time. In the trial scene, the play's audience is invited, with Bassanio, Portia and Antonio to "void its collective rheum" upon Shylock-to spit out, in other words, the Jewish taint that semiotically inflected the idea of the merchant in the early modern period.

- The vicious absurdity of Shylock's literalism encourages the view of the Jew as a resurrection not only of the Jewish usurer of England's past but also of the short-sighted economic logic of the Middle Ages. Unlike the new ethic of speculation that allowed for the formation of the merchant-adventurer, Shylock is framed as a mad literalist-assigning the letter of the bond a sanctity that is incompatible with a capitalist ethos of continual transvaluation. Shylock's exchange with Portia, when disguised as a judge, exaggerates the former's bloodthirsty literalism and its attendant villainy:

Por. Why this bond is forfeit
And lawfully but this the Jew may claim
A pound of flesh, to be by him cut off
Nearest the merchant's heart: be merciful
Take thrice thy money, bid me tear the bond.
Shy. When it is paid, according to the tenour.
It doth appear you are a worthy judge,
You know the law, your exposition
Hath been most sound: I charge you by the law,
Whereof you are a well-deserving pillar,

Proceed to judgment: by my soul I sear,
There is no power in the tongue of man
To alter me,-I stay here on my bond.

Ant. Most heartily I do beseech the court
To give the judgment.

Por. Why then thus it is,—
You must prepare your bosom for his knife.

Shy. O noble judge! O excellent young man!

Por. For the intent and purpose of the law
Hath full relation to the penalty,
Which here appeareth due upon the bond.

Shy. 'Tis very true: O wise and upright judge,
How much more elder art thou than thy looks.

Por. Therefore lay bare your bosom.

Shy. Ay, his breast,
So says the bond, doth it not noble judge?

"Nearest his heart,"
those are the very words
[my italics]. (IV. i. 227-250)

Portia's apparent descent into a similarly implacable literalism has been characterized by critics negatively, who see her as "sinking" to the level of Shylock's medieval madness. I would argue, however, that Portia's entrapment of Shylock is more of a cathartic staging of purging and expulsion to which I alluded earlier. By catching Shylock in the web of his own making, Portia resurrects the pleasing historical memory of the expulsion of the Jews from England under the direction of Edward I. Forbidden usury yet prevented from practicing any other profession, medieval English Jews were necessarily doomed by their own actions (of money-lending), much as Shylock is condemned by the bond that he himself creates with Antonio. In begging for mercy, Shylock acknowledges the way in which his livelihood and his life are interconnected-much as they were for Antonio and other "victims" of (Jewish) usury for which Shakespeare stages retribution:

Nay, take my life and all, pardon not that, —
You take my house, when you do take the prop

That doth sustuin my house: you take my life
When you do take the means whereby I live.
(IV. i. 370-374)

The play achieves a further victory that eluded the medieval English in their relations with the Jews. Shylock is made to convert-albeit against his own will. Through this forced conversion, the "voiding of collective rheum" is complete-not only is Jewish usury defeated and the new merchant-class freed from its uncomfortable tainting, but Shylock is ontologically eradicated and made to subsist within a quintessentially Christian economic order in which the merchant-formerly known as Jew-no longer exists.

Many thanks to the "Artist Formerly Known as Prince" for inspiring this article's title. I should note that this title has been used in a different form by Linda Charnes in her discussion of Hamlet; this article is entitled "The Hamlet Formerly Known as Prince," and may be found in *Philosophical Shakespeares,* edited by Hugh Grady.

For a detailed discussion of post-Holocaust representations of Shylock (and attendant controversies) see Robert King's "Shylock After Auschwitz" *Chicago Review* 40:4 (1994): 59-67 and John Gross, *Shylock: A Legend and its Legacy* (1994).

Of course, historiographically, the economic and historical contexts are inseparable; however, much literary criticism of this play tends to telescope the issues of usury and alienness rather than contextualizing these two critical trouble spots within a sustained consideration of the play's economic horizon, i.e. early modern capitalism. For a very recent example of the problem I mention, see Stephen Greenblatt's recent reading of the *Merchant of Venice* in his book, *Will in the World: How Shakespeare Became Shakespeare* (Norton, 2004).

A notable exception to this relative lack of discussion of capitalism in its various forms in *The Merchant of Venice* is a recent collection edited by Linda Woodbridge entitled, *Money and the Age of Shakespeare: Essays in New Economic Criticism* (Palgrave, 2003). Three articles in this collection are devoted to *The Merchant of Venice.* All consider the influence of monetary and economic theory upon the portrayal of the

Christians of the play: ie, Antonio, Bassanio and Portia. None of the articles, surprisingly, considers Shylock in light of the emergent capitalist market in early modern England. And, although Eric Spencer in his fine article, "Taking Excess, Exceeding Account" acknowledges the ontological quandaries of the new economy, noting that money was a "great equivocator", and appropriately citing the famous speech in *Timon of Athens* (4.3. 28-30) to buttress his point, he does not consider the way in which Shylock's character-as usurer par excellence-works to differentiate the new breed of Christian capitalists from their Jewish forbearers. It is this concern that is the focus of my article and which is critical for a complete understanding of the role of Shylock in *The Merchant of Venice* in particular and the English collective imaginary in general.

Until the late sixteenth century, the word usurer was synonymous with both merchant and Jew. Consequently, a semantic ellipsis resulted wherein the word merchant was intimately associated with Jew since Jews fulfilled this function for hundreds of years before the advent of Christian usury. For a more detailed discussion of the etymology of usurer and merchant, see Bernard Grebainer, *The Truth About Shylock*, especially chapter 3 "Jingler of the Guinea: The Usurer."

The debate around readmission also occasioned frequent expressions of anti-Semitic fear and suspicion: One such example is William Prynne's *Short Demurrer* where he writes passionately against readmission: "the Jews themselves in all ages having been principle firebrands of sedition both in their own land, and all places where they have dispersed (qtd in Shapiro, *Shakespeare and the Jews*, 61). For a detailed discussion of English perceptions of Jews from the Middle Ages to their return in the 1650's, see David Katz, *The Jews in the History of England: 1475-1650.*

There is an interesting epistemological slippage here that rendered the "merchant" and the "Jew" as ontologically identical. Since mercantile activity was so closely associated with usury in the popular imagination, and since the usurer was always already the Jew, the merchant was necessarily "Jewed" by his assumed participation in usury. Thus, we have the following logical fallacy that recurs in discussions of merchants: All usurers are Jews; all merchants are usurers, therefore all merchants are "Jews." For a discussion of the etiology of this conception see Pollins, *The Economic History of the Jews,* Roth, *History of the Jews in the Renaissance* and Andrew McCall, *The Medieval Underworld,* esp. 281 and Joshua Trachtenberg's *The Devil and the Jews.*

In transvaluation of any kind, value becomes embedded in a particular semiotic of value; the twenty dollar bill, for example, is not itself worth twenty dollars; the bill is simply a semiotic of value-its value resides elsewhere (in our collective agreement about the value of particular denominations). In renaissance writings about language, symbols (such as metaphors) were frequently suspect as mechanisms for the perversion of meaning (see George Puttenham, *The Art of* Poesie); this suspicion also extended to other sign systems of value.

Cotgrave's 1611 definition of the "cabal" affirms the common connection between Jews and magic:

Cabale: [f.] The Jewes Caball; or, a hidden science of diuine mysteries, which the rabbies affirme, was reuealed, and deliuered, together with the Law, unto Moses, and from him deriued, by successiue relation, vnto posteritie; (yet is it, in truth, no better than a vaine rabble of their owne tradition.)

For a thorough discussion of questionable contemporary analyses of Shakespeare, Jewishness and *The Merchant of Venice,* see Shapiro's *Shakespeare and the Jews,* especially pages 80-88.

This folklore was primarily composed of Chronicle sources from the Middle ages and renaissance, such as those of William of Norwich noted above, as well as the chronicles of Ralph Holinshed and John Foxe and especially the medieval guild plays that dramatized the life of Christ.

For a fuller discussion of the effect of professionalization upon Jewish life in Eastern Europe, see Jonathan Israel's fine study, *European Jewry in the Age of Mercantilism.*

While Walter Cohen's article "The Merchant of Venice and the Possibilities of Historical Criticism" is an exhaustive account of the play within the context of emerging capitalism, it does not consider the way in which capitalism complicated understanding of the identity of the merchant and as such, imbricated figures like Antonio within an anxiety-producing nexus of rhetorical instability occasioned by this economic revolution.

In the sixteenth and seventeenth centuries there was a concerted attempt to reframe the merchant in heroic terms. Some pertinent examples may be found in John Wheeler's *A Treatise of Commerce* (1601) and Daniel Price's "The Merchant: A Sermon Preached at Paul's Cross." Wheeler claims that merchantry is the cornerstone of England's financial well-being: "[T]his kind of life [merchantry] may be exercised and used with commendations, and without loss of one jot of honour in those who are honorable, or of eminent degree... Whereunto I add this further, that without merchandise, no ease or commodious living continueth long in any state or commonwealth... (*Merchant* 232).

And lest we object that Wheeler, as the secretary of the Society of Merchant Adventurers, had a compelling motivation to defend the merchant against disparagement, similar glorification came from different primarily religious directions. Daniel Price's "The Merchant: A Sermon Preached at Paul's Cross" also characterizes the merchant as the hero of the English state: "The doctrine I observe out of the word merchant, is this: that the state of a Christian is not in idle vain speculation, but must be a careful, painful, diligent, walking in his vocation.... The fool foldeth his hands, and eateth up his own flesh.... But contrariwise, the wise merchant, the true Christian, he seeketh, he taketh pains, he laboreth, he endeavoreth to follow hard to the mark... no peril, no danger... can confront him" (*Merchant* 237).

Even Tubal, Shylock's friend and the only other Jew in the play, is presented as a relatively sympathetic character. In his exchange with Shylock, Tubal remarks that like Shylock, Antonio also has also had "ill luck" (III.i.73). Tubal thus likens Shylock's anguish to Antonio's and thereby insinuates an empathetic bond between the two.The following soliloquy from Marlowe's *Jew of Malta* is perhaps the best example of the "bogey-man" that a figure like Barabas represented for the early modern English audience:

I walk abroad o' night
And will kill sick people groaning under the walls;
Sometimes I go about and poison wells...
Then after that was I an usurer,
And with extorting, cozening, forfeiting,
And tricks belonging unto brokery,
I fill'd the jails with bankrupts in a year,
And with young orphans planted hospitals,
And every moon made some or other mad,
And now and then one hang himself for grief,
Pinning upon his breast a long great scroll
How I with interest tormented him
(II. iii. 167-214)

Lisa Freinkel notes Shylock's particularist epistemology in her article, "*The Merchant of Venice*: 'Modern' Anti-Semitism and the Veil of Allegory." Commenting upon the punning of gentle/Gentile that occurs throughout the play, Freinkel writes, "The pun on gentle/Gentile... reveals that ways in which Shylock stands for a resistant particularity-for the principle of difference itself" (Hugh Grady, Ed. *Shakespeare and Modernity*, 134). While I agree with Freinkel's characterization of Shylock as "standing for difference itself," I think it is important to consider the context of this difference-making.

It is the task of this chapter to assert that the particularism of Shylock-his medieval bond-making-marks him as different from the newly emerging merchant-class-the Christian merchant-adventurers who must be "de-Jewed" in the English popular imagination. Thus, Shylock's difference is a particular difference, specifically relating to the philosophy of exchange and valuation. Shylock is monstrous to the play's audience because he refuses to convert *economically* and religiously.

The discourse of the marketplace and the way it which it threatened to sunder not only value from its material expression (gold, silver) but muddied the reliability of communication even in a non-economic context was remarked by such writers as Francis Bacon. In his *Organum,* Bacon focuses on the marketplace's creation of "idols" of discourse that obstruct the clear understanding of meaning and message, "There are also Idols formed by the intercourse and association of men with each other, which I call Idols of the Market-place, on account of the commerce and consort of men there. For it is by discourse that men associate; and words are imposed according to the apprehension of the vulgar. And therefore the ill and unfit choice of words wonderfully obstructs the understanding..." Later in the same section of the *Organum,* Bacon continues, "[T]he idols of the market-place are the most troublesome of all: idols which have crept into the understanding through the alliances of words and names... Whence it comes to pass that the high and formal discussions of learned men end oftentimes in disputes about words and names; with which (according to the use and wisdom of mathematicians) it would be more prudent to begin, and so by means of definitions reduce them to order" (87). Thus, Bacon ends up prescribing a return to strict ontological correspondence to clear away the obfuscations caused by the proliferation of ambiguous signs in the context of economic and human commerce.

As Ferber explains in "The Ideology of the Merchant of Venice," the distinction between landowner (seigniors) and rich merchants (burghers) was not very clear. "In the real Venice, it is true, 'seigniors and rich burghers' were the same people: the noble families in the closed Venetian oligarchy were nearly all 'royal merchants.' On the other hand, these same oligarchs whether in commercial, political or military affairs... were renowned for their gravity, caution and hard bargaining" (Ferber).

For Antonio's reaction to Shylock's Biblical rationalization of usury (the Jacob/Esau story), see I. 3. 67-8. In regards to the suspicion of sorcery that fed English anxiety about Jewish money-lending, it is important to note that alchemy was said to originate with a Hellentistic Jew, known as "Maria the Jew". The writings of Maria were familiar to early modern readers, so much so that her theories were said to influence such minds as Newton and Goethe (Patai 5). And, although alchemy and magic were distinct "specialities" to their respective practitioners, alchemists were commonly perceived as magicians in the Western early modern imaginary. Also, alchemists frequently practiced as physicians, a profession which was clearly associated with Jewishness in Shakespeare's time especially given the collective trauma around the alleged conspiracy against Elizabeth by a Jewish doctor, Roderigo Lopez. (For an interesting discussion on the epistemological interrelationship between alchemy and medicine in the Middle Ages and the renaissance, see Raphael Patai, *The Jewish Alchemists,* Princeton: 1994).

The argument that usury defies natural law dates back to Aristotle:

The most hated sort of money-making, and with greatest reason, is usury, which makes gain out of money itself, and not from the natural use of it. For money was intended to be used in exchange, but not to increase at interest. And this term usury, which means the birth of money from money, is applied to the breeding of money from money because the offspring resembles the parent. Wherefore of all modes of making money this is the most unnatural (qtd in *The Truth about Shylock,* 79).

For a detailed discussion of Christian usury in England, see Cecil Roth, *History of the Jews in England.*

The "state" is here implicated because of their role in assisting the Jews in collecting debts, of which the governing authority took a large percentage.

The chronicle of William of Norwich, an infamous blood libel in English-Jewish chronicles, stresses the dangers inherent in associating with Jews in their homes or communities: "So it came to pass that when the holy boy, ignorant of the treachery that had been planned, had frequent dealings with the Jews, he was taken to task by Godwin the priest... and he was prohibited from going in and out among them any more. . . . But the Jews, annoyed at the thwarting of their designs, tried with all their might to patch up a new scheme of wickedness... Accordingly, they found a man... who was a most treacherous fellow and just the fitting person for carrying out their execrable crime... they sent him out to find and bring back with him the victim, which, as I said before, had slipped out of their hands".The chronicle continues by detailing the ways in which William was first feasted at the Jewish home during Passover and then subjected to the tortures of a mock circumcision. The site of terror and helplessness for the non-Jew in these chronicles is the Jewish home; once captured and taken into the home and community, there seems to be no escape-like the spider that entangles the fly in her web.

For a further description of the particular form the Jewish question took in the early modern English imaginary, see James Shapiro, *Shakespeare and the Jews*.

It is important to note that Portia is also economically positioned *vis á vis* her home, Belmont. Like Shylock's, her value is literally encased within the halls of Belmont. This metynomic conflation is indicated by Bassanio's first mention of Portia to Antonio: "In Belmont is a lady richly left..." (I. i. 161). This collapse is further confirmed by the casket game in which choosing the correct encasement (of Portia's image) functions performatively as marriage. The fact that Portia's image is hidden in a leaden casket, however, differentiates the Christian-Portia from the Jewish Shylock in terms of the logic underlying this metonymical equivalency. Portia, unlike Shylock, has value in and of herself.

In her article, "Portia's Ring: Unruly Women and the Structure of Exchange" Karen Newman reveals how even the love plot is inflected with a mercantile ethos. In her betrothal to Bassanio, for example, Newman discusses how Portia refers to herself in the third person-as a thing to be exchanged; as such her persons becomes synechdocally conflated with the ring she gives Bassanio: "[Portia's] account of herself [to Bassanio] ... illustrates the exchange between the erotic and economic that characterizes the play's representation of human relations. The rhetorical distance created by the mercantile metaphor shifts the speech from her more personal commitment to a more formal bond marked by the giving of the ring. *Shakespeare Quarterly* (38)1: (Spring 1987), 25.

Of course, Antonio's bond does not come without an "interest" payment of its own. In some sense, Bassanio's flesh (the arrow) is what Antonio claims at the end of the play, the exchange of which is signified by the former's willingness to part with Portia's ring on behalf of Antonio.

Chapter 17

Important Quotations Explained

Quotation

> *I am a Jew. Hath not a Jew eyes? Hath not a Jew hands, organs, dimensions, senses, affections, passions; fed with the same food, hurt with the same weapons, subject to the same diseases, healed by the same means, warmed and cooled by the same winter and summer as a Christian is? If you prick us do we not bleed? If you tickle us do we not laugh? If you poison us do we not die? And if you wrong us shall we not revenge? If we are like you in the rest, we will resemble you in that. If a Jew wrong a Christian, what is his humility? Revenge. If a Christian wrong a Jew, what should his sufferance be by Christian example? Why, revenge. The villainy you teach me I will execute, and it shall go hard but I will better the instruction.*
>
> (III.i.49–61)

Explanation

This passage from Chapter 4 describes the beginnings of Roger's cruelty to the littluns, an important early step in the group's decline into savagery. At this point in the novel, the boys are still building their civilization, and the civilized instinct still dominates the savage instinct. The cracks are beginning to show, however, particularly in the willingness of some of the older boys to use physical force and violence to give themselves a sense of superiority over the smaller boys. This quotation shows us the psychological workings behind the beginnings of that willingness. Roger feels the urge to torment Henry, the littlun, by pelting him with stones, but the vestiges of socially imposed standards of behaviour are still too strong for him to give in completely to his savage urges. At this point, Roger still feels constrained by "parents and school and policemen and the law"—the figures and institutions that enforce society's moral code. Before long, Roger and most of the other boys lose their respect for these forces, and violence, torture, and murder break out as the savage instinct replaces the instinct for civilization among the group.

Quotation

What if my house be troubled with a rat,
And I be pleased to give ten thousand ducats
To have it baned? What, are you answered yet?
Some men there are love not a gaping pig,
Some that are mad if they behold a cat,
And others when the bagpipe sings i'th' nose
Cannot contain their urine; for affection,
Mistress of passion, sways it to the mood
Of what it likes or loathes....
So can I give no reason, nor I will not,
More than a lodged hate and a certain loathing
I bear Antonio, that I follow thus
A losing suit against him. Are you answered?

(IV.i.43–61)

Explanation

This important snippet of conversation from Chapter 3 finds Atticus giving Scout the crucial piece of moral advice that governs her development for the rest of the novel. The simple wisdom of Atticus's words reflects the uncomplicated manner in which he guides himself by this sole principle. His ability to relate to his children is manifested in his restatement of this principle in terms that Scout can understand ("climb into his skin and walk around in it"). Scout struggles, with varying degrees of success, to put Atticus's advice into practice and to live with sympathy and understanding toward others. At the end of the book, she succeeds in comprehending Boo Radley's perspective, fulfilling Atticus's advice in Chapter 3 and providing the novel with an optimistic ending despite the considerable darkness of the plot.

Quotation

> *You have among you many a purchased slave*
> *Which, like your asses and your dogs and mules,*
> *You use in abject and in slavish parts*
> *Because you bought them. Shall I say to you*
> *'Let them be free, marry them to your heirs.*
> *Why sweat they under burdens?...*
> *You will answer*
> *'The slaves are ours.' So do I answer you.*
> *The pound of flesh which I demand of him*
> *Is dearly bought. 'Tis mine, and I will have it.*
>
> (IV.i.89–99)

Explanation

In Chapter VI, when Nick finally describes Gatsby's early history, he uses this striking comparison between Gatsby and Jesus Christ to illuminate Gatsby's creation of his own identity. Fitzgerald was probably influenced in drawing this parallel by a nineteenth-century book by Ernest Renan entitled The Life of Jesus. This book presents Jesus as a figure who essentially decided to make himself the son of God, then brought himself to ruin by refusing to recognize the reality that denied his self-conception. Renan describes a Jesus who is "faithful to his self-created dream but scornful of the factual truth that finally crushes him and his dream"—a very appropriate description of Gatsby. Fitzgerald is known to have admired Renan's work and seems to have drawn upon it in devising this metaphor. Though the parallel between Gatsby and Jesus is not an important motif in The Great Gatsby, it is nonetheless a suggestive comparison, as Gatsby transforms himself into the ideal that he envisioned for himself (a "Platonic conception of himself") as a youngster and remains committed to that ideal, despite the obstacles that society presents to the fulfillment of his dream.

Quotation

The quality of mercy is not strained.
It droppeth as the gentle rain from heaven
Upon the place beneath....
It is enthronèd in the hearts of kings;
It is an attribute to God himself,
And earthly power doth then show likest God's
When mercy seasons justice. Therefore, Jew,
Though justice be thy plea, consider this:
That in the course of justice none of us
Should see salvation. We do pray for mercy,
And that same prayer doth teach us all to render
The deeds of mercy.

(IV.i.179–197)

Explanation

These words are spoken by Lady Macbeth in Act V, scene i, lines 30–34, as she sleepwalks through Macbeth's castle on the eve of his battle against Macduff and Malcolm. Earlier in the play, she possessed a stronger resolve and sense of purpose than her husband and was the driving force behind their plot to kill Duncan. When Macbeth believed his hand was irreversibly bloodstained earlier in the play, Lady Macbeth had told him, "A little water clears us of this deed" (II.ii.65). Now, however, she too sees blood. She is completely undone by guilt and descends into madness. It may be a reflection of her mental and emotional state that she is not speaking in verse; this is one of the few moments in the play when a major character—save for the witches, who speak in fou-foot couplets—strays from iambic pentameter. Her inability to sleep was foreshadowed in the voice that her husband thought he heard while killing the king—a voice crying out that Macbeth was murdering sleep. And her delusion that there is a bloodstain on her hand furthers the play's use of blood as a symbol of guilt. "What need we fear who knows it when none can call our power to account?" she asks, asserting that as long as her and her husband's power is secure, the murders they committed cannot harm them. But her guilt-wracked state and her mounting madness show how hollow her words are. So, too, does the army outside her castle. "Hell is murky," she says, implying that she already knows that darkness intimately. The pair, in their destructive power, have created their own hell, where they are tormented by guilt and insanity.

Quotation

> *The man that hath no music in himself,*
> *Nor is not moved with concord of sweet sounds,*
> *Is fit for treasons, stategems, and spoils.*
> *The motions of his spirit are dull as night,*
> *And his affections dark as Erebus.*
>
> (V.i.82–86)

Explanation

These words are uttered by Macbeth after he hears of Lady Macbeth's death, in Act V, scene v, lines 16–27. Given the great love between them, his response is oddly muted, but it segues quickly into a speech of such pessimism and despair—one of the most famous speeches in all of Shakespeare—that the audience realises how completely his wife's passing and the ruin of his power have undone Macbeth. His speech insists that there is no meaning or purpose in life. Rather, life "is a tale / Told by an idiot, full of sound and fury, / Signifying nothing." One can easily understand how, with his wife dead and armies marching against him, Macbeth succumbs to such pessimism. Yet, there is also a defensive and self-justifying quality to his words. If everything is meaningless, then Macbeth's awful crimes are somehow made less awful, because, like everything else, they too "signify nothing."

Macbeth's statement that "life's but a poor player / That struts and frets his hour upon the stage" can be read as Shakespeare's somewhat deflating reminder of the illusionary nature of the theater. After all, Macbeth is only a "player" himself, strutting on an Elizabethan stage. In any play, there is a conspiracy of sorts between the audience and the actors, as both pretend to accept the play's reality. Macbeth's comment calls attention to this conspiracy and partially explodes it—his nihilism embraces not only his own life but the entire play. If we take his words to heart, the play, too, can be seen as an event "full of sound and fury, / Signifying nothing."

Bibliography

Baker, Susan. "Sex and Marriage in The Dutch Courtesan," in *In Another Country:*

Feminist Perspectives on Renaissance Drama. Eds. Dorothea Kehler and Susan

Baker. Metuchen and London: Scarecrow Press, 1991.

Bakhtin, Mikhail. M. *The Dialogic Imagination: Four Essays.* Trans. Caryl Emerson and

Michael Holquist. Ed., Michael Holquist. Austin: University of Texas Press, 1981.

Rabelais and His World. Trans. Helene Iswolsky. Bloomington: Indiana University Press, 1984.

Bourdieu, Pierre. *Language and Symbolic Power.* Trans. Gino Ryamond and Mathew

Adamson. Ed., John B. Thompson. Cambridge: Harvard University Press,1991.

Bowers, Fredson. Ed., *The Dramatic Works of Thomas Dekker.* Cambridge: Cambridge UP,1969.

Brown, John Russell. *Shakespeare and His Comedies.* London: Methuen, 1964.

Cohen, Walter. "*The Merchant of Venice* and the Possibilities of Historical Criticism," in *English Literary History,* 49, 765-89.

Comensoli, Viviana. 'Household Business': *Domestic Plays of Early Modern England.*

Toronto: University of Toronto Press, 1996. de Lauretis,

Teresa. *Technologies of Gender: Essays on Theory, Film, and Fiction.* Bloomington: Indiana University Press, 1989.

Dekker, Thomas. *The Gull's Hornbook.* London, 1609. Rpt. New York: AMS Press, 1971.

With Thomas Middleton. *The Honest Whore.* In *The Dramatic Works of Thomas*

Dekker. Ed., Fredson Bowers. Cambridge: Cambridge UP, 1969.

The Honest Whore part II. In *The Dramatic Works of Thomas Dekker.* Ed.,

Fredson Bowers. Cambridge: Cambridge UP, 1969.

With John Webster. *Westward Ho* and *Northward Ho.* In *The Dramatic Works of Thomas Dekker.* Ed., Fredson Bowers. Cambridge: Cambridge UP, 1969.

Deleuze, Gilles and Felix Guatarri. *Anti-Oedipus: Capitalism and Schizophrenia.* Trans.

Robert Hurley, Mark Seem, Helen R. Lane. Minneapolis: University of Minnesota Press, 1983.

Engle, Lars. "'Thrift is blessing': Exchange and Explanation in *The Merchant of Venice*" in *Shakespeare Quarterly,* 37 (1986) 1. 20-37.

Evèns, G. Blakemore. Ed., *Elizabethan-Jacobean Drama: The Theatre in Its Time.* New York: New Amsterdam, 1988.

Frazer, Russell A. and Norman Rabkin. Eds., *The Drama of the English Renaissance: II*

The Stuart Period. New York and London: MacMillan Publishing, 1976.

Frye, Susan and Karen Roberston. Eds., *Maid and Mistresses, Cousins and Queens:*

Women's Alliances in Early Modern England. Oxford and New York: Oxford University Press, 1999.

Foucault, Michel. *History of Sexuality: An Introduction.. Vol. I.* New York: Vintage Books, 1978.